Under the Mask

AN ANTHOLOGY ABOUT
PREJUDICE IN AMERICA

Selected, edited, and arranged by

KAREL WEISS

87

DELACORTE PRESS / NEW YORK

LIBRARY OF CONGRESS CATALOG CARD NUMBER: 71-176035
MANUFACTURED IN THE UNITED STATES OF AMERICA
FIRST PRINTING

Library of Congress Cataloging in Publication Data

Weiss, Karel, 1929–   comp.
    Under the mask.

    1. U.S.–Race question–Collections. 2. Mi-
norities–U.S.–Collections. 3. Prejudices and
antipathies–Collections. I. Title.
E184.A1.W36   301.45'0973   71-176035

Grateful acknowledgment is given to the following for permission to use excerpts from copyrighted material.

ADDISON-WESLEY PUBLISHING COMPANY, INC.
The Nature of Prejudice by Gordon W. Allport, 1954. Reprinted by permission of Addison-Wesley, Reading, Mass.

A. D. PETERS & COMPANY
Journey Down a Rainbow by J. B. Priestly and Jacquetta Hawkes. Published by Heinemann. Reprinted by permission of A. D. Peters & Company.

AMERICAN COUNCIL ON EDUCATION
Children of Bondage by Allison Davis and John Dollard. © 1940, 1968 American Council on Education, used by permission.

ATHENEUM PUBLISHERS, INC.
"Prayer for Peace" from *Selected Poems* by Léopold Sédar Senghor, translated by John Reed and Clive Wake. Translation copyright © Oxford University Press 1964. Reprinted by permission of Atheneum Publishers and Oxford University Press.

ATLANTIC-LITTLE, BROWN AND COMPANY
Children of Crisis by Robert Coles. Copyright © 1964, 1965, 1966, 1967 Robert Coles. "Supermarket Sweep" from *Supernation at Peace and War* by Dan Wakefield. Copyright © 1968 Dan Wakefield. Reprinted by permission of the publisher.

KNOX BURGER ASSOCIATES
Island in the City by Dan Wakefield. Copyright © 1957, 1958, 1959 by Dan Wakefield. Reprinted by permission of the author and his agent, Knox Burger Associates.

iv

CHICAGO SUN-TIMES

"The DAR Says Crispus Attucks Was a Rioter, Not a Revolutionist" by Betty Flynn. Reprinted with permission from the *Chicago Sun-Times* and the *New York Post*.

COLUMBIA UNIVERSITY PRESS

"Racial Myths" by Juan Comas, from *The Race Question in Modern Science* and *Unesco: Race and Science,* used by permission.

CONGRESS OF RACIAL EQUALITY

"Dinner at Stoner's" by George Houser, from *Negro Protest Thought in the Twentieth Century,* edited by Francis L. Broderick and August Meir. © 1965 The Bobbs-Merrill Co., Inc. Reprinted by permission of Congress of Racial Equality.

DODD, MEAD & COMPANY, INC.

"The Man Inside" from *Rendezvous With America* by Melvin B. Tolson. Copyright 1944 Dodd, Mead & Company, Inc. Reprinted by permission of the publisher.

DOUBLEDAY & COMPANY, INC.

Indians of the United States by Clark Wissler. Copyright © 1940, 1966 Doubleday & Company, Inc. Reprinted by permission of the publisher.

DOVER PUBLICATIONS, INC.

"Love-Song" from *The Indians' Book: Indian Lore, Musical and Narrative* by Natalie Curtis Burlin. Reprinted with permission of the publisher.

E. P. DUTTON & CO., INC.

The Centuries of Santa Fe by Paul Horgan. Copyright © 1956 Paul Horgan. Reprinted by permission of the publisher.

GROVE PRESS, INC.

Excerpts from "Nightmare" and "Homeboy" from *The Autobiography of Malcolm X.* Copyright © 1964 Alex Haley and Malcolm X; Copyright © 1965 Alex Haley and Betty Shabazz. Reprinted by permission of Grove Press, Inc.

HARCOURT BRACE JOVANOVICH, INC.

"Racial Exercise" from *Two Cheers for Democracy* by E. M. Forster. Copyright 1951 E. M. Forster. Reprinted by permission of Harcourt Brace Jovanovich, Inc. and Edward Arnold (Publishers) Ltd.
"The Artificial Nigger" from *A Good Man Is Hard to Find and Other Stories.* Copyright © 1955 Flannery O'Connor.
"The Mexicans" and "The Unwritten Law" from *Not With the Fist* by Ruth D. Tuck. Copyright 1948 Ruth D. Tuck.
"Walls" from *The Complete Poems Of Cavafy,* by C. P. Cavafy, translated by Rae Dalven. Copyright 1949 Rae Dalven. Reprinted by permission of Harcourt Brace Jovanovich, Inc.

HARPER & ROW, PUBLISHERS, INCORPORATED

Indians and Other Americans by Harold E. Fey and D'Arcy McNickle. Copyright © 1959 Harold E. Fey and D'Arcy McNickle.
Dark Ghetto by Kenneth B. Clark. Copyright © 1965 Kenneth B. Clark.
From Many Lands by Louis Adamic. Copyright 1939, 1940 Louis Adamic.

v

to

MY MOTHER

and

THE MEMORY OF MY FATHER

CONTENTS

Part Three: REMOVAL

Part Four: GHETTOS OF THE MIND

Part Five: BEHIND THESE WALLS

Part Seven: THE BREAKING POINT

Epilogue

Acknowledgments

To Jan Wahl, who believed that there could be a book, and without whom this book would never have been begun, I owe an incalculable debt of gratitude.

Special thanks to Joanne Dolinar, whose sound editorial insights and extraordinary patience did much to bring order out of chaos; to Jane Greenspan for her counsel and because her initial enthusiasm for the book never wavered; to Robert Wyatt and Deborah Baker; and to Pamela Roman and Marta Celorio, who performed an almost impossible task with exemplary skill; as well as to all the other members of the Delacorte staff involved in the project.

I am very grateful to Ruth Wilcox of the Library of the Museum of the American Indian, New York City, and to the staffs of the Schomburg Collection, the American History Division, and the General Research and Humanities Division (in particular, Anthony Warren) of the New York Public Library. My appreciation goes also to the librarians of the Cadman Plaza branch of the Brooklyn Public Library, Brooklyn, New York, and to Mrs. Joan Sigerist, bibliographic assistant, Rutgers University Center of Alcohol Studies, New Brunswick, New Jersey. Without their efforts much of the material in this book might never have been found.

To Donald E. Wheeler for having introduced me to the writings of Alice Marriott, to Una Corbett for knowledge, graciously given, and to Dr. Emanuel Peterfreund and the late William Raney, whose encouragement helped make this book possible, I should like to express my appreciation.

Finally, to Warren Means, whose critical perceptions during the many stages of the book were of invaluable help, deep appreciation.

FOREWORD

Without the aid of dozens of sociological and psychological works this book could never have been completed. Yet it is precisely because of the limitations of these sciences that the book was begun. Though the social sciences have done much to uncover injustices, they have also left much unsaid. Objectivity of appoach can never come to terms with the human heart. The most carefully documented case history can not convey the frustration of an Indian girl caught between two worlds—but a story by Alice Marriott can. All the charts and statistics of all the government-sponsored housing commissions can never capture the anguish of one lifetime in El Barrio —but *Diary of a Rent Striker* can. With a minimum of sociological trappings I have set out to let the people speak for themselves.

Much consideration went into the unconventional arrangement of the material. Minority groups are too often seen with a provincial eye. There is only one prejudice. The growing militancy of the southwestern *Chicanos* is paralleled by the platform of the Young Lords in New York. Poverty is the same on an Indian reservation and in Jimtown, Kentucky. A statement made by W. E. B. Du Bois in 1910 becomes more pertinent when read with an article written in the 1960s—the past illuminating the present, the present the past.

We live in a time of growing separatism and alienation, but I hope that in these pages Langston Hughes says as much to the Indian of New Mexico as he does to the blacks of New Orleans, and C. P. Cavafy as much to the *Chicanos*, whom he could never have known, as to the citizens of Alexandria.

PROLOGUE

Promises and Performances

*We promise according to our hopes
and perform
according to our fears.*

La Rochefoucauld

DECLARATION
OF INDEPENDENCE

We hold these truths to be self-evident, that all men are created equal,

The profile of Indian poverty is as follows:

Schooling ...... 5 years
Life-span .... 43 years
Family income .. $1,500
Unemployment . 45 percent
Housing .... 90 percent
below acceptable
standards

Association on American Indian Affairs, Inc. 1968

that they are endowed by their Creator with certain unalienable rights, that among these are Life,

DOCTOR FROM BOMBAY FINDS
RICKETS IN BRONX

An Indian doctor from Bombay detected a rare case of rickets a few months ago in the Bronx.

The victim of this childhood disease, characterized by soft deformed bones and recognized to be largely, if not entirely, the result of a deficiency of vitamin D, was an eighteen-month-old Negro girl.

Dr. Srihari Sakadeo of the Montefiore Neighborhood Health Center recalled that the rachitic infant had been

3

breast-fed, but the mother's milk had low-level vitamin D. The center serves one of the poorest sections of the Bronx—Morrisania and Bathgate. The neighborhood, according to Dr. Harold B. Wise, has a tuberculosis rate of 8.1 a 1,000, more than double the boroughwide rate of 3.7 a 1,000.

New York Times, 24 March 1969

Liberty,

The Spaniards pursued the Indians with bloodhounds, like wild beasts; they sacked the New World like a city taken by storm, with no discernment or compassion; but destruction must cease at last and frenzy has a limit: the remnant of the Indian population, which had escaped the massacre, mixed with its conquerors and adopted in the end their religion and their manners. The conduct of the Americans of the United States toward the aborigines is characterized, on the one hand, by a singular attachment to the formalities of law. Provided that the Indians retain their barbarous condition, the Americans take no part in their affairs; they treat them as independent nations and do not possess themselves of their hunting grounds without a treaty of purchase; and if an Indian nation happens to be so encroached upon as to be unable to subsist upon their territory, they kindly take them by the hand and transport them to a grave far from the land of their fathers.

The Spaniards were unable to exterminate the Indian race by those unparalleled atrocities that brand them with indelible shame, nor did they succeed even in wholly depriving it of its rights; but the Americans of the United States have accomplished this twofold purpose with singular felicity, tranquilly, legally, philanthropically, without shedding blood, and without violating a single great principle of morality in the eyes of the world. It is im-

possible to destroy men with more respect for the laws of
humanity.

Alexis de Tocqueville, from *Democracy in America*

and the pursuit of Happiness.

The City University study by Leonard S. Kogan and
Morey J. Wantman estimated median income for all city
families at $6,684 in 1966—$3,949 for Puerto Ricans,
$4,754 for nonwhites, and $7,635 for whites. Puerto Ricans
gained only $49 in two years, compared with a white
gain of $927. But Puerto Rican leaders yesterday thought
the figure for four-member Puerto Rican families should
be closer to $3,500 a year.

In an analysis for the Puerto Rican Forum, Richard
Lewisohn, now head of the city's Economic Development Administration, estimated Puerto Ricans on relief
had risen in percentage more than any other group from
29.5 percent of the welfare rolls in 1959 to 33 percent
last year.

Experts in the city Department of Social Services believe Puerto Ricans may now be 35 to 40 percent of the
relief recipients, with perhaps nearly 40 percent of the
city's Puerto Ricans getting welfare help, often, however,
to supplement low wages of working fathers.

White-collar employment among New York City
Puerto Ricans actually declined for men from 17 to 12
percent between 1960 and 1965, according to Lewisohn,
although increasing for women from 18.7 to 24.9 percent. Unemployment in Puerto Rican areas such as East
Harlem, South Bronx, and South Brooklyn ran at 12 percent last winter, triple the national rate.

A Puerto Rican Forum analysis said half of the Puerto
Ricans over twenty-five years of age had less than an
eighth-grade education, with those reaching ninth grade
often four years behind in reading. Of those finishing

high school, 90 percent have been getting a general diploma, 8 percent a vocational certificate, only 1.2 percent the academic diploma opening the way to college.

Peter Kihss, *New York Times, 25 July 1968*

CONSTITUTION
OF THE UNITED STATES,
AMENDMENT 4

The right of the people to be secure in their persons,

CIVILIAN EXCLUSION ORDER, NUMBER 27
30 APRIL 1942

I. Pursuant to the provisions of Public Proclamation numbers 1 and 2, this headquarters, dated 2 March and 16 March 1942, respectively, it is hereby ordered that from and after 12 o'clock noon, P.W.T., of Thursday, 7 May 1942, all persons of Japanese ancestry, both alien and nonalien, be excluded from that portion of Military Area Number I . . .

Allan R. Bosworth, from *America's Concentration Camps*

houses, papers, and effects, against unreasonable searches, and seizures,

The house-to-house search for stolen weapons in a Negro section of Plainfield, New Jersey, conducted by state troopers and national guardsmen Wednesday under gubernatorial proclamation but without warrants lasted less than two hours.

But the arguments concerning the legality of the

searches are certain to last for many months, perhaps years, in and out of the courts.

Undoubtedly, history will be consulted both by those who support the action of Governor Richard J. Hughes and those who condemn it. The central question: was his declaration of a state of emergency in the riot-beset city sufficient legal justification for the searches?

The answer may ultimately be decided by the courts. The American Civil Liberties Union said yesterday that it will file a federal court suit next week, challenging the constitutionality of the action, requesting money damages for those whose homes were searched, and demanding an injunction against further searches without warrants.

Sidney E. Zion, *New York Times*, 22 July 1967

shall not be violated . . .

STATUE OF LIBERTY

Give me your tired, your poor,
Your huddled masses yearning to breathe free,
The wretched refuse of your teeming shore.
Send these, the homeless, tempest-tost to me,
I lift my lamp beside the golden door!

Emma Lazarus, from sonnet
engraved on the Statue of Liberty

4 MEXICAN MIGRANTS FOUND
SLAIN IN TEXAS

DEL RIO, Tex., April 17 (UPI)—Four Mexicans were found beaten and stabbed to death near a highway in southwest Texas today.

Two unidentified children, one shot between the eyes and the other stabbed, were found alive but critically hurt. They were semiconscious and spattered with blood and gravel when found.

The dead—one man, two women, and a child—all carried passports and apparently were the victims of a motorist who picked them up yesterday when their car blew a tire. All six were from Piedras Negras, across the Rio Grande from Eagle Pass, Texas. City, county and state law enforcement men set up roadblocks.

"They were evidently beaten to death," said Justice of the Peace Warren Hutt of Rocksprings. "The baby was stabbed. The others were pretty well beaten up around the head."

He said one of the victims, a 19-year-old girl, had apparently been raped.

The victims were a part of a large migrating labor force that lives in Mexico but works in the United States. They carried green cards that were their passes to and from the United States.

The slayings took place in one of the more isolated sections of Texas. It is 90 miles from Sonora to Del Rio along U.S. Highway 277, with nothing in between except a country store and gasoline station.

New York Times, 18 April 1968

PART ONE

In the Beginning

Tired of living, afraid of dying, like
The lost brig, plaything of the waves,
My soul sets sail toward fearful disasters.

Paul Verlaine

THE INDIANS

"There is a new land over there. Across some water. Somebody has been there, and come back again. So we hear. They had all the meat they could eat. It is a plentiful land. Life is easy."

The world was full of rumors just then. A marvelous thing had happened. A new land had been discovered, just when it was needed too. The people had wandered to the end of the world, in quest of food and safety.

Somewhere in their rear, in their dim racial memory, were scenes of mortal struggle, in which they had been vanquished and driven away. Somewhere back there was a fearful dream they wanted to escape from and forget. So they had worked their way northward, into the outer darkness. Life got thinner as they went along. Forests thinned, then disappeared. Game animals were found less easily. The people had to keep moving and they had to divide their camps into even smaller numbers. Yet they could never turn back, but must move ahead, hoping to come upon a kindlier country. This wandering had continued, now, for generations so numerous the old people could not count them. It seemed to have lasted from the beginning of time.

Now, there were these rumors. A new land. A plentiful land. Life was easy over there, across some water. The older people, sitting in their crudely made tents of skin, their eyes blinded by smoke and snow gazing, were inclined to shrug their shoulders. They had heard of such things before: only a little farther ahead, things would be different, keep moving. It was a fable.

The young ones though would not be put off. They had

been told these tales by wanderers who had talked to other wanderers who had talked to some of the very people who had crossed that water and had come back to tell of it. The tales were true. If the old people refused to believe, that was too bad; but they, the young ones, would not wait forever. They would go themselves and find out.

Across many campfires the matter was argued. The old people saw that they had no choice but to go along, if they could keep up. Wolf packs waited for them if they stayed. If they died on the march, at least the tribe would be together.

So they drifted northward, ever northward and eastward, toward land's end. The only living things it seemed were these few people and the wolves who followed behind. Each day brought death. In all the ragged tents death was a fireside companion. The people's strength grew thin. Even the strongest among the leaders began to question the faith that carried them along. In their councils, voices rose in sharp anger.

How they endured it, no one can say. Finally, they were there. They knew the place at once, from the way it had been described. The sea was below them, at the bottom of a rock cliff. Staring eastward in clear weather, they could see the low-lying, dark stretch of shore. After that first long look, they turned their eyes back upon each other. Perhaps then and there they saw each other for the first time and realized that they were a people apart. They had survived together and the knowledge of that would never leave them.

Like sand in an hourglass, pouring grain by grain. Over many thousands of years, wandering bands of people drifted toward the end of one world and crossed over into another. Both worlds were nameless, the old from which they came and the new into which they crossed. For that matter, so were they a nameless people.

A handful of people standing in the new world!

It seemed at first that they had stumbled upon an entirely empty land. They saw mountains blocking out the horizon; broad rivers coming out to breast the sea; prairies that stretched on like the waters of ocean; forests that darkened areas greater than the eye could encompass—and in all that region, no living human folk. But wait! Here was an old campfire! And here, a rock shelter. Someone had been there before them. The land was less lonely then.

Ages passed, generations of men—children born, maturing, and dying as old men—thousands of such simple cycles, and the people who first crossed over were followed by others and still later ones. They moved with their faces to the noontime sun, ever southward. With all the new world to roam in, it was natural to move along. Always in their minds was the vague thought that only a little ways on, perhaps beyond the next mountain range, they would find that fabulous land, the land where life would be easy.

It must almost have come true. Exploring southward, life did become more abundant. Wild fruits flowered and bore. Edible roots were savored. Most gratifying of all were the animals roaming in small bands and in prairie-darkening herds, upon which they might spend their lives in feasting. It was almost the very end of the quest. Here they might have settled for all time.

But quests are never ended. Beyond the next mountain range or the next forest barrier—who knows what may not yet be found!

On all of this migration, the how and when, we can only speculate. Motives can only be guessed at. A stone weapon or tool shaped by a human hand can tell us only so much. Men passed there. A bed of charcoal buried under tons of sediment earth suggests that they camped and cooked food. By studying the movement of glaciers and the building up and wearing away of the earth's crust, we arrive at crude timetables.

They had no name for the land they left and no name either for the land they discovered and entered. That, of course, is a surmise. Probably they made the basic distinction: the Old Land, the New Land, but it is not likely that they used encompassing terms such as Asia and America. They had only their limited experience as a handful of people by which to measure the world. No man knew the earth beyond the reaches of what he or other wanderers might cover in a lifetime on foot. Rivers and mountains and seacoasts were nameless, except that a man in his own family or his own camp might lend his notion of what the thing looked like to him. In time, some of these private notion words would stick and be passed on until they became part of common speech.

Even in speaking of themselves, they had no common use term by which they recognized that they were all one people. Each group had its own name, and when two strange groups met by the greatest chance and found that they had no common speech, their amazement was mutual. Each had thought that no other such body existed. Each in its own tongue, not understanding the other, would say: "I am Inunaina. . . . I am Taneks haya. . . . I am Hasinai. . . . I am Ani-yunwiya. . . . I am Dzitsiistas. . . . I am Leni-lenape. . . . I am Inuit. . . . I am Dine. . . ." By which they meant, "I am of *The People*, or *The First People*, or *Our Own Folk*, or *The Real People.*" It did not sound strange or presumptuous.

In the beginning, then, a band of people, scarcely more than one strong man and his wives, his sons and daughters with their wives and husbands, perhaps his brothers as well and all their womenfolk, and the children of all these, and their dogs. Without horses. Without wheeled vehicles. With only such tools and weapons and clothing as a man and his womenfolk could carry. Just such a band crossed from one world into another and sent back word. Perhaps a beacon fire burning at night was the signal that the crossing had been made, from one nameless world into another nameless world, by a people still nameless.

One day the land would be called America, and the people Indians.

Before passing from generalizations to particulars, we make this last generalization: that somewhere in the interior of Asia, back in the distance, was the very beginning point of the human race. People very like those who went northward, and eventually crossed over into America, also went southward and westward, some of them, and emerged as the wild tribes who peopled the caves of the Mediterranean basin, Africa, and western Europe. In time they brushed away their wild habits and began to build the early cultures of the world.

Those who made the passage through the northeastern (Asiatic) corridor, across what in modern times we call Bering Strait, they too adapted themselves to the land and the climate and made a place for themselves. In time, they had pried into every corner of the two continents; a few miserable ones even reached to the terrible loneliness of Tierra del Fuego and stared into the south polar sea, land's end again. They were the first to come, the first discoverers, the first settlers.

D'Arcy McNickle, from *They Came Here First*

THE BLACKS

If the weather was clear, they were brought on deck at eight o'clock in the morning. The men were attached by their leg-irons to the great chain that ran along the bulwarks on both sides of the ship; the women and half-grown boys were allowed to wander at will. About nine o'clock the slaves were served their first meal of the day. If they were from the Windward Coast, the fare consisted of boiled rice, millet, or cornmeal, which might be cooked with a few lumps of salt beef abstracted from the sailors' rations. If they were from the Bight of Biafra, they were fed stewed yams, but the Congos and the Angolans preferred manioc or plantains. With the food they were all given half a pint of water, served out in a pannikin.

After the morning meal came a joyless ceremony called "dancing the slaves." "Those who were in irons," says Dr. Thomas Trotter, surgeon of the *Brookes* in 1783, "were ordered to stand up and make what motions they could, leaving a passage for such as were out of irons to dance around the deck." Dancing was prescribed as a therapeutic measure, a specific against suicidal melancholy, and also against scurvy —although in the latter case it was a useless torture for men with swollen limbs. While sailors paraded the deck, each with a cat-o'-nine-tails in his right hand, the men slaves "jumped in their irons" until their ankles were bleeding flesh. One sailor told Parliament, "I was employed to dance the men, while another person danced the women." Music was provided by a slave thumping on a broken drum or an upturned kettle, or by an African banjo, if there was one aboard, or perhaps by a sailor with a bagpipe or a fiddle. Slaving captains sometimes advertised for "a person that can play on the bagpipes, for a Guinea ship." The slaves were also told to sing. Said Dr. Claxton after his voyage in the *Young Hero*, "They sing, but not for their amusement. The captain ordered them to sing, and they sang songs of sorrow. Their sickness, fear of being beaten, their hunger, and the memory of their country, and so forth, are the usual subjects."

While some of the sailors were dancing the slaves, others were sent below to scrape and swab out the sleeping rooms. It was a sickening task, and it was not well performed unless the captain imposed an iron discipline. James Barbot, Sr., was proud of the discipline maintained on the *Albion-Frigate*. "We were very nice," he says, "in keeping the places where the slaves lay clean and neat, appointing some of the ship's crew to do that office constantly and thrice a week we perfumed betwixt decks with a quantity of good vinegar in pails, and red-hot iron bullets in them, to expel the bad air, after the place had been well washed and scrubbed with brooms." Captain Hugh Crow, the last legal English slaver, was famous for his housekeeping. "I always took great pains," he says, "to promote the health and comfort of all on board, by proper diet, regularity, exercise, and cleanliness, for I consider that on keeping the ship clean and orderly, which was always my hobby, the success of our voyage mainly depended." Consistently he lost fewer slaves in the Middle Passage than the other captains, some of whom had the filth in the hold cleaned out only once a week. A few left their slaves to wallow in excrement during the whole Atlantic passage.

At three or four in the afternoon the slaves were fed their second meal, often a repetition of the first. Sometimes, instead of African food, they were given horse beans, the cheapest provender from Europe. The beans were boiled to a pulp, then covered with a mixture of palm oil, flour, water, and red pepper, which the sailors called "slabber sauce." Most of the slaves detested horse beans, especially if they were used to eating yams or manioc. Instead of eating the pulp, they would, unless carefully watched, pick it up by handfuls and throw it in each other's faces. That second meal was the end of their day. As soon as it was finished they were sent below, under the guard of sailors charged with stowing them away on their bare floors and platforms. The tallest men were placed amidships, where the vessel was widest; the shorter ones were tumbled into the stern. Usually there was only room for them to sleep on their sides, "spoon fashion." Captain William Littleton told Parliament that slaves in the ships on which he sailed might lie on their backs if they wished—"though perhaps," he conceded, "it might be difficult all at the same time."

After stowing their cargo, the sailors climbed out of the hatchway, each clutching his cat-'o-nine-tails: then the hatchway gratings were closed and barred. Sometimes in the night, as the sailors lay on deck and tried to sleep, they heard from below "a howling melancholy noise, expressive of extreme anguish." When Dr. Trotter told his interpreter, a slave woman, to inquire about the cause of the noise, "she discovered it to be owing to their having dreamt they were in their own country, and finding themselves when awake, in the hold of a slave ship."

More often the noise heard by the sailors was that of quarreling among the slaves. The usual occasion for quarrels was their problem of reaching the latrines. They were inadequate and hard to find in the darkness of the crowded hold, especially by men who were ironed together in pairs.

In each of the apartments [says Dr. Falconbridge] are placed three or four large buckets, of a conical form, nearly two feet in diameter at the bottom and only one foot at the top and in depth about twenty-eight inches, to which, when necessary, the Negroes have recourse. It often happens that those who are placed at a distance from the buckets, in endeavoring to get to them, tumble over their companions, in consequence of their being shackled. These accidents, although unavoidable, are productive of continual quarrels in which some of them are always bruised. In this situation, unable to proceed and prevented from going to the tubs, they desist from the attempt; and as the necessities of nature are not to be resisted, they ease themselves as they lie.

In squalls or rainy weather, the slaves were never brought on deck. They were served their two meals in the hold, where the air became too thick and poisonous to breathe. Says Dr. Falconbridge, "For the purpose of admitting fresh air, most of the ships in the slave trade are provided, between the decks, with five or six air-ports on each side of the ship, of about six inches in length and four in breadth; in addition to which, some few ships, but not one in twenty, have what they denominate windsails." These were funnels made of canvas and so placed as to direct a current of air into the hold. "But whenever the sea is rough and the rain heavy," Falconbridge continues, "it becomes necessary to shut these and every other conveyance by which the air is admitted. . . . The Negroes' rooms very soon become intolerably hot. The confined air, rendered noxious by the effluvia exhaled from their bodies and by being repeatedly breathed, soon produces fevers and fluxes which generally carry off great numbers of them."

Dr. Trotter says that when tarpaulins were thrown over the gratings, the slaves would cry, "Kickeraboo, kickeraboo, we are dying, we are dying." "I have known," says Henry Ellison, a sailor before the mast, "in the Middle Passage, in rains, slaves confined below for some time. I have frequently seen them faint through heat, the steam coming through the gratings, like a furnace." Falconbridge gives one instance of their sufferings.

> Some wet and blowing weather having occasioned the port-holes to be shut and the grating to be covered, fluxes and fevers among the Negroes ensued. While they were in this situation, I frequently went down among them till at length their rooms became so extremely hot as to be only bearable for a very short time. But the excessive heat was not the only thing that rendered their situation intolerable. The deck, that is, the floor of their rooms, was so covered with blood and mucus that had proceeded from them in consequence of the flux, that it resembled a slaughterhouse. . . . Numbers of the slaves having fainted they were carried upon deck where several of them died and the rest with great difficulty were restored. It had nearly proved fatal to me also. The climate was too warm to admit the wearing of any clothing but a shirt and that I had pulled off before I went down; notwithstanding which, by only continuing among them for about a quarter of an hour, I was so overcome with the heat, stench, and foul air that I nearly fainted; and it was only with assistance that I could get on deck. The consequence was that I soon after fell sick of the same disorder from which I did not recover for several months.

Not surprisingly, the slaves often went mad. Falconbridge mentions a woman on the *Emilia* who had to be chained to the deck. She had lucid intervals, however, and during one of these she was sold to a planter in Jamaica. Men who went insane might be flogged to death, to make sure that they were not malingering. Some were simply clubbed on the head and thrown overboard.

While the slaves were on deck, they had to be watched at all times to keep them from committing suicide. Says Captain

Phillips of the *Hannibal*, "We had about twelve Negroes did willfully drown themselves, and others starv'd themselves to death; For," he explained, " 'tis their belief that when they die they return home to their own country and friends again." This belief was reported from various regions, at various periods of the trade, but it seems to have been especially prevalent among the Ibo of eastern Nigeria. In 1788, nearly a hundred years after the *Hannibal's* voyage, Ecroide Claxton was the surgeon who attended a shipload of Ibo. "Some of the slaves," he testified, "wished to die on an idea that they should then get back to their own country. The captain in order to obviate this idea, thought of an expedient, viz., to cut off the heads of those who died intimating to them that if determined to go, they must return without heads. The slaves were accordingly brought up to witness the operation. One of them by a violent exertion got loose and flying to the place where the nettings had been unloosed in order to empty the tubs, he darted overboard. The ship brought to, a a man was placed in the main chains to catch him, which he perceiving, made signs that words cannot express expressive of his happiness in escaping. He then went down and was seen no more."

Dr. Isaac Wilson, a surgeon in the Royal Navy, made a Guinea voyage on the *Elizabeth* [commanded by] Captain John Smith, who was said to be very humane. Nevertheless, Wilson was assigned the duty of whipping the slaves. "Even in the act of chastisement," Wilson says, "I have seen them look up at me with a smile, and in their own language, say, 'presently we shall be no more.'" One woman on the *Elizabeth* found some rope yarn, which she tied to the armorer's vise; she fastened the other end round her neck and was found dead in the morning. On the *Brookes* when Thomas Trotter was her surgeon, there was a man who, after being accused of witchcraft, had been sold into slavery with his whole family. During his first night on shipboard, he tried to cut his throat. Dr. Trotter sewed up the wound, but on the following night the man not only tore out the sutures but tried to cut his throat on the other side. From the ragged edges of the wound and the blood on his fingers, he seemed to have used his nails as the only available instrument. His hands were tied together after the second wound, but he then refused all food, and he died of hunger in eight or ten days.

"Upon the Negroes refusing to take food," says Falconbridge, "I have seen coals of fire, glowing hot, put on a shovel and placed so near their lips as to scorch and burn them. And this has been accompanied with threats of forcing them to swallow the coals if they persisted in refusing to eat. This generally had the required effect." But if the Negroes still refused, they were flogged day after day. Lest flogging prove ineffective, every Guineaman was provided with a special instrument called the speculum oris, or mouth opener. It looked like a pair of dividers with notched legs and with a thumbscrew at the blunt end. The legs were closed and the notches were hammered between the slave's teeth. When the thumbscrew was tightened, the legs of the instrument separated, forcing open the slave's mouth; then food was poured into it through a funnel.

Even the speculum oris sometimes failed with a slave determined to die. Dr. Wilson reports another incident of his voyage on the *Elizabeth*, this one concerning a young man who had refused to eat for several days. Mild means were used to divert him from his resolution, "as well as promises," Wilson says, "that he should have anything he wished for; but still he refused to eat. He was then whipped with the cat but this also was ineffectual. He always kept his teeth so fast that it was impossible to get anything down. We then endeavored to introduce a speculum oris between his teeth but the points were too obtuse to enter and next tried a bolus knife but with the same effect. In this state he was for four or five days when he was brought up as dead to be thrown overboard. . . . I, finding life still existing, repeated my endeavors though in vain and two days afterward he was brought up again in the same state as before. . . . In his own tongue he asked for water, which was given him. Upon this we began to have hopes of dissuading him from his design but he again shut his teeth as fast as ever and resolved to die and on the ninth day from his first refusal he died."

Daniel P. Mannix and Malcolm Cowley,
from *Black Cargoes*

THE PUERTO RICANS

It is no good to be poor.

Ricardo Sánchez, a
Puerto Rican migrant

Ricardo Sánchez came from where the sugarcane is higher than a man to the plaza in old San Juan where the buses marked *Aeropuerto* stop. He came with his wife and two daughters and three suitcases and a paper bag and the promise from a brother in Harlem, New York, that there was work to be found in *fábrica*. The work in the sugarcane was over for the season and Ricardo had found nothing else. The government would pay him $7 every two weeks for thirteen weeks before the season began again, and then with the season he would get $3.60 a day for eight hours in the sun. He had done it before, as his fathers had done it, but this time he told himself he wanted something more. "It is," he said, "no good to be poor." His lean brown face was twisted in a grimace of disgust as he said the words, and remained that way, in the memory of poverty, slowly relaxing as he fingered the three fountain pens neatly clipped to the pocket of his new brown suit, and turned to face the dark from where the buses come.

Christopher Columbus, migrant by trade, stood by frozen in the stone of a statue, the accidental patron saint of the plaza that serves as a boarding place for those who go away. Even more practically, Columbus's weathered figure serves those who stay, for around it sit the old men who sit around the statues of the plazas of the world; these by the chance of Columbus's mistaken discoveries (and Ponce de León's mistaken hopes) speaking the language of his creditor the queen. But the queen is four centuries dead, and the island's highest ruler is a president from Kansas—a place whose name and language are totally foreign to the old men who sit by the statue.

Their fathers before them were Indians here, called Borinqueños, and Spanish followers of Ponce de León, seeker after gold and youth and captor of neither. His body is buried up the street. Their fathers were Negro slaves from Africa, brought here to fill the vacuum left when the Indians painfully vanished, by death and escape, from the Spaniards' rule. The Spaniards built great forts and repulsed the futile attacks of the French and the Dutch and Sir Francis Drake and ruled until 1898. It was then, a year after Spain had finally granted the people of the island a form of self-government, that Admiral Sampson bombarded San Juan and General Nelson Miles led his troops to the island soil with the news that he had brought "the advantages and blessings of enlightened civilization from the United States of America" and the island again was a colony without self-rule. The old Spanish walls of the city were broken at last, and to the east of the plaza of Christopher Columbus there stands today a building of the YMCA where there once stood one of the four city gates. The only gate remaining is used now not to keep enemies out but to draw tourists in. Across from the *Alcaldia*—the city hall—constructed by the Spanish in 1604, is the New York Department Store, proclaiming in Spanish a sale in which "Everything Goes." Below the iron grillwork balconies of the Old San Juan Bar and Grill a sign in the window reads Real Italian Pizza. A taxicab crawls through the narrow stone streets like an insect caught in a maze, turning the high-walled corners with painstaking care. The city is quiet, and the old men who sit in the plaza seem unconcerned. Their fathers are gone and their sons are free to go.

For more than a century the sons have left the plazas and the dust-and-green towns of the interior to come to New York. Ricardo Sánchez is young, but his journey is old. The first Puerto Ricans came to New York in the early 1800s, along with other men of good hope from the underfed islands of the Caribbean who decided that "it is no good to be poor." From Cuba and Santo Domingo they came, from San Juan and Haiti and Jamaica. Some survived and others were lost, and in 1838 the men from Puerto Rico who had managed to make themselves merchants of New York City formed a Spanish Benevolent Society for those of their brothers who had failed and were hungry.

Others went west, and by 1910 there were Puerto Ricans living in thirty-nine states of the Union. Twenty years later the people of the island were in every state, though the great majority were still in New York City. The journey north from the Caribbean became a regular route for those seeking something better (and having the money to make the search), and for most of the first half of the twentieth century an average of 4,000 came from Puerto Rico to the mainland every year.

No one seemed to notice. It was not until near the end of World War II that the quiet, steady migration became the great migration—the promise of the mainland suddenly expanding with more new jobs than ever before and the word passing on from relative to relative, friend to friend, employment recruiter to unemployed. During the war there was little transportation available for Puerto Ricans who wanted to leave the island, but toward the end of it the U.S. War Manpower Commission brought workers up in army transports to help fill the booming job market. In the first year after the war, 39,900 Puerto Ricans came to the mainland, and the annual stream reached an average of roughly 50,000 in the postwar decade. As it has throughout its history, the Puerto Rican migration curve followed the business curve on the mainland, and the start of the greatest postwar recession in 1957 was reflected by a 28 percent decrease in migration from the year before. Downturns in the volume of business on the continent have always meant downturns in migration from the island, and during the worst depression years of the thirties, the flow of migrants actually reversed itself, with more returning annually to the island than came from it. But barring an extreme and prolonged depression, the total of 600,000 first- or second-generation Puerto Ricans in New York City in 1958 was expected to rise to a million by the early 1970s. And, for the first time, the great migration had begun to spread more heavily in cities and towns throughout the country. In 1950, 85 percent of the entering migrants settled in New York City, but by 1956 and 1957 the average was down to 65 percent, with others going to expanding Puerto Rican settlements in cities such as Philadelphia (New York's largest Spanish-language newspaper now carries a special column of Puerto Rican news from Philadelphia), Chicago, Cleveland, Ashtabula, Bridgeport, Milwaukee, and others farther west.

The journey from the island had become not only more promising because of the market for jobs after World War II but also much easier to make because of the airplanes that rose from San Juan and landed at Idlewild, New York City, sixteen hundred miles up the ocean, in only eight hours and for only $75 on regular airlines instead of the former price of $180. Besides the approved commercial lines that opened up regular service after the war, there were secondhand planes making unscheduled flights for $35—they could charge that price because they were paid off later by men from the states who came to Puerto Rico and charged "employment agent" fees that often consumed life savings sweated from sugarcane as payment for nonexistent jobs in New York City. Some of the victims never found out because they first became the victims of ill-equipped planes that crashed in the ocean. After several such tragedies the government outlawed the small, unscheduled airlines from making the San Juan—New York run.

But the regular, legal air travel flourished—not only giving a boost to the old migration to the mainland cities but also opening up a new migration. Cheap and fast plane travel made it possible to transport idle agricultural workers from Puerto Rico during the heavy harvesting season on the mainland in the spring, and back again to the island when the sugarcane season began in the fall. A new seasonal migration began on that basis after the war and has grown to an annual flow of about 30,000 workers (not counted in the regular migration figures of those who come and plan to stay). Contrary to popular belief, the great majority of Puerto Ricans who come to New York and other U.S. cities are not laborers but city people who have held city jobs on the island.

Ricardo Sánchez, who waited in the dark for the bus marked *Aeropuerto*, was one of the small but slowly growing number of Puerto Ricans who have left the sugarcane fields for the city. The desire to escape from the backbreaking work of the cane cutting is still not easily fulfilled, but the dream has become much more widespread since many young men saw the world in service with the U.S. Army in Korea, and returned home with higher aspirations. Frank Ruiz, the secretary-treasurer of the *Sindicato Azucarero* (Sugar Workers Union) in Puerto Rico says that it is harder now to get the young men to work in the cane fields because "the army has refined them."

Ricardo Sánchez was able to make at least a partial transition in his work before the drastic change from the island fields to the New York fabric shops. During the idle season a year before, he had found a job doing piecework in a garment shop in the small town of Vega Baja. But the work didn't last, and after another season in the fields he decided to try his luck—and his brother's help—in the *fábrica* shops of New York City.

Ricardo held for himself and his family tickets on the $52.50 night coach thrift flight to Idlewild airport. It leaves six nights a week from San Juan at eleven o'clock and arrives the next morning at Idlewild at seven. The adjective *thrift* is the only term of distinction between this flight and the other night coach flight, which costs $64, leaves a half hour later, and arrives in New York City two hours earlier. The thrift flight is not recommended—or even suggested at the ticket counters—to non-Puerto Rican travelers. English-speaking people who ask about it are told that it is better to spend the extra money and go on the eleven-thirty flight.

There were only Puerto Ricans on the *Aeropuerto* bus that Ricardo Sánchez boarded in the plaza of Christopher Columbus. They stayed together when they reached the San Juan airport, checking in baggage and then joining friends and relatives and watchers in the crowd on the observation deck. When the flight was called, it was as if a troop plane were leaving for a war, or a group of refugees being shipped of necessity out of their native country. It is that way every night around eleven o'clock at the San Juan airport—the women crying and the men embracing them; the old people staring out of wrinkled, unperceiving faces and the young engrossed with the wonder, rather than the pain of it, pressing up against the iron rail of the observation deck and squinting through the dark to watch the line of human travelers move as if drawn by a spell through the gate below and into the still, silver plane that swallows them, closing silver on silver to complete itself, and then slowly moves toward the dark and disappears.

Dan Wakefield, from *Island in the City*

THE JAPANESE

For three days they had been sailing off the southern Japanese coast in search of fish when, twenty miles from shore, they ran into a great school of mackerel and sea bream. Manjiro, fifteen and youngest of the five, saw them first.

Six buckets of nets they cast, and their nets were full when a corner of the sky grew suddenly black and a monkey-and-cock wind began to blow, first with a pulsing breath then with a fierce steadiness. Then borne on the wind came a swift, stinging rain. Denzo, head of the crew, dropped the sail of the little sampan and raised a smaller one while the other men —two of them but boys—tried to keep the boat from foundering. He had no more than raised it when the wind carried away mast and sail together. As the boat tossed, all their oars but one, much of their spare canvas, and their rudder were washed away. Death was on the other side of a thin wall of leaking planks.

At night the wind froze their wet clothes into stiff boards. Icicles formed on their sleeves and in the knots of their sashes. They ate of the cold raw fish lying in the bottom of the boat. Sleet, blown in at the neck of their loose-fitting jackets, melted and ran down the channel of their spines. For water they gnawed the icicles from their sleeves.

On the fourth day the wind still blew as hard as ever, still drove the rain in their faces. They tried to roof themselves in with canvas. Hour after hour they lay in the bottom of the boat, half-frozen, surrounded by the slimy remainder of their catch, peering out at the empty, storm-beaten sea, shuddering when a strong gust tore the canvas out of their numbed hands and drove a sheet of rain full against them. The constant plunging of the boat had numbed their minds as the wind their bodies. Misery had occupied them; no space was left for the sharp thud of fear.

On this day the wind began to be warmer, and on the next the rain seemed to lessen a little. White birds flew over the rudderless boat. At evening they looked out upon an island whose sharp cliffs dropped beachless to the sea.

At daybreak they cut their anchor, which they could not lift, and with rudder and oars made of planks headed for the cliffs. Driven by a high wave, the boat swept forward and up. As it smashed against a rock two of the men leaped out. Manjiro and the other two, borne under by the surf, were lifted on the next wave and thrown bruised but safe upon the rock.

Though the sea had delivered them up, it had delivered

them to hopeless solitude. The island was not more than two miles around, its steep slopes rising everywhere directly from the sea. For six months the five Japanese lived on albatross, seaweed, and shellfish until early in June 1841 an American whaling vessel sent in a boat looking for turtle, found them, and brought them safely off.

Thus the story of the Japanese in America begins in the logbook of a New England whaling captain who on 27 June 1841 wrote:

This day light wind from SE. Isle in sight at 1 P.M. Sent in two boats to see if there was any turtle, found five poor distressed people on the isle, took them off, could not understand anything from them more than that they was hungry. Made the latitude of the isle 30° 31′ N.

For another six months the Japanese learned the art of whaling until the ship put in at Honolulu. There four of them stayed. But Manjiro begged Captain Whitfield to let him stay aboard the *John Howland* and to go to America. The fifteen-year-old lad, christened plain John Mung, had already become popular with the crew. So he had his wish.

For three years more the voyage continued—to the Kingsmill group, to Guam, even into Japanese waters, before the holds were full of whale oil. When Captain Whitfield finally brought his ship into New Bedford harbor in 1844, he had been five years absent. This was a long voyage, even for a whaler, but New England harbors in those days were accustomed to the sight of ships returning from the other side of the world.

This time, however, Captain Whitfield had stayed too long. When he brought the *John Howland* into her berth that winter morning, the residents of New Bedford paid little attention to the Chinese-looking fellow who followed him off the ship. Crew members from Polynesia, shipwrecked men from China were not unusual sights here. No one knew that this boy of the captain's was the first Japanese to set foot in

America. Nor could they know that his arrival would, in its consequences, prove historic.

Captain Whitfield took young Manjiro across the great bridge to Fairhaven, to his home, to the wife and children he had not seen for five years.

Only his wife was not there. She had died during his absence.

Manjiro Nakahama, the first Japanese to reach the United States, came at a time when Japan had chosen a rigid policy of exclusion, when foreign ships were driven away with no sign of the courtesy that later was accounted a Japanese trait, and when Japanese who had the ill fortune to be shipwrecked were subject to prompt execution if they returned home. No American, no European—except for a few Dutch traders who were virtually prisoners on a small island in Nagasaki harbor —had been allowed to live in Japan since the rigid exclusion policy had been put in force about 1640.

Manjiro came to America voluntarily, knowing that he must always remain cut off from his native land or, returning, risk death. His plea to Capain Whitfield that he be brought to America is symbolic of a later wave of Japanese arrivals that came to be a subject of humor in America—the Japanese schoolboy. For Manjiro wanted to see and learn. The traits of eager curiosity and avid learning were apparently already present in the Japan of a hundred years ago.

Everything in Fairhaven was new and strange to Manjiro —the prim white houses seeming angular and cold to one familiar with curving roof lines where thatch and unpainted wood blended into the landscape; the sharp clank of church bells so unlike the mellow bronze temple bell; the stiffness of dress so different from the flowing kimono. Yet he fitted into the town's life, probably as a result of that nervous eagerness to harmonize with his surroundings that is a familiar trait to those who know the Japanese—a trait that has been transmitted to Americans of Japanese ancestry.

Whatever John Mung thought of New England culture,

he kept his eyes open during the years he spent in Fairhaven. Captain Whitfield, marrying again, took the boy into his own home and treated him as a son. John not only went to school, but like the son of any practical Yankee he learned a trade— that of cooper. In later years schoolmates remembered him as an industrious and scholarly fellow with a flair for mathematics and navigation. That their memories are correct is borne out by the fact that in 1857 Manjiro completed his translation of Bowditch into Japanese. They also remember his deep yearning to return and see his mother.

If Manjiro wanted to see his mother so badly, why had he come to America? The answer has its roots in some basic traits of Japanese temperament—traits that, contrary to popular opinion, are far from inscrutable.

Climate and geography have had a good deal to do with molding the Japanese. Earthquakes, typhoons, and other natural disasters have given them a stoic and fatalistic turn of mind. Isolation for centuries has made them both stubbornly suspicious of foreigners yet at the same time markedly curious about the foreign and unfamiliar, sensitive to any change in environment, and often eager to acquire the new for their own. Isolation also fostered a naïve belief in their own invincibility, their own explanations of the physical world, and their central position in it. Because they lived close together, the Japanese developed conformity and repression of the individual to an extreme. The long feudal period with its firm bonds between lord and vassal encouraged an absolute and unquestioning obedience to higher authority whether in the family or the nation. Individual enterprise and opinion are at a discount: to be submerged in the group is to be safe. Yet the individual is always responsible for upholding the family honor. A failure on his part is also a family, perhaps even a national, disgrace. Fear of failure spurs many a Japanese to effort beyond his strength and sometimes to suicide. It also prevents the timid from undertaking anything that does not promise sure success.

Because the nation's resources never provided quite enough to keep everyone alive, self-denial became one of the cardinal virtues. Industriousness, hard work, a meager subsistence are taken for granted and even wealthy men live simple lives. Thus almost every influence on the Japanese is repressive rather than expansive. The one truly happy situation a Japanese remembers is that of his preschool childhood when his indulgent mother permitted him to nurse when he chose, carried him on her back, and warmed him in her bed. The impossible dream of a return to such a state lies deep in Japanese character; mother is the symbol for a lost world, for happiness too complete to last.

In Fairhaven, Massachusetts, Manjiro showed those Japanese traits that a foreign environment would be most likely to bring out—industry, a quick and sensitive adaptability, an eagerness to learn. Even the casual memory of his schoolmates caught that duality of character in Manjiro—the steady industry in assimilating a new environment and the thought of his mother.

Manjiro saw the best of America. The kindness of a whaling captain rescued him from ultimate starvation or madness on an uninhabited island. In Fairhaven he lived as the adopted son of a man respected in the community. He must have come to know the town well; its flamboyant individualists must have been a source of amazement to this boy from a small fishing village.

And when he did return to Japan—by way of the California gold rush, Honolulu, and a whale boat launched from an American ship off the shores of the Loo Choos (Okinawa)— this knowledge served him and his country well. The Japanese government kept him prisoner for thirty months before deciding that he might live, and when he was finally permitted to return to his mother in January 1853 it was only for three days. The government had need of him in Yedo (now Tokyo) where the pressure of Western civilization had become too strong to resist. Within a few months his knowledge of English was turned to good account when in July Commodore

Perry steamed into the bay of Yedo and Japan's long exclusion was forcibly brought to an end. As interpreter between Perry and the officials of the shogun, Manjiro played an important part. His understanding of American ways, his memory of the kindness shown him by Captain Whitfield and the people of Fairhaven gained on this occasion historic importance.

Although Manjiro returned to America in 1860 as a government official, he did not see Captain Whitfield until 1871 when he came again, this time as member of a commission on its way to Europe to study military science during the Franco-Prussian War. Then for a day he revisited the town that had been his home thirty years before.

After his return to Japan, he became a university professor. By the time of his death in 1898, thousands of his countrymen had emigrated to Hawaii and were beginning to come to the mainland in increasing numbers.

Japan's entrance into the modern world would have happened without Manjiro Nakahama; historical process does not stand still for want of individuals. Yet Manjiro's presence at the critical moment was at the very least a lubricant without which Japan might not have been so successfully launched.

It would be stretching things to call Manjiro the first Japanese American. But with him the story really begins. He was probably the first Japanese to learn English, certainly the first to reach the United States and to live and study here. His thirst for American learning found echo in many a Japanese student of later days, and his four months in the gold mines ("Average eight dollars per day beside expenses," he wrote the captain) are in a way a realization of the dream many a Japanese had in later years—to make a modest fortune in America and return to Japan.

Other Japanese had been picked up by American ships and had come ashore at Honolulu before Manjiro's day. Eight survivors out of twenty-two shipwrecked men were brought to Hawaii in 1806, the other fourteen having been washed overboard or killed and eaten after drawing lots. Although Captain Amasa Delano, an ancestor of Franklin Roosevelt,[1] returned the remaining eight to Canton, only one finally reached Japan. But these and all the other shipwrecks scarcely belong in the main stream of the story. Manjiro, by simple force of character and achievement, does.

Bradford Smith, from *Americans from Japan*

THE MEXICANS

Juan Pérez is, of course, an abstraction; no one exactly like him exists, but many people very similar to him do. His story is a composite of life histories and reminiscences of those who spent their youth in Mexico and their adult lives in the United States. No attempt has been made to present his life in daily detail; while it could be done, it would make a book in itself, and one whose perusal would be of more interest to the sociologist or anthropologist than to the general reader. This brief story only tries to suggest how he was conditioned in childhood, the ideals and sanctions of the society that surrounded him, the techniques he was taught for launching himself in adult life. These things constituted his cultural heritage, the extra baggage that he brought with him to the United States.

Juan Pérez was born in Celaya in 1894, in a barrio called

[1] President Roosevelt's grandfather, Warren Delano, was part owner of the ship that brought Manjiro to America. To Manjiro's son Franklin Roosevelt once wrote: "Your father lived, as I remember it, at the house of Mr. Tripp, which was directly across the street from my grandfather's house, and when I was a boy, I well remember my grandfather telling me all about the little Japanese boy who went to school in Fairhaven and who went to church from time to time with the Delano family. I myself used to visit Fairhaven and my mother's family still owns the old house."

Los Conejos. There had his father been born, and his mother too. The family home was a three-room adobe, with a flat tile roof, dirt floors, and slits in the adobe work for windows. It had a small yard, carefully walled off from the street, ornamented with flowering plants set in old jars and dishes and swept daily. In back were the storehouses, the hen houses, and when the family was prosperous, a pig in the stockade. The barrio had fifty or sixty such houses, two *tienditas*,[2] and a small chapel. Almost all the families in the barrio had lived there for a generation or two; some of them were laborers at haciendas five to ten miles outside Celaya, many owned and worked tiny tracts outside the town, others were woodcutters or muleteers. A few were artisans. It was a poor district, but it had its own life, ambitions, and standards.

Juan was his mother's fourth child; she was assisted as usual by neighbors, one of whom had a reputation as a *partera*, or midwife. She was delighted with another baby—children were welcomed and loved in the barrio—but she was glad to be free of some of the troublesome restrictions of pregnancy. For nine months she had not been able to touch or dress an open cut or to handle fresh meat, for the touch of a pregnant woman on blood was supposed to be poisonous. She had to avoid standing pools of water, particularly at night, because of the evil spirits lurking in them, and she had worried over her cravings for certain foods that were unobtainable, but whose lack might cause a miscarriage. One ordeal remained, *la dieta*,[3] the forty days following parturition during which women with any pretense to status remained strictly within their own homes. And she had to be careful not to eat onions or citrus fruit while she was nursing Juan, although she would begin early to supplement his diet with bits of tortilla, *atoles*,[4] and even fruit.

[2] *Tienditas:* very small grocery stores.
[3] *La dieta:* literally, the diet, but referring to the length of time the newly delivered woman remains within doors, whether or not her diet is restricted.
[4] *Atoles:* gruel.

The Sunday following the fortieth day of Juan's life was an important one. His mother took him to Mass—this was *la presentación*.[5] He had received a lay baptism shortly after birth, but now he had the official—and expensive—church ceremony. His godparents, who had been selected with great care, vowed to give him material as well as spiritual care. They were important, these godparents. If his father and mother died, they would rear him; in many other crises of life, they would be at hand with gifts, advice, and aid. If they failed to do so, they would lose face with the entire barrio, for no obligation was taken more seriously. Juan would always have a second set of parents, an extra complement of relatives; no child stood alone in his society. He was given the name of the saint of that day, John, although his family had already begun calling him *El Rincón*,[6] because of his shy way of burrowing into his mother's shoulder. That afternoon, half the barrio celebrated the christening with a party at the Pérez home. This expenditure, added to the baptismal fee, was to put a crimp in the Pérez finances for some time, but one had to do it if one possibly could. Only *cualquieras*[7] evaded these obligations.

Before Juan could speak or scarcely understand, he was aware that there was another galaxy of persons, almost like relatives, who stood ready to aid him. He would hear his father, gesturing toward the ceiling, refer to *El Patron Arriba* as though the deity hovered somewhere immediately above the roof tile. He was aware of his mother's close, personal relationship with the Virgin; she conversed with her, while doing household tasks, almost as if she had been another woman sitting by the hearth. There was his own saint, and those of his brothers and sisters, and those of the barrio, the city, and the region. They were all human, intimately known,

[5] *La presentación:* the presentation, to the church and to the public, of an infant.
[6] *El Rincón:* the corner, literally; it is a common nickname for a shy child, one who hides in a corner.
[7] *Cualquieras:* persons of no account.

even to be seen occasionally by those of sufficient faith. They understood everything, fears, sins, disappointments, meannesses, hopes, and triumphs, and one could talk things over with them—far more easily than with the priests, with their perpetual demands for money. In fact, it was often more comfortable to divorce them in one's mind from their representative on earth; deep religious feeling was not incompatible with considerable antagonism toward the church. Many a time, Juan heard his father say, angrily, "All priests are wolves!" Juan was not to lose this sense of having heavenly intimates, supernatural friends who were always at hand, until after he came to the United States. It may be that the loss was great, but he does not admit it now. Those were things of yesterday.

Juan had colic throughout the first two years of his life. Neither his mother's milk nor the adult tidbits, including green fruit, with which it was supplemented, seemed to agree with him. The *curandera* [8] was constantly in consultation with his mother. First they thought it might be *el daño*, a sickness caused by a glance from someone who had an evil eye; it might be the strange woman in the market who had smiled at the baby in his mother's arms. His mother broke an egg on a plate and left it overnight. In the morning, the white and the yolk had separated—yes, that meant it had been the woman. Someone found out where she lived, someone else managed to secure a cloth that she had used but had not washed. Little Juan was rubbed with it, while the confiteor was recited over him, and by morning he could hold food on his stomach again! But later his complaint was thought to be *el empacho*, [9] just plain overstuffing himself. For this the *curandera's* remedies were different—we would say more rational. She gave him a herbal cathartic and massaged his small stomach with a warm herbal effusion. These herbal remedies seemed to be effective, too, when he had sore eyes, when he had a rash, and when his foot was infected from a stone bruise. They did not always work,

[8] *Curandera:* a woman skilled in the folk remedies for disease.
[9] *El empacho:* the surfeit, apparently indigestion.

however; three out of Mrs. Pérez's nine children died in infancy, but Juan, by the time he was five, was as healthy and lively as the goats he helped to herd.

Juan's father had title to about two hectares of land (about four and a half acres) outside Celaya; his uncles had some adjoining pieces. With agricultural methods hardly improved since the conquest, they wrested a subsistence crop of corn, beans, peppers, squash, and other vegetables from the land. By pasturing a few goats, they had milk for cheese and an occasional kid to barbecue. But it was always necessary to supplement the products of the two hectares with some cash money. Juan's father was proud of the fact that he "never worked for anybody, just for myself," meaning that he was not in peonage to a mine or hacienda owner, but he had some close calls. He hired out as muleteer on the road to Irapuato one dry season, and cut wood in the mountains during another. One year he made a lucky sale of surplus chilies, another he got several bags of beans for helping a neighbor build a house. He would have liked to accumulate sufficient capital to work as an *arriero* or even a *viajero* part of the time, but it never seemed to come his way.

Juan cannot remember when he could not hear the sound of his mother's *metate*, or grinding stone. There was a gristmill in Celaya, but it was too expensive; besides, women of his mother's class took pride in being able to grind their own corn clean and fine. Between times, she was at the mortar and pestle, grinding chilie, or at the public washing fountain, rubbing clothing clean on the stones. In her spare time, her strong, quick hands would turn in the patting circular motion necessary to produce a thin, perfectly round, tortilla. Before fiestas or celebrations, the sounds of grinding, patting, and chopping rose to a crescendo in Juan's barrio; all the good festival recipes, like those for *moles*,[10] or tamales, required hours of reducing ingredients to a paste.

---

[10] *Mole:* a highly spiced sauce, served with pieces of boiled meat.

Juan's mother sewed, too. All the men's work clothes, *cal-zones*,[11] *camisas*,[12] and *blusas*,[13] were made at home from white cotton yardage bought in the market, as were Mrs. Pérez's full, swinging skirts (*enaguas*) and blouses. Juan's father, who had worked for a shoemaker in his youth, could do a creditable job making and repairing leather sandals. Of course, no one wore them much, except in very cold weather, for work on rough ground, or for travel to a distance.

From the time Juan was two until he was five, he was in the care of his older sister, for by this time his mother had another baby to nurse. It was from this sister that he first heard the folklore of his region. There was the woman in his barrio who was supposed to be a *bruja* (witch), able to change herself to an animal at will; she had bathed in a secret lake in a mountain cave and then rolled in an anthill to gain this power. His sister pointed out the curiously shaped hill, which looked like a sitting figure. That, she said, was all that was left of a bad little boy who refused to stand when his elders spoke to him! Juan soon learned that implicit obedience and instant respect to his elders was part of his role in life; he learned it so early that he cannot remember how he was taught. True, there were occasional stinging slaps and sharp words—and he knew that serious misbehavior could bring a severe beating— but he had no sense of being under heavy-handed authority. For the most part, he was loved, played with, and petted. Why did he obey? "I never thought of doing otherwise," he said. "No child did." He is puzzled and saddened today because his own children do not give him the same unquestioning respect and cooperation.

He was expected to make himself useful early. There were tasks, such as husking nuts and peeling seedpods, which baby hands could do, and errands that small feet could run. When

[11] *Calzones:* loose, white cotton trousers.
[12] *Camisas:* shirts.
[13] *Blusas:* blouses, buttonless, worn with the lower ends tied together at the front.

he was five, he was taken into the men's world for his apprenticeship in life. After all, it was not uncommon in his barrio for boys to marry at fourteen or fifteen, and ten years was none too long a time in which to learn the techniques of a householder. He helped his cousin herd goats; he could care for stock by the time he was eight; and when he was ten, he put in long days pushing seed corn into the ground with a pointed stick. During the dry season, he spent interminable, wriggling hours learning to recite his *doctrinas*, his catechism, by rote, so that he could be properly confirmed. One year, he and his cousin even went for a few hours a week to the house of a woman who could read and write; they learned the alphabet, the general shape and form of about twenty-five simple words, and how to scrawl Pedro and Juan, their names, laboriously. This was the only schooling he ever had.

Juan loved his mother devotedly—she lives in his home in Descanso today, and he addresses her as *madrecita* [14] in the tone of a small boy; he was close to the sister who had been his foster-mother, and he admired the fat baby Concha, but he soon learned that men's and women's worlds lay far apart. Men were leaders, women followers, and one's own women must be protected from other men. It was his job to see that his sisters never left the yard without an escort; he trotted dutifully beside them on the streets or in the fields, conscious that they were never to be left alone a moment. Boys and girls, after babyhood, did not play much together, although they encountered one another thousands of times in the course of work or barrio celebrations. When boys began hanging around the gate, attracted by his pretty sister Blanca, it was Juan's job to see that they got no farther. Finally, after much family consultation, the most promising of them, Socorro Vargas, was permitted to come to the door or window and talk to Blanca, under the supervision of the entire household; he did not cross the threshold, however, until he came with an older friend to

---

[14] *Madrecita:* a little mother, an affectionate diminutive.

ask for Blanca's hand in marriage. As it turned out, Blanca and Socorro lived together for some time without a church marriage, in fact, until after their second child was born. There had been some bad years; money was scarce and a priest's fees high. No one thought the less of them for this; there were many such unions, referred to in later years as *casamientos del tiempo de Porfirio*.[15] The important thing was that community custom and sanctions had been satisfied. Everyone knew that Blanca had conducted her courtship properly and that she had been virgin at marriage—the old women who made these things their business had examined the nuptial sheets and announced the happy fact to the barrio.

If girls were to be protected, young men were to have their experience as soon as possible. Very often, their fathers would supervise the arrangements. One day, he saw his uncle stop to greet a widow of the barrio on the street; as Juan passed by, he heard the uncle say, "It's all right. It's time." Soon thereafter, Juan was aware, his cousin had his first sexual experience. There were always a few women in each barrio who, while outwardly respectable and even devout, were known to be open to advances—deserted wives, widows, or girls without adequate protection. They were not outcasts; they were tolerated, even by other women, whose comment was likely to be a shrug and a caustic, *"En puerta abierta hasta un ángel peca."* [16] Juan had his own experiences, not unlike his cousin's: they apparently moved him neither toward guilt nor toward sentiment. At fourteen, he had witnessed death, birth, and probably procreation, in a three-room house where numerous persons of assorted ages and sexes slept on *petates* [17] on the floor. His parents were not careless—they had given him training in

[15] *Casamiento del tiempo de Porfirio:* marriage in the time of Porfirio Diaz, when there was no legal substitute for the comparatively expensive church marriage.
[16] *"En puerta abierta hasta un ángel peca":* "If the door is open, even an angel sins."
[17] *Petates:* plaited mats, used as beds.

modesty of speech and action—but the accidents of crowded living made it inevitable that he should see more than they intended.

By the time Juan was seventeen, he was ready to marry. In spite of the confusion and want the civil war had brought, the Pérez family was not doing badly. They had not starved and they still had their land. True, Juan's hotheaded older brother had joined the rebel forces and been killed; and Blanca's husband, always eager for money, had gone to work in a mine, where he had been crippled in an accident. But Juan felt that he was equal to these family problems; he could do every sort of man's work, from shoeing mules to harvesting crops; he had even spent two seasons with his uncle, the *arriero*, on the road, so he knew the world. His help was badly needed on the family plots; with his share from them, plus what he could earn by outside work during the dry season, he could maintain a family of his own. He asked his uncle to act as *señor grande* [18] for him with the family of Lola Ramos.

His family had not approved of his interest in Lola. Her father was one of those who "worked for someone else," as a laborer on a hacienda about five miles from town, although he maintained his family in a poor house in the barrio. That, however, was not so important as the fact that Lola's mother had once been involved in a scandal. Even Juan's mother had to admit, however, that Lola seemed to be virtuous and hardworking; Juan assured them that Lola had been properly careful during his courtship, that she had never seen him alone, and that she had demurred the customary five or six times before accepting his proposal.

That evening, the uncle and Juan dressed up and went to the Ramos house. Juan waited outside, but he knew what was happening in the house. Everyone but Lola's father would leave the room immediately. The uncle would then say, "I come on a matter of business." The father would pretend he

[18] *señor grande:* an important man, in this case applied to an older friend or relative of the suitor.

did not know what the business was; the uncle would explain. If the father consented, he would call in the mother and she would set the date. Everything went well, except that Lola's family committed one breach of etiquette; they set the date too soon, just a month ahead. Juan's mother said that anyone could see the Ramos family was anxious to marry off its girls; a family mindful of the proprieties would have set a date six months ahead, no matter how pleased they were with the match.

Like Blanca and Socorro, Lola and Juan went to live together without benefit of a church ceremony. There had not been a priest in Celaya for several months now; no one knew when he would return. And if he had, the combined families could not have scraped together money for the fee; the burial of Juan's grandmother and the baptism of Blanca's child a year ago had exhausted their funds. This did not mean that the new home did not have community sanction. The Ramos family gave a fiesta, poor enough, but sufficient in its way. All the godparents and relatives brought gifts of household goods; Juan gave his bride some simple *donas;* [19] the parents-in-law pledged one another as *consuegros,* [20] promising mutual friendship and aid in making the new household a success. That night, Juan took Lola to the abandoned house, which he had repaired, of his dead brother.

That season was the hardest the barrio of Los Conejos had ever known. There was too much rain, and half of the seed corn spoiled in the ground. Juan's uncle, the *arriero,* was robbed and half killed by drunken soldiers. Another band of soldiers drove off the goats, every one of them, and slaughtered them for meat. The Pérez family was saved by the fact that Juan had gone into business with a *viajero;* they had made some money buying corn in another district and reselling it in

[19] *Donas:* gifts which the groom gives to the bride; in classes somewhat higher than Juan Pérez's, they include her trousseau.
[20] *Consuegros:* parents-in-law with respect to the parent of his son or daughter-in-law.

Celaya, but the trips were dangerous. Juan felt himself losing heart in spite of his comparative success. He thought of his father's life, so hard, so subject to accident and whims of fate —why, a man could work like a burro and then see it all swept away someday. His cousin, who was now working for a railroad in Texas, earned as much as two dollars a day, people said. The man he had talked to in Irapuato said you could get more, if you were hardworking. Juan was sure he was hardworking. Quite suddenly, without consulting anyone, he sold one or two blankets and some blacksmith tools. That night, he walked slowly with Lola, who was pregnant, over to his mother's house; when they were inside, he made his announcement: *"Me voy lejos—a los Estados Unidos."* [21] When the weeping and astonishment had subsided, he outlined the arrangements he had made. Lola would stay with his mother until after the baby was born; by that time, he would have money to send for her and, perhaps, for any of the others who wanted to come. The younger brother, now fifteen, could take his place on the family plots; with the help of the now retired *arriero*, there would be enough men. He could get a place on a mule team going to Irapuato; from there he would take the train.

When they were returning from his mother's, Lola wept again. Was it right, she asked, that a man should just leave when he wanted to? "Yes," Juan said firmly. She knew as well as he did that it was the man who was the head of the house, who made the decisions and took the risks. On matters of the heart, those connected with the welfare of children or relatives, husband and wife consulted together; but on matters of business, the husband stood alone.

Two weeks later, when Juan, just eighteen, climbed over the little hill at El Paso, heard the shouts of the labor coyotes, and felt the impact of an alien and indifferent world strike him, he wondered whether he had decided right. Never in his life

---

[21] *"Me voy lejos—a los Estados Unidos"*: "I'm going far off—to the United States."

had he been so alone or felt so helpless, but it was too late to turn back. He shrugged and quoted a *refrán* [22] to the man nearest him. "When one is blind in the house of a money changer, who does the counting?" "*Aie!*" said his neighbor, who appreciated an apt turn of speech, "this is like being in the house of the soapmaker. He who does not fall, slips."

Ruth D. Tuck, from *Not With the Fist*

[22] *Refrán:* a saw or proverb.

PART TWO

Between Two Worlds

*In the beginning, God gave to every people
a cup, a cup of clay, and from this cup
they drank their life. . . . Our cup is broken now.
It has passed away.*

Quoted by Ruth Benedict

THE AMERICAN
NATIONALITY

(neither in justice, nor in charity . . .)

There is, say what you will, such a thing as American nationality . . . Whether it be for good or for evil, the American nationality will be determined by the Anglo-American portion of our population. The speculations of some German writers that it must ultimately become German, and of some Irish editors that it must ultimately become Celtic are worthy of no attention. No nationality here can stand a moment before the Anglo-American. It is the all-absorbing power, and cannot be absorbed or essentially modified by any other. This, quarrel with it as you will, is a "fixed fact." . . .

This is to be considered as settled, and assumed as their starting point by all immigrants from foreign countries. They should understand in the outset, if they would avoid unpleasant collision, that they must lose their own nationality and become assimilated in general character to the Anglo-American race . . . It is not attachment to American soil, or sympathy with the American nationality, spirit, genius, or institutions, that brings the great mass of foreigners to our shores. No doubt we derive great advantages from them, but the motive that brings them is not advantage to us or service to our country. They come here solely from motives of personal advantage to themselves; to gain a living, to acquire wealth, or to enjoy freedom denied them in their own country, or believed to be more easily obtained or better secured here than elsewhere. The country, therefore, does not and cannot feel that it is bound either in justice or in charity to yield up its nationality to them, or to suffer the stream of its national life to be diverted from its original course to accommodate their manners, tastes, or prejudices.

Orestes Brownson, from *A Few Words*
on Native Americanism, 1854

THE UNWRITTEN LAW

As Juan Pérez started up the back streets of El Paso, in company with the gang of railroad workers with whom he had signed, the forces of his new environment began to operate. He was unaware of them, except that he felt uneasy and helpless, certain that the old traditions and habits would be of little aid here, but ignorant of what lay before him and what he could do about it. It is interesting to speculate on how the absorption of our immigrant groups might have been different, had they been officially oriented into the ways of life in the United States. What if those who could read had been handed little booklets, printed in their own languages, similar to those used by American armed forces abroad—"How to Act in the United States" or "The Customs and Habits of the North Americans," or "The Immigrant Handbook"? What if those who could not read had been held in immigration centers while they received careful instruction on the laws, currency, social habits, taboos, and idiosyncrasies of the society in which they were to make their home, along with enough language instruction to give them command of useful, simple phrases? What if there had existed some official agency called, perhaps, the Commission for Immigrant Affairs, to which they could go for advice, protection, and guidance?

Even with these safeguards, transition would have been painful enough, but it might not have been so flagrantly wasteful of human emotions and talents. The result might have been a more harmonious whole than exists today. Needless to say, Juan Pérez received no such attention . . . America was a place where they were darned lucky to be, ran the popular thought, and if they couldn't learn to act like other folks, it just proved they were dumb. With the whole previous pattern of his life shattered by the act of crossing the border, Juan Pérez set about piecing together bits of the new. In the bunkhouse at night, he and his companions shared scraps and tags of information, many of them incorrect, many of them set in the wrong context, but a few, by sheer luck, right. It was a great deal like working a jigsaw puzzle when you don't know what the picture is supposed to be, and you are sure that several of the important pieces are missing. It cannot be said of Juan Pérez that, in his late forties, after twenty-eight years of living here, he has ever succeeded in getting the whole puzzle together. But in certain sections of it he has done well.

There was one thing that impressed Juan and his compadres as they talked in bunkhouses, around picking fires, or in the cheap cafés of El Paso's poor districts. The life they had led before was valueless to them here. No American was interested in it; no one considered it anything but low or savage or funny; manifestations of another culture were likely to be met with reactions ranging from aversion to ridicule to incarceration. Juan had not enjoyed high status in his own country; he had known both exploitation and injustice; but he had been able to feel a certain sureness in his way of life. The little pattern of Los Conejos was part of the big pattern of Mexico; it had its place, its validity, and its worth. But in the United States it had no worth; he began to feel powerful pressures on him to make him into something he was not prepared to be, a person he hardly understood—the man who was "just like everybody else." He could refuse, he could hang back, or he could fail. The penalties would not be obvious. He would not be sent to prison or deprived openly of his few possessions. He would just be pushed into a half world, a place reserved for the foreigner and the half-assimilated, where advantage, opportunity, and recognition were sharply limited. He would be hung between his old world and the new, with no place except among other dwellers in the half world.

Juan Pérez had lived under a dictatorship; he was familiar with force and coercion. If Porfirio Díaz had decided that the barrio of Los Conejos was to contribute 50 percent of its income to the building of a new Palacio Municipal or that its adult males should go off to forced labor in the tropics, his *rurales* probably could have accomplished both objects very summarily. Four hundred years ago, the Spaniards had checked a civilization in mid-career and forcibly imposed European institutions upon it. Folk memories of that event are implicit in the way Juan Pérez draws back his lips when he says "*Gachupin!*" [23] Conformity induced by violence was a historical fact in his country, but the United States was different. It was the land of the free—even the residents of Los Conejos knew that. Why, then, did he feel under constraint and compulsion—under disapproval?

There are no signs in Descanso [24] that say The State Has a Penalty for Speaking Broken English or By Decree, Preferential Hiring Will Be Given to Native Sons, or By Civic Ordinance, All Persons of Mexican Descent, with Certain Exceptions, Will Be Housed West of the Railroad Tracks. Descanso's best instincts would be outraged by such tactics. Committees of protest would be formed. The law would be evaded in a thousand ingenious ways. The person of Mexican descent would find himself the focal point of warm and agitated sympathy. There would be some angry talk about trying to regiment people. What if a law read, "All persons of Mexican origin, after five years' residence in the United States, shall cease to display, in action or manner, recognizable signs of their former culture, under penalty of forfeiting access to equal employment opportunity, use of public recreation, service in restaurants or hotels, and rental or purchase of property in

[23] *Gachupin:* a spur-wearer; a Spaniard.
[24] *Descanso:* an imaginary name representing a typical California town.

prescribed areas"? A tornado of protest would engulf the unfortunate administration that had engineered such a law; cries of "bureaucracy" and "dictatorship" would rend the air. It would be said—with justice—that every phrase of the offending legislation was an insult to the spirit and letter of our Constitution.

But Descanso, having accomplished practically the same ends by indirection, considers its methods, not regimentation, but "common sense." Its practices toward its Mexican group actually constitute a large unwritten body of law. This law, in effect, says, "Those of different culture and/or race, particularly if they lack economic power, are to be treated by standards inferior to those prevailing for residents of the United States at large." In carrying out the unwritten law, Descanso found it necessary to abridge a constitutional amendment, certain sections of the civil code of the state, as well as a civic ordinance or two of its own. The unwritten law, or any intimations of it, never stood a chance of getting on a statute book. Public opinion would not have stood for seeing it in black and white, for Descanso's assertion that it wants to be fair is not an idle one. If the cards had been laid on the table, in the form of crystallization of practice into law, Descanso would have been sickened by the sight of the marked deck it was dealing. This was one folkway it could not have stood seeing embodied in a stateway. If, however, Descanso could claim that the unwritten law did not exist, or if it could rationalize its practices on the ground that the group concerned was low or different or inferior, a bad conscience was thereby eased. Juan Pérez, however, felt the impact of the unwritten law every day of his life; the price of not being "just like everybody else" was underprivilege, often inequality before the existing law. That is why he did not feel as free as he had expected to, north of the border; he was puzzled by the presence of a force he could not understand, one not so simply explained as Don Porfirio and the *rurales*. In a thousand ways, at countless points, this force determined the nature and quality of his assimilation into American life. Combined with the cultural luggage he had brought with him, it produced the results that can be observed in Descanso's *colonia* today.

Ruth D. Tuck, from *Not With the Fist*

The march of the white man across the continent has been the flowing of a stream. As the stream flowed, it overwhelmed the life that stood in its way. All life opposing was swept within its general current. But also, the varied life that had made up the stream, had given to it its force, soon lost its variance and was merged.

Waldo Frank, from *Our America*

THIS DECREE OF GOD

It is a great problem in statesmanship wisely to control the mingling of races into one nationality. The dominant race must regulate the incoming class. Such is political destiny, and history proves it. It is the only salvation of both. It is the compact of the incoming race. Legislation must cooperate with time and circumstance in working out this decree of God, this axiom of political philosophy, this theory of nationality.

To dispel from popular use every foreign language—so great a preserver of unassimilating elements of character—to print all public documents in the English tongue alone, to ordain that all schools aided by the state shall use the same language, to cultivate a living and energetic nationality, to develop a high and vital patriotism, to Americanize America . . . to nationalize before we naturalize . . . all these constitute a work transcending the ordinary platform of party . . .

The alien-born who has lived among foreign customs and institutions, however honest and well disposed, cannot be competent to enter into the spirit and comprehend the genius of our institutions like one born and educated amid them.

. . . let him [the alien] freely avail himself of all the blessings his industry and our laws can give him; but we must insist that we ourselves shall continue to administer those laws untrammeled, according to our own judgment and the example of our fathers . . .

Henry J. Gardner, from an address
to the Massachusetts legislature, 1855

HOW TO BECOME
AN AMERICAN

A Puerto Rican friend who came up in the twenties as a small boy recently gave me his views on this, and they were not tender.

"How do you become an American?" he asked. "Why, you give up your background and language. You are changing from one culture to another, and the price you pay is to become colorless."

He told me that he had been raised in his early years on a Long Island farm, by an Anglo-Saxon Protestant family with whom his father had left him because he—the father—had had no home of his own then. Later he had remarried, though, and had brought my friend, still a small boy, to live in a cold-water flat in East Harlem.

"I'll never forget the first time I stood on the stoop there," my friend told me. "I knew only two words of Spanish when I crossed the East River, and I was much more of an American culturally than the immigrant boys around me in the street. I stood there and watched the young men and teen-agers playing. Some were playing stickball and some were throwing dice —things I had never seen and didn't understand. Later I saw boys stealing potatoes from the horse-drawn wagons that went by. They would put them in the cans and cook them over fires in empty lots—making mickeys, they called it. I learned to make them too, and they were very nourishing.

"I learned fast in those days. I remember a freckle-faced boy coming up to me and saying, 'Hey you, what are you?' 'I'm an American,' I said. 'Yeh, yeh, I know that,' he answered, 'but what *are* you?' Finally, it came out that I was a Puerto Rican. 'Oh, so you're a spik?' he said, and then we had to fight. Everybody was spiks and wops and micks and kikes in those days. A kid would have this pounded into him, and he would try to hide his nationality and be like everyone else. An Italian kid would be ridiculed as a spaghetti-bender, and he would get ashamed and turn away from his parents."

Today it was the same with the Puerto Rican children, my friend went on. "In school the teacher will say, 'Don't speak Spanish.' She really means 'Speak more English,' but she puts it in the negative way and the kids feel ashamed. Or a nutritionist will say, 'Tell your mother not to give you rice and beans.' She really means, 'Tell her to give you other things too,' but the way it is put sounds like criticism, and the kids get the idea their parents are in the wrong. And then they keep hearing all the city's ills blamed on the parents—you know how the talk against Puerto Ricans goes here. So of course they reject them. Or else they retreat into their own group."

My friend warned against trying to assimilate the Puerto Ricans too quickly in New York. "If you say, 'Don't read a Spanish paper,' they won't read any paper," he said. "And if you say, 'Don't join a Spanish-speaking group,' they won't join any group. So it is better to get them adjusted within the Puerto Rican community, and not try to make them leave it entirely."

Christopher Rand, from *The Puerto Ricans*

LEARNING
NOT TO SPEAK

In the bundle of issues that is called "the Mexican problem" none has occasioned more discussion and controversy than the language issue in the schools. Both the history and latter day ramifications of this issue are most complex. Prior to 1846 the borderlands were without schools, public or private; illiteracy was the rule, literacy the exception. The first school systems were dominated, in administration and personnel, by Anglo-Americans who knew little or no Spanish. While official concessions were made to Spanish speech in New Mexico, school officials in the Southwest have always insisted upon English as the language of instruction. They still invest their position, on this issue, with an emotional halo of moral and patriotic self-righteousness. To a generation of American teachers trained in the normal schools of the period from 1890 to 1910, it seemed both heretical and disloyal, despite the guarantees of the Treaty of Guadalupe Hidalgo, to tolerate any form of bilingualism. In some areas, the issue has even been colored by religious prejudices of one kind or another. According to Dr. Ortega, Anglo teachers have actually changed the names of Spanish students on the first day of school, to some English equivalent by way of emphasizing the "terrible handicap" that Spanish speech is supposed to be. In other cases, Hispano teachers in rural schools made up of Spanish-speaking children have used Spanish surreptitiously for fear of being called on the carpet by some irate Anglo administrator.

The natural consequence of this official attitude has been to foster a generation illiterate in both languages, for the teaching of Spanish has been as systematically neglected as instruction in English has been systematically stressed. Spanish-speaking children often come to the schools without a word of English and without the environmental experience upon which school life is based. In many cases, they are not even familiar with the concepts for which they are supposed to learn English names. The use of standard curricula, books, and instruction materials in such schools has been ludicrously inept.

Once Anglo-American teachers had "retarded" Spanish-speaking students, they sought to rationalize their incompetence as teachers by insisting on segregated schools that only aggravated the problem. Notoriously bad linguists, Anglo-American teachers have been known to show an unreasoning irritation over the mere sound of a Spanish word or phrase spoken in their presence. This irritation is often reflected in a hostile attitude toward Spanish-speaking students. Over a period of many years, I have heard Anglo-American teachers in the Southwest complain bitterly about the "stubbornness" of Mexican-American youngsters who just *will* persist in speaking Spanish on the playgrounds and so forth.

Carey McWilliams, from *North from Mexico*

FROM
"AMERICAN LETTER"

America is alone: many together
Many of one mouth, of one breath,
Dressed as one—and none brothers among them:
Only the taught speech and the aped tongue.
America is alone and the gulls calling.

Archibald MacLeish,
from *Collected Poems, 1917–1952*

LOVE-SONG, 1907

In the present state of transition from the old life to the new, Indian children often are educated by the government at a distant boarding school, where they must remain for five years without returning home. Not infrequently the pupil stays in school for a longer period than the five years, and on going home finds the life of his people completely strange to him. It is not at all uncommon for the Indian child to have forgotten his own language during the school period, and so, on his return, to be unable to speak with his parents. The going away to boarding school, with its parting from parents and friends, is a distinct era in the life of the Indian. The following song shows how throughout the changing conditions of his life the Indian retains the instinct to embody experience in song. It is supposed to be sung by a young maid just setting out for school.

LOVE-SONG
For the last time, come greet me again,
For the last time, come greet me again,
Dear friend, I loved thee alone!
Now to school I'm going away;
For the last time, come greet me again,
For the last time, come take my hand!

Natalie Curtis Burlin, from *The Indians'
Book: Indian Lore, Musical and Narrative*

BACK TO THE
BLANKET

Leah sat on the train and wondered. When you were going back to something that you didn't remember, except that it was there, you had much to wonder about. Her parents had sent her to school in the East when she was nine, and all that she could remember before that was blurred, with a few sharp points sticking out of it, like tablelands coming up out of the plains.

There was no knowing what she was going back to. There would be space all around her, that she knew. Even in these past years, set in the warmly curled Pennsylvania valleys, she had missed that feeling of flat width. But what would be inside the space was what made her uneasy—maybe nothing and maybe something.

Her stepmother and her father and older sister were clear enough, but they had come East to see her twice. Her father was a smile—what she thought of as a good smile—and a square, chunky, brown block. Her stepmother was short and thin and quick, like a bird. Even coming East she wore her blanket, and her hair was in two smooth, flat braids. Never shoes, always moccasins for both of them.

It was her sister for whom Leah felt sorry. She had had too many babies, too soon. On the trips east she had tried to dress up and do Leah credit. She wore white woman's store-bought dresses and shoes that hurt. But she never could give up her braids, and she knew herself that the dresses were ugly. She was always looking for an excuse to say she was chilly so that she could wrap up in her shawl. All her English seemed to leave her and go back to the mission school where she had learned it. Father and mother did all right, because when their English gave out, they could smile at people and get along that way; but it was bad for Jane because she thought she ought to talk to people and the words weren't there to be said.

This was the ending of the second day on the train. The people at the school were generous about these things. When the students went home, they were sent first-class, in the sleeping cars. It amounted to something, coming home in style like that. When you got off the train, people knew you amounted to something.

She had slept all right the first night, but this second one was harder. Sleep kept running away from her, and she tired herself out trying to catch it. When morning came, she couldn't be sure whether she had slept or not, and it made her slow and uncertain in her dressing not to know.

Girdle, brassiere, bloomers, slip, blouse, skirt, jacket. Her hair braided, and the braids twisted around her head. A pin at the throat of her blouse, and then her hat and gloves. She looked at herself and pulled her veil down. The outfit really was stylish. Now that you couldn't see the color of her skin, she could pass anywhere for a white girl.

The school people had given her money for her meals, and when she had had breakfast, she went back to her seat and looked out of the window. It was half-past eight, and the train would be in at ten. Already they were running through space that opened beside and beyond the train and where nothing ever seemed to end or begin. She was a little afraid of the space, and glad of the train window that held it back, but at the same time she was eager and glad to see it, excited by it, wanting to plunge into it.

When the train stopped, she walked squarely and solidly, like her father, down the aisle and carefully got off. The platform was flat ugliness blotting the clean space about it. Beyond it the earth spread red as the Pennsylvania barns. She had forgotten that anything in the world could be so red. Down under the air ran a current of coolness that wasn't wind, but that made everything feel like moving.

The wagon stood beside the station, and was as ugly. It was painted a green that was the only green in the world that would fight with the red of the earth. The paint ponies, with their homemade harness, drooped their heads and pulled up a foot apiece and looked two-thirds asleep. There was a general feeling that the wagon and the ponies were waiting. When something happened, they would go along, but not because they wanted to.

The three of them, mother, father, and sister, sat on the high seat of the wagon, crowded close together. Behind them there were two chairs fitted into the wagon box. They were old chairs and broken down, and you knew that even when they were new, they weren't good. Packed into the wagon box around the chairs were what looked to Leah like all the groceries in the world.

Father threw the lines over the ponies' backs to touch the ground. He got down from the wagon seat one muscle at a time and fitted himself to the ground as if to be sure that his feet hit the right places. Then he came across to her and stood and looked straight at her. It gave her a funny feeling, as if nobody had ever looked straight at her before. As far as she could remember, her father never had.

"Is this Leah?" he asked in Kiowa.

She got her name and nodded, looking at the ground as if there were nowhere else to put her eyes. Then she heard her name again, and her stepmother's arms went around her.

"Na-na-na-na! Na-na-na-na! How big she is! And dressed like a white girl. But this is Leah. Couldn't be anybody else."

They stood there a moment, all three of them, smiling and talking in Kiowa. All of a sudden, Leah found words coming back to her. She had thought they were all gone, but she could understand what her stepmother and her father said, and she even began to make little easy words with her tongue and throat herself. It was funny to do it, because in the East, when they came to visit her at school, she had had no words and no understanding of them.

Then she remembered her sister and went toward her with her hand out. Jane had pulled her shawl clear over her head, with just her little hand, as little as people said their grandfather's had been, showing. When Leah spoke to her in English, she let go of the shawl and held out the little hand to shake. She didn't say a word.

Leah turned then, back to her parents. They were bringing her luggage. It startled her to see her little stepmother carrying one end of the trunk like a man. She went over and tried to push her away and take it, but her mother shook her head and went on with the trunk. Father was carrying his end of the trunk and the suitcase, and between them they put the things into the back of the wagon. The train was gone. She was here to stay.

Leah fitted herself into one of the chairs in the back of the wagon, and her stepmother took the other. They had to crawl over a hundred-pound sack of flour, a fifty-pound sack of cornmeal, and a big bag of sugar to get there. The sacks of food were just tumbled into the bed of the wagon. Beyond them were sacks of feed for the horses and a can of coal oil and a quarter of beef that wasn't even in a sack.

Father said something in Kiowa. Jane moved on the seat as if she were turning to face her sister, and explained.

"Old man say you got excuse things in the wagon. He don't get to town only once a month, got to get lots groceries then."

"That's all right," said Leah. "I don't mind."

She minded that quarter of beef terribly. It hurt her to see the meat lying out like that with the flies all over it. Everything that she had been taught about germs and keeping things clean and keeping coal oil away from groceries was piling into her head and bothering her. She wanted to turn around and look at the meat, but she knew if she did, it would make her sick.

She looked ahead and around, and then she remembered. The earth curved just right, not flat, but running away to the foot of the mountains as if it were alive. Underneath, it was red, always red; but on top it was green, the right greens to go with the red. The mountains were the edge of the world. Not big, high mountains like the Alleghenies, but little, warm, round, gray white mountains that could be big and cold and gray black sometimes. There was a creek to the right of them, running south, and out ahead she could see the big bend of the Washita River and the corner that the creek made emptying into it. The ponies were coming to life and stepping as if they liked the feeling of earth instead of cinders under their feet. There was warmth in the day and there was warmth among them in the wagon. Only Jane sat on the edge of it and let herself be cold with shyness.

It was a long trip home. Going along in the wagon, it took all day. There was time for thinking and time for talking. Sometimes Jane spoke, pulling Leah's mind back from its secret place with a jerk, but most of the time mother or father just talked easily.

"The missionaries will be looking for you," her father said, and she answered, "I want to see them."

"They're sure proud of you, what you done. First Kiowa girl going away to college like that. They want you to work at the mission. Make translations. Put Bible stories and church songs into Kiowa."

"That's good," said Leah.

"They think it's pretty important, what you do now. Got to set an example to everybody. Got to show everybody what to do. You're pretty important, all right."

Her stepmother spoke, "That's right, pretty important. Grandmother says she's going to make war whoop for you, like for a young man coming back from the raids in the old days." She laughed. "Then you have to give her a horse."

Father laughed too. "Where's she going to get a horse? Took all her horses to keep her in school. Had to sell all her horses to buy those good clothes she's got on."

That was a new thought. Leah had never wondered much about where her clothes came from. She leaned forward and spoke directly to Jane in English.

"Is that true? Did they have to sell my horses?"

"We all had to sell some horses," Jane said. "You don't get good clothes, lots books, all like that, without money. Sometimes missionaries writing us. You got to have things. You needing them. Then we sell horses, send the money to the school."

Leah had never had any money herself, except her dollar weekly allowance. The missionaries said they gave the students an allowance to teach them responsibility and the use of money. She had never thought about how she was kept in school. The missionaries had said they were sending her to a mission school, and she had supposed it was like the mission church, kept up by the white people to help the Indians. It didn't seem fair to tell people you were doing things to help them and then make them pay for it.

"I'm sorry you had to sell horses," she said to Jane, and Jane said quietly, "That's all right. We sold them to the soldiers. They weren't very good horses, just workhorses. Couldn't run."

Leah wondered about selling off the workhorses and keeping the ones that could run, when you lived on a farm and needed workhorses for plowing. That wasn't what she had been taught at school, but that was why she had gone to school, so that she could come back and educate her people. She'd have to start doing it, but this didn't seem a good place to begin.

Jane let her shawl go back over her shoulders so that it lay in soft folds, like her stepmother's. She seemed easier now. She began to talk a little more.

"What they teaching you at that school? Just books?"

"Lots of things," Leah answered.

"What things?" Jane persisted.

"How to work in the house, scrubbing and sweeping and dusting. How to take care of things, mending and washing and ironing. Making clothes last a long time."

"That's good," said Jane. "Those clothes you got on won't last long out here. Dust just cuts through that soft cloth. Won't have any hem left on your skirt in four days."

That was about right too. The dust had got through her clothes to her skin already, and the various layers of clothing were all rubbing against each other and against her and against every separate grain of dust. It felt like things crawling over each other and over her. It was bad, and she wanted to scratch.

"I got wash dresses in my trunk," she said.

"You got shawl too?" Jane wanted to know. "You going to need shawl. Hat's blowing off, getting lost out here."

It was a mean, mischievous wind. There had been none all morning, and now it came out of the noon that was drawing the mountains close. It twisted up handfuls of dust from the red earth and twined them around the wagon like vines going around a tree trunk. When it was gone, Leah's hat was gone with it.

"Na-na-na-na!" mother cried, and father stopped the wagon and got ready to move himself down to earth to go after it.

"That's all right," Leah said. "Let it go. Don't go after it. It's a heavy hat anyhow. Makes my head ache."

Father chuckled deep down and got back on the wagon seat. "Maybe she's some Indian anyhow," he said to Jane.

"She looks like an Indian," mother said. The braids would never stay up against her head without her hat to hold them, and already they were slipping down and hanging to her waist. They felt better that way, lighter and not so thick.

"I guess we better eat," father said, and stopped the wagon.

They had gone over one of those sudden folds in the earth and had come upon a creek that you didn't expect, going through a grove of cottonwoods and willows that surprised you too. It was all green and cool and quiet, held in the clear space as if nothing could touch it.

They all got down from the wagon, and father unhitched and turned the ponies loose. Mother and Jane went off up the creek, and when they came back, their shawls were over their shoulders, full of little limbs and branches and dead stuff.

"Pecan wood," mother said. "That's what makes a good cooking fire. Flavors the meat like salt."

Leah watched while Jane built the fire. She was neat and quick about it, with small, tidy gestures that seemed to waste neither wood nor movement. Leah turned to see what her mother was doing. She had pulled the piece of meat across the floor of the wagon and was whittling off some of the ribs.

The fire was like perfume, but Leah knew that however

sweet the smoke smelled, she could never eat any of that meat. She took off her jacket and folded it carefully on the chair, and said to Jane, "Is there anything I can do?" as if she were speaking politely to one of the lady teachers at the school.

"You can get water," Jane told her, and jerked her chin toward a bucket that hung under the wagon.

"Where's the well?" Leah asked.

"Down there." Jane jerked her chin toward the creek.

"You drink creek water?"

"Sure. That's all the water there is around here."

"But it isn't safe. It might be infected."

Jane forgot about the fire for a moment. "What's that?"

"It might have germs in it."

"What's germs?"

"Little animals that you can't see that make you sick."

"Hum." Jane went back to her fire. "If you can't see them, what makes you know they're there?"

"You can see them through the microscope."

"What's a microscope?"

"It's a thing to make little things look bigger."

"Like missionary's glasses?"

"Sort of."

"Missionaries need glasses to see things they want to see," said Jane. "It's the things they say they don't want to see they spot without no glasses. I guess they want to see those old germs all right if they look at them with glasses. You got one of them things with you?"

"A germ?"

"One of them 'scope things."

"No. They cost too much. Just a few people have them."

"I guess you could have one if you wanted it. We can always sell more horses."

That hurt. Leah took the bucket and, germs or no germs, went down to the creek for water. It was hard, coming back to this life. The missionaries made it sound easy. You went away for most of your life and forgot your own language, but you learned lots of other things to take the place of it. Then you went back and taught all the new things to the people at home, and they did better and lived better, like you. There was just one danger that you had to look out for. That was going back to the blanket. If you ever went back to the blanket, you were lost. Then there was no hope for you anymore. You would be just Indian all your life.

It was really hot when she came back through the sun to the shade with the bucket. At first she thought it was the fire that made things hot, but all of its heat was going into cooking the meat. It was just time moving around to noon that made the heat. Nobody else seemed to be hot. Jane was watching the meat, and mother had got a paper bag of things from the wagon and was spreading out store bread and some oranges and stick candy.

The meat and the smoke together smelled good. It was cooler in the shade, and Leah found that she was hungry. She still didn't want to eat that meat, but when Jane gave her a piece laid on a slice of store bread, she didn't want to hurt her sister's feelings and she bit into it.

"Look out for germs," Jane warned her.

"I guess maybe cooking will kill them. Scalding water will."

She hadn't said "I guess maybe" since the first year she was at school. You could say it two ways. One way was when you made up your mind to do a thing and nothing could change you. The other way was, as now, when it meant you were making a joke. The English teacher said "I guess maybe" was redundancy and you didn't need all those words. Jane must have thought you did need them, because it made them both feel easier.

They ate, and then they rested against the grass. Leah wondered if she slept and thought she did because she hadn't last night, and knew she didn't because she knew everything that was around her. She had never thought about the shapes of grass blades or that they had different colors on their two sides before. She had always thought of shadows as gray or black but they were blue when father got up off the grass and began to hitch up the ponies.

It was cooler than at noon, but she didn't put the jacket on. She still felt hotter than her mother or sister looked. She asked Jane, "What you got on underneath?"

Jane just turned and looked at her feet. "Nothing," she said.

You couldn't have told it. She looked perfectly well covered up in the straight cotton dress with full sleeves. Of course the overskirt kept her legs from showing through. It was just as modest as anybody else's clothes, even if it wasn't stylish. It looked all right in this country.

The house had been built by the missionaries to be a model Indian home. It was square and solid, with its fields around it. There was a high porch on the front, looking south to the mountains that dusk was pushing away from them again. Under the porch was storage space for canned goods. It had some in it, but there was a lot of harness there too, because it was closer to where they unhitched the wagon than the barn was.

They ate again, and then slept on their beds. The bed was hard, just a thin mattress over boards, but it was sleep that Leah had forgotten that took hold of her and held her. It let her go with the first movements of morning. She wondered which moved first, her mother or the mockingbird in the tree outside the kitchen.

It would be hot again today. It would be hot every day until the rains came, and then it would be cool suddenly and quickly. Jane had been sleeping in the arbor, and she came in now for a clean dress.

"You got another dress?" Leah asked her.

"Sure," said Jane. "I got four dresses." She opened the dresser drawer. Showing off, like women in the old days who had lots of buckskin clothes. All Indian.

"You lend me one?" Leah asked.

"What you want with it?" Jane sounded suspicious.

"I'm hot," Leah replied. "These clothes are hot. I want to put on something cool. Then I'll make over some housedresses to be like yours. That way's cooler, and you don't need a slip."

Jane handed her the dress and overskirt. "Sure is funny," she said. "You go away, learn to be white woman. First thing when you come back, you put on Indian clothes."

"Indian clothes are better here. You got to wear clothes you can work in."

"That's right," Jane said. "I got to work today too. Got to dry that beef."

She went about it after breakfast, slicing the meat away from the ribs in sheets as thin as tissue paper, then gashing each sheet against the grain of the meat. She threw them up over a bar in the sun as she finished, and the sun and the flies fought over them.

Leah wanted to help her, but when she said so, Jane said, "This is Indian way. Gets lots germs on the meat. That's what makes it taste good," and Leah went off to unpack her trunk.

That took all day, and when she had finished, she had just repacked it, with her books and heavy clothes at the bottom and her cotton dresses at the top where she could get at them. Even in the thin cotton of Jane's dress she was hot and sweaty, with her braids tied together at the back of her neck making her even hotter. She went out on the porch and unbraided her hair and got ready to brush it before supper. Father sat down on the steps.

"Wagon coming," he said presently.

Mother was sitting on the porch floor behind Leah's chair. "Missionaries' wagon," she said.

Leah could see a spot in movement, that was all. It could have been a horse or a cow until she squinted her eyes up. Then she could see a small spot ahead of a big one—a horse pulling a wagon.

The spots turned across the fields head-on, and lost their two shapes and became one big one. A blue roan was pulling a black wagon. The black looked worse against the fields even than father's green wagon. The roan plopped his feet up and down in the dust until he came to the steps and stopped there.

"Hello, there," said the man missionary. "Good evening."

"Get down, friend," said father, and the missionary laughed and repeated the Kiowa words and got down. He went around to the side of the wagon and helped his wife to the ground. Leah remembered her mother, climbing down all by herself yesterday and felt ashamed of her father for not helping his wife. Jane came and stood in the door behind them.

"Where is Leah?" asked the lady missionary. "My, I can hardly wait to see her. Such a little thing when she went away, and a grown-up young lady now. We're so proud of her. I said to father this morning, 'We'll just harness up in the cool of the evening and drive right over and get Leah,' that's what I said; and he said, 'Mother, you're just right,' he said. Where is she?"

She was coming up the steps with little nervous hoppings all the time she was talking and now she was standing right in front of Leah, looking at that sheet of black hair pouring down and hiding her face.

"That's her," said Jane, pulling her chin around to point.

Leah shook back her hair and stood up.

"Good evening, Mrs. Gaines," she said.

"Why, Leah! Why my dear child! Why, what has happened! Look at her, father. Look at this poor creature. Something terrible must have happened. Where are your clothes, my dear? Did you lose your trunk? What happened to your hair?"

"I was unpacking my trunk, and I got hot. I took down my hair to brush it."

"Oh, that's all right then. I thought something had happened. I thought maybe— Where did you get that dress?"

"That's her dress," said Jane suddenly from the door. "I made it for her."

"You made her a squaw dress? Jane, that was wrong. You had no right. You know she's educated. She wouldn't want to wear those clothes."

"She's Indian," Jane's voice was stubborn. "She's just educated Indian."

This was harder than anything Leah had dreamed. She thought she would come home, go to the mission, work to uplift her people. It would all be easy. Then she would marry some good young man, not an Indian, a missionary, and go away and do good all her life. And here was her own sister calling her Indian.

"That's just it," said Mrs. Gaines. "She's educated. She's got intelligence. She knows better than to dress like that and run around like everybody."

The English teacher at school had said intelligence was capacity for learning, and that having learned was knowledge. Jane had capacity for learning all the things Leah had learned. She just hadn't learned, and so she lacked knowledge. But the missionary woman didn't seem to know the difference between the two. She couldn't be very intelligent herself.

"Get your bag, Leah," said Mr. Gaines. It surprised you to hear him because most of the time his wife drowned him out. "We want to get home at six o'clock in time for supper."

Why, supper was when you were hungry. That was the time to eat. They had all been working and were hot, and they wouldn't eat until they had cooled off. It was silly to say you must be hungry at six o'clock or ten o'clock or any other one time. It had always seemed silly, even at the school. Leah shook her head.

"I guess I won't go," she said. "I guess I'll stay here awhile. I haven't seen my folks for a long time."

"But we have your room all ready for you and the things laid out for you to go to work." That was Mrs. Gaines all right, making plans and making everybody stick to them. Too many plans kept you from living. You were all the time trying to catch up with the things you'd planned to do.

"Maybe Leah wants a little visit with her folks first," said

Mr. Gaines more quietly. He wasn't so tied down to living in a certain line. "It's been a long time since she saw them. Maybe she wants to get acquainted again."

"Of course it's a long time since she saw them! That's the whole plan of Indian education. How can these children learn to be good, upright men and women and set a good example if they aren't given an opportunity? If they have to see the old things going on around them all the time and live the old way, how are they going to make the others change for anything better?"

Well, father and mother had changed all right and had done it without going away, although father had gone to the school at Fort Sill. They had a house instead of a tepee, and they rode in a wagon instead of on horseback. They could buy flour and bread and sugar and cloth in stores instead of going out and killing something to eat and tanning its hide for clothes—those were all things the white people meant when they talked about being progressive—and they had learned staying at home.

"I guess I better stay here awhile," she said. "You want me to translate some things, but I couldn't right now. My Kiowa's not good enough. I better stay home and learn it again."

"It'll come back to you," Mrs. Gaines said determinedly. "When you've been here a month, you'll find you remember it. You don't have to stay at home to learn it. Why, you'll pick it up from father, here. He preaches in Indian once a month."

Leah's father just didn't smile, but it was only because he was too polite. Leah remembered one thing they had said about Mr. Gaines, years ago when she was just a little girl. "He thinks he's talking Kiowa, but all he's doing is shaking the arbor poles." They had even named him after that. That was one of his names Mr. Gaines didn't know about. He always told visiting missionaries about the name he did know, because he was proud of it. It meant "Loud Talking Man."

"Thank you for asking me," Leah told them. "I bet I could

learn a lot from Mr. Gaines. But this is where I belong. I think I had better stay here and learn."

"If you stay here, you ought to teach. That's what you're equipped for. There's nothing these people can teach you, they have everything to learn from you."

Leah didn't like that, calling her family "these people," with all of them standing there understanding every word. "I guess maybe I stay here," she said. Jane came out of the door and stood beside her. They were suddenly alike. You knew they had to be sisters.

"I can't do good to people if all they think about when they see me is how different I am," Leah said. "You have to be enough like people so that they will stop thinking about how you look and just remember that your mind feels right to them. I have to stay here until we all feel that."

"That's the way it is," said Mrs. Gaines. She didn't sound angry so much as tired and hurt. She went back to the wagon and stood waiting for her husband to help her up to the seat. She looked little and old and sharp, like an old flint arrow in a museum.

"You take these children away and put them in a good environment. You do everything in the world for them that you can. Just when you think you've changed them and made something out of them, they fool you. They'll go back to the blanket every time, even the best of them."

Mr. Gaines helped her into the wagon and turned the blue roan. At the corner of the fence, he turned to call, "Try to come to church Sunday," and they went away, with the two spots of the wagon and horse getting smaller until they turned into one spot.

Leah sat down again. Her knees folded under her and she missed the chair and sat on the floor. The sun was sloping across from the west end of the porch, and she sat in a puddle of it with her hair still down around her shoulders.

So she had gone back to the blanket. She had quarreled with her sister, and they had hurt each other's feelings. She had tried to get near her stepmother and her father, and there was always something between them that prevented her. She was different from them and they all knew it, and none of them felt right about it. Mrs. Gaines said she had gone back to the blanket because she wouldn't come and live at the mission.

What good would it do to live at the mission? There was no warmness from her to Mr. and Mrs. Gaines. There was respect, that was all. Here there was warmness toward the people around her and toward her, anyway. Yes, and there was the beginning of respect. They hadn't tried to hold her back or force her to go. They had left it up to her to make her own decision. That was what people did when they had respect for each other. Then they could sit still together and think things out too, as now. There was privacy in that way. You didn't have to go into another room to be alone. People knew without telling when your mind needed leaving alone and were careful not to touch it with theirs.

She got up then, and braided her hair. Jane stood up too. "Come on," said Leah. "I guess maybe we better bring that meat in for the night. Dew might make it spoil."

"That's right," said Jane. They went toward the drying bar.

"That old Mrs. Gaines," said Jane. "She's got a lot to learn. All these years she's living in Indian country, and she still looks right at us when she's talking to us."

Leah began taking down the meat and piling it on a piece of canvas. Jane went on talking. "But we got things to learn too. All that talk about germs. Makes things sound like they're dirty, animals crawling all over them. Maybe they are. Maybe we better learn things like that. Indians sure like to have things clean."

Alice Marriott, from *The Ten Grandmothers*. Copyright 1945 by the University of Oklahoma Press.

REMEMBERING

As a child I understood how to give; I have forgotten this grace since I became civilized. I lived the natural life, whereas I now live the artificial. Any pretty pebble was valuable to me then; every growing tree an object of reverence. Now I worship with the white man before a painted landscape whose value is estimated in dollars! Thus the Indian is reconstructed, as the natural rocks are ground to powder and made into artificial blocks, which may be built into the walls of modern society.

Charles Alexander Eastman,
from *The Soul of the Indian*

THE HAIRCUT

I needed a haircut, and went to a barbershop. The barber glowered at me. What did I want? I told him. "Nothin' doin'; get out!" In the town I had come from I never had a hint of anything like this, so I asked for an explanation. He sneered and said, "We don't cut any Jap's hair here, see? This is an American establishment!" I said I was not a Jap, but an American. He said, "Aw, go tell it to the marines!" I said I was born in this country, right here in California, and that made me an American. "To me it don't!" he shot back. For a moment I saw red, and I wanted terribly to sail into him. That would have been the thing to do at the home; here, something told me, it was not.

I walked out, hurt and bewildered. Goddamnit, I *was* an American, *not* a Jap!

Then I discovered that the signs Rooms to Let were not addressed to me. The landlady of the fifth house where I applied for lodging took me in. She was an Armenian woman who spoke very little English.

I had arrived in San Francisco with twenty dollars. For two weeks I walked about twelve hours every day. No job—

Off and on, I found a curious comfort in the thought (accurate enough) that I failed to get employment not merely because I had a Japanese face but also because of the country-wide depression and the recent general strike and other capital-labor troubles that kept industry and business in San Francisco in a state of jitters. I felt a wavering, indirect gratitude to Harry Bridges, whom the newspapers and the big employers blamed loudly for the situation.

Of course I could not live on this consolation, even if I gave up the idea of entering college at once. I had to begin to earn something. I tried to get ordinary labor. . . . *"Nothin' doin'!"* . . . One labor boss informed me casually, "I wouldn't have anything for you even if you was an American."

Walking about, I came upon the rather shabby, run-down district that is Japanese Town in San Francisco. There were Japanese signs over all the stores. I could not read them. Most of the people in the streets were Japanese. They spoke Japanese. Arches, with lights on them, were rigged up over the streets as I supposed they were in the cities in Japan. . . . I felt a stranger, a foreigner.

I entered a barbershop. The barbers were women, and after I got into the chair I was sorry I had gone in. The woman talked to me in Japanese; she knew no English. I indicated with pantomime that I wanted my hair cut only in back and around the sides. She nodded, then talked to her fellow barber, no doubt about me: how strange it was that I did not understand Japanese. I tried not to listen; did not like the sound of the language—but I could not help hearing them, and there was the rumble of meaning in my head, similar to that I had experienced when the lawyer visited me at the institution; only it was even more remote. Touching a residue of understanding in me, their words made me miserable. And the barber's touch on my neck, as she put the towel about me, sent shivers all through me.

I had felt intensely strong and compact when I arrived in San Francisco; now, in this chair, having my hair cut, I felt as though I were cracking up, falling to pieces, turning soft and weepy.

Louis Adamic, from *From Many Lands*

HELP US BELIEVE

That our ancestors are still remembering.
Go back to them with sacred meal, go back
Down through the earth, oh be our messengers!
Tell them with reverence, tell them our lack;
Tell them we have no roots, but a sap that stirs
Forever unrooted upward to the sky.
But tell them also, tell them of our song
Downward from heaven, back where we belong.
Oh north, east, west, and south, tell them we die!

Witter Bynner, from *Indian Earth*

PART THREE

Removal

*They that hate you
shall reign over you.*

Leviticus 27:17

Racial and ethnic conflicts are often resolved when one group expels another from the territory in which it resides. For the victors the end result is comparable to that attained by annihilation, but the process is somewhat more humane. We say "somewhat" more, because mass expulsion is often carried out in an atmosphere of massacres, riots, and other forms of violence, though there are instances where the dominant group has manifested a degree of consideration for those who were being expelled, permitting them to convert their properties into movable wealth and affording them protection from mob attack. Mass expulsion, moreover, has often been resorted to when other methods have failed. There are instances where a minority group has been driven from a country only after a policy of extermination has failed, for one reason or another. On the other hand, mass expulsion has been adopted after concerted efforts to assimilate a minority have proved fruitless.

Brewton Berry, from *Race and Ethnic Relations*

THE TRAIL OF TEARS

A classic example of mass expulsion, taken from our own history, is that of the forced removal of the Cherokees from their homeland in the East. The magnitude of the injustice and the toll of lives have caused the Indians to call this incident the Trail of Tears.

The Cherokees were a powerful people who lived in that region where Georgia meets Tennessee and North Carolina.

Their first contact with the whites came in 1540, when de Soto marched through their country; but there was nothing in the conduct of the Spaniards to make the Indians regard them as superior, and they hoped they would see no more of such people. A century and half later the whites came again, this time the British. The initial contacts were friendly, for the Indians were far removed from the settlements and the white visitors were bent upon establishing cordial relations for reasons of trade and security. But as the frontier advanced, the Cherokees began to feel the encroachment of the land-hungry Europeans. There was friction; the Indians lost some of their territory; but in the meantime they had learned many things from the whites that had made them a stronger, more prosperous, even a civilized people.

By 1825 there were more than thirteen thousand Cherokees living in their eastern home, while approximately seven thousand others had been induced to migrate across the Mississippi. Contact with the whites, then, had greatly stimulated the growth of their population. They had willingly received into their group many white men and women who had taken Cherokee spouses. They still owned seven million acres of land. Schools and churches had been established, their farms were prosperous, they managed their political affairs well, the nation was out of debt, they were at peace, and they owned more than one thousand Negro slaves. One of their number, Sequoya, among the truly great men of American history, had invented a Cherokee alphabet, and he was on his way to turning them into a literate people.

The tide was turned when gold was discovered in the Georgia hills, for the whites were determined to get possession of it. On 19 December 1829 the legislature of Georgia passed an act appropriating a large area of the Cherokee lands. It provided also that the laws of the Cherokees would henceforth be null and void in that area, and all persons living therein would be subject to the laws of the state of Georgia. Finally, the act provided that "no Indian or descendant of an Indian . . . shall be deemed a competent witness in any court of this state to which a white person may be a party." The governor warned the Indians that they would be liable to punishment if they mined the gold on the lands the state had appropriated. A lottery system was set up to distribute the Indian lands among the whites.

The Cherokees appealed to President Andrew Jackson; but he was no friend of theirs, old Indian fighter that he was. In fact, it was he who had been responsible for having Congress enact the Indian Removal Act, which placed upon his shoulders the task of driving all Indians to lands beyond the Mississippi. The Cherokees then appealed to the Supreme Court, but the court declared that it was not its function to meddle in such affairs. The various branches of the government, far from seeing justice done to the Indians, actually connived in the theft. The president's commissioners, in fact, illegally persuaded a handful of the tribe's members to sell all of its seven million acres to the government, and the Senate quickly ratified this "treaty." The Cherokees, however, denounced the treaty, and remained on the land.

General Winfield Scott moved in with seven thousand troops and an unruly rabble of civilians. Men, women, and children, the Indians were rounded up; homes and barns were burned; cattle and household goods were seized by the mob. Even graves were opened, and the silver and other valuables, which by Indian custom were buried with the dead, were taken with the loot. The captives were herded into stockades, conducted under guard down the Tennessee, Ohio, and Mississippi rivers and up the White, and shoved into the territory that is now Oklahoma. The cost of all this was charged to the Indians.

The details of this mass expulsion and of the westward trek are revolting. The suffering was intense, and the toll of life staggering. More than ten thousand Cherokees were driven west, and of that number it is estimated that four thousand perished along the way.

Brewton Berry, from *Race
and Ethnic Relations*

ENFORCED REMOVAL

In spite of the pressure upon the Indians, only about two thousand of the eastern Cherokee had removed by 23 May 1838, the expiration of the time fixed for their departure. The remaining nearly fifteen thousand could not believe that they would soon be driven out of the country; not from a fatuous reliance on the ultimate rectitude of the government—they had no such illusion. But their fixed habits, devoted attachment to their homes, and their unfamiliarity with any other life and country prevented their comprehension of what was soon to happen to them.

Their enforced removal was entrusted to General Winfield Scott, who was ordered to take command of the troops already in the Cherokee country, together with reinforcements of infantry, cavalry, and artillery, with authority to call upon the governors of the adjoining states for as many as four thousand militia and volunteers. The total so employed was seven thousand. The Indians had already been disarmed by General Wool.

General Scott established headquarters at New Echota, the capital of the Cherokee nation, whence, on 10 May, he issued a proclamation to the Cherokee people, warning them that the emigration must begin at once and in haste and that before another moon had passed every Cherokee man, woman, and child must be in motion toward the West as commanded by the president, whose orders he, General Scott, had come to enforce. The proclamation concludes: "*My troops already occupy many positions . . . and thousands and thousands are appearing from every quarter to render assistance and escape alike hopeless . . . Will you, then by resistance compel us to resort to arms . . . or will you by flight seek to hide yourself in mountains and forests and thus oblige us to hunt you down?"*—reminding them that pursuit might result in conflict and bloodshed, ending in a general war. Even after this Ross [25] endeavored, on behalf of his people, to secure some slight modification of the terms of the treaty, but without avail.

Grant Foreman, from Indian Removal

THE WAY
INTO EXILE

The history of this Cherokee removal of 1838, as gleaned by the author from the lips of actors in the tragedy, may well exceed in weight of grief and pathos any other passage in American history. Even the much-sung exile of the Acadians falls far behind it in its sum of death and misery. Under Scott's orders the troops were disposed at various points throughout the Cherokee country, where stockade forts were erected for gathering in and holding the Indians preparatory to removal. From these, squads of troops were sent to search out with rifle and bayonet every small cabin hidden away in the coves or by the sides of mountain streams, to seize and bring in as prisoners all the occupants, however or wherever they might be found. Families at dinner were startled by the sudden gleam of bayonets in the doorway and rose up to be driven with blows and oaths along the weary miles of trail that led to the stockade. Men were seized in their fields or going along the road, women were taken from their wheels, and children from their play. In many cases, on turning for one last look as they crossed the ridge, they saw their homes in flames, fired by the lawless rabble that followed on the heels

[25] John Ross, Cherokee chief.

of the soldiers to loot and pillage. So keen were these out-
laws on the scent that in some instances they were driving
off the cattle and other stock of the Indians almost before
the soldiers had fairly started the owners in the other direction. Systematic hunts were made by the same men for Indians' graves, to rob them of the silver pendants and other
valuables deposited with the dead. A Georgia volunteer,
afterward a colonel in the Confederate service, said: "I fought
through the Civil War and have seen men shot to pieces and
slaughtered by thousands, but the Cherokee removal was
the cruelest work I ever knew."

To prevent escape the soldiers had been ordered to approach
and surround each house, as far as possible, so as to come
upon the occupants without warning. One old patriarch when
thus surprised calmly called his children and grandchildren
around him, and kneeling down, bid them pray with him in
their own language, while the astonished soldiers looked on
in silence. Then rising he led the way into exile. A woman, on
finding the house surrounded, went to the door and called
up the chickens to be fed for the last time, after which, taking
her infant on her back and her two other children by the hand,
she followed her husband with the soldiers.

Camp Hetzel, near Cleveland, 16 June. The Cherokees are
nearly all prisoners. They had been dragged from their houses,
and encamped at the forts and military places, all over the
nation. In Georgia especially, multitudes were allowed no
time to take anything with them, except the clothes they had
on. Well-furnished houses were left a prey to plunderers,
who, like hungry wolves, follow in the train of the captors.
These wretches rifle the houses, and strip the helpless, unoffending owners of all they have on earth. Females, who have
been habituated to comforts and comparative affluence, are
driven on foot before the bayonets of brutal men. Their feelings are mortified by vulgar and profane vociferations. It is
a painful sight. The property of many has been taken, and
sold before their eyes for almost nothing—the sellers and
buyers, in many cases, having combined to cheat the poor

Indians. These things are done at the instant of arrest and consternation; the soldiers standing by, with their arms in hand, impatient to go on with their work, could give little time to transact business. The poor captive, in a state of distressing agitation, his weeping wife almost frantic with terror, surrounded by a group of crying, terrified children, without a friend to speak a consoling word, is in a poor condition to make a good disposition of his property, and is in most cases stripped of the whole, at one blow. Many of the Cherokees, who, a few days ago, were in comfortable circumstances, are now victims of abject poverty. Some, who have been allowed to return home, under passport, to inquire after their property, have found their cattle, horses, swine, farming tools, and house furniture all gone. And this is not a description of extreme cases. It is altogether a faint representation of the work that has been perpetrated on the unoffending, unarmed, and unresisting Cherokees.

New York Observer, July 1838

JAPANESE EXPULSION

A more recent case of mass expulsion occurred during World War II, when some 110,000 persons of Japanese ancestry were forcibly evacuated from the area bordering the Pacific Ocean, and including parts of Washington, Oregon, California, and Arizona. Ostensibly this was nothing more than a wartime measure undertaken in the interest of national security. But actually, as we gain the perspective of time, it appears to be simply one more chapter in the long conflict between whites and Japanese. Let us review that conflict.

The Japanese are among the most recent immigrants to

enter the United States. For a long time Japan was opposed to its citizens leaving their own country. Prior to 1854 emigration was a crime punishable by death, and the construction of ocean-going vessels was forbidden by imperial decree. Then an occasional shipwrecked sailor or stowaway found his way to these shores. Their numbers were negligible, however, for there were only 55 Japanese here in 1870, and 148 in 1880. But the Hawaiian Sugar Planters' Association, in 1884, prevailed upon the Japanese authorities to reverse their traditional opposition to emigration, and immediately the numbers of Japanese in other countries began to swell. They went to Hawaii in droves, and many came to Canada, the United States, and South America. There were 2,039 here in 1890; and in the first decade of the present century some 55,000 arrived from Japan, and another 37,000 from Hawaii.

They were never warmly received in the United States, even though their labor was needed in the West where they settled. At the time they began to arrive in large numbers, Japan was emerging as a world power; and many Californians regarded the Japanese immigration as the spearhead of invasion. An anti-Japanese meeting was held in San Francisco on 7 May 1900; and in 1905 the Hearst newspapers launched a major attack upon them. Various repressive and discriminatory measures were adopted. In 1907 President Roosevelt, by executive order, stopped Japanese immigration from Hawaii, Canada, and Mexico; and he negotiated the famous Gentleman's Agreement with the Japanese government, putting an end to immigration from that source, except for the so-called picture brides. These measures, however, did little to halt the tide of anti-Japanese prejudice. Hostile bills and resolutions were introduced in a number of state legislatures, California placed restrictions upon ownership of land by Japanese, and several other states followed her example. The culmination of the struggle came in 1924, when Congress passed a law barring the immigration of persons "ineligible for citizenship," which was intended, and interpreted, as a blow to the Japanese.

The Japanese have never been one of our large minorities, being greatly outnumbered by the Negro, Jewish, Mexican, and even the Indian groups. On the eve of World War II, there were only 126,947 in the continental United States, two-thirds of whom, by virtue of their having been born on American soil, were citizens. They were concentrated, however, and this was a factor contributing to the misfortune they later suffered. At the outbreak of the war, 43 percent of those gainfully employed were in agriculture, more particularly in the production of vegetables and fruits for the local urban markets; 23 percent were engaged in the wholesale and retail trade, chiefly the distribution of Japanese-grown products; 17 percent were employed in service industries—domestic service, cleaning and dyeing, and the operation of hotels, barbershops, and restaurants; and others owned stores or were engaged in the professions. In these latter areas, as a result of discrimination and boycotts, the patrons and clients were chiefly Japanese.

The attack upon Pearl Harbor gave the anti-Japanese forces their great opportunity. They began to clamor for expulsion. The Hearst newspapers took up the cry. Rumors of espionage and sabotage began to circulate, entirely without foundation in fact, for Japanese Americans, both in Hawaii and in the United States, have a clear record on that score. Lobbyists went to work, and West Coast representatives in Congress recommended to the president "the immediate evacuation of all persons of Japanese lineage." Accordingly, the War Department was authorized in an executive order to set up military areas and to exclude from such areas any persons regarded as dangerous. Mr. Stimson, secretary of war, delegated this authority to General J. L. DeWitt, who was commanding officer of the Western Defense Command.

Brewton Berry, from *Race
and Ethnic Relations*

PROCLAMATION,
30 APRIL 1942

On 2 March General DeWitt's Public Proclamation Number One designated the western half of the West Coast and the southern half of Arizona as Military Area Number 1 and set up prohibited and restricted zones from which residents of Japanese ancestry would be required to move.

Some ten thousand did move, voluntarily, some to stay with friends or relatives, many to discover that they were not welcome in Colorado or Utah. Those who had gone just outside the restricted zones were dismayed shortly afterward when creation of Military Area Number 2 forced them to move again.

General DeWitt ordered cessation of voluntary evacuation on March 29 and resumed writing civilian exclusion orders. Between February and 30 April there had been twenty-seven such orders; the paper war went on until there was a total of 108 civilian exclusion orders.

Number 27, on April 30, said in part:

1. Pursuant to the provisions of Public Proclamations nos. 1 and 2, this headquarters, dated 2 March and 16 March 1942, respectively, it is hereby ordered that from and after 12 o'clock noon, P.W.T., of Thursday, 7 May 1942, all persons of Japanese ancestry, both alien and nonalien, be excluded from that portion of Military Area Number 1 . . . [description follows]

2. A responsible member of each family, and each individual living alone . . . will report between the hours of 8:00 A.M. and 5:00 P.M., Friday, 1 May 1942, or during

the same hours on Saturday, 2 May 1942, to the Civil
Control Station. . . .
[Instructions given the people included the following:]
   Evacuees must carry with them on departure for the
assembly center, the following property:
   (a) Bedding and linens (no mattress) for each member of the family;
   (b) Toilet articles for each member of the family;
   (c) Extra clothing for each member of the family;
   (d) Sufficient knives, forks, spoons, plates, bowls, and cups for each member of the family;
   (e) Essential personal effects for each member of the family. . . . No pets of any kind will be permitted. . . .

J. L. DeWitt, Lieutenant General, U.S. Army
Commanding

Allan R. Bosworth, from *America's
Concentration Camps*

THE DOG
THEY LEFT BEHIND

"My cousin's dog . . . was a big colly. He knew something
was wrong because my cousin said we will be back soon. He
said we're going shopping, but somehow the colly knew it
was not so and he also knew that he wanted to go with us.
He suspected because we were carrying our suitcases. When
we were going down our garden, the dog followed us. I
told him to go home. He just sat and howled. My cousin and
I got mad at him but we love him almost as if he were a human
being. He seemed to be one that day because he seemed to
understand what we were saying to him. I got down to the
sidewalk (I was the last one) and looked back and I could

see him but he was still following me. His name was Spruce. The lady that rented our house said she would take good care of him. When we drove away from the front of the house, he was sitting inside the fence looking out."

quoted by Carey McWilliams, from Prejudice

NO ONE
WOULD BE WRONGED

A Pasadena citizen suggested that the internment camps be operated by a board of control composed of representatives of each of the veterans' organizations. A correspondent of Portsmouth, Virginia, urged separate camps for the sexes pending an exchange with American prisoners of war in Japan. A Berkeley, California, housewife saw healthful benefits in her suggestion that the Japanese be made to live in tents, because "the weather is wonderful and they should enjoy the change." But a central California resident (who spoke for "many others") had no regard for physical culture and ordered: "Move them back into the desert and feed them rice."

Alternatives for keeping the Japanese under guard were frequent. A Florida correspondent, for example, suggested that the Japanese could be employed in building the Alaska highway; he didn't approve of "mistreating the Jap women" but demanded they also be made to work. As for the men, "have a guard with instructions to shoot to kill—put road builders over them of the Simon Legree type and let them use the whip when needed."

Even more unusual solutions were contained in letters to the Justice Department that fell outside the sample analyzed for content: ". . . exterminate them. If the powers that be don't want to kill the women and children, then sterilize them so that they can never produce any more of their kind." An elderly California woman also had a unique and bloodthirsty idea: "Last night the plan enclosed came to me in all the detail as plain as though written and then I went to sleep. . . . You may be horrified, *but all loyal Japs* will be eliminated so why should we not take them *all secretly* and *silently;* securely blindfold them and bind their hands behind them, then make them 'walk the plank' into the ocean . . . *no one* would be *wronged.*" Several persons urged using the Japanese as shields rather than hostages by erecting concentration camps "behind highly charged wire fences" in the shadow of defense plants "so if the plants are bombed, the Japs will be bombed."

Morton Grodzins, from *Americans Betrayed*

I SHALL NEVER
BECOME BITTER

Mike Masaoka, reared in the Mormon Church of the Latter Day Saints in Salt Lake City, was about as American as anybody could be, and twice as sharp as most. He was early hailed as a prodigy, breezed through college, and became the underpaid secretary of the then young Japanese American Citizens League.

Mike Masaoka wrote the Japanese American creed in 1940 to inspire the Nisei to be better citizens. It was first read to the Senate by U.S. Senator Elbert D. Thomas of Utah, then chairman of the Senate Military Affairs Committee, and was published in the *Congressional Records* of 9 May 1941. It was an expression of patriotism that sustained thousands of Nisei during the difficult days of the evacuation; it was the Bible for the heroes of the 442nd Regimental Combat Team. It remains the creed of the Japanese American Citizens League today. It reads:

I am proud that I am an American citizen of Japanese ancestry, for my very background makes me appreciate more fully the wonderful advantages of this nation. I believe in her institutions, ideals, and traditions; I glory in her heritage; I boast of her history; I trust in her future. She has granted me liberties and opportunities such as no individual enjoys in this world today. She has given me an education befitting kings. She has entrusted me with the responsibilities of the franchise. She has permitted me to build a home, to earn a livelihood, to worship, think, speak, and act as I please—as a free man equal to every other man.

Although some individuals may discriminate against me, I shall never become bitter or lose faith, for I know that such persons are not representative of the majority of the American people. True, I shall do all in my power to discourage such practices, but I shall do it in the American way—above board, in the open, through courts of law, by education, by proving myself to be worthy of equal treatment and consideration. I am firm in my belief that American sportsmanship and attitude of fair play will judge citizenship and patriotism on the basis of action and achievement, and not on the basis of physical characteristics.

Because I believe in America, and I trust she believes in me, and because I have received innumerable benefits from her, I pledge myself to do honor to her at all times and all places; to support her Constitution; to obey her laws; to respect her flag; to defend her against all enemies, foreign and domestic; to actively assume my duties and obligations as a citizen, cheerfully and without any reservations whatsoever, in the hope that I may become a better American in a greater America.

Mike Nasaoka and thousands of other Nisei kept their faith under this creed. The American government betrayed them.

Mike went to North Platte, Nebraska, on 7 December 1941, to make a talk to Japanese Americans there—the descendants of those three hundred Issei who used to ice the refrigerator cars on transcontinental express trains. The North Platte authorities said, "We are at war with Japan," and promptly threw him into jail—under no actual charge, at all.

Such arrests were common for several weeks. The mountain states wanted none of the Japanese. After three days, Mike was finally permitted to get in touch with Utah's U.S. Senator Elbert D. Thomas (mentioned previously). Then his jailers unlocked his cell door with a begrudging but wholesome respect, and said, "Well, you must be all right, when a U.S. senator vouches for you!"

A little later the army in California sent Mike, his five brothers, and their widowed mother to internment camps, where Mike's faith in American ideals and benefits was put to a severe test, indeed. As a leader of the Japanese American Citizens League, he was allowed to do considerable traveling east of the military zone to help loyal Nisei resettle. He was still arrested frequently, sometimes as an enemy spy. He worked tirelessly for the right of the Nisei to bear arms in defense of their country, and this brought him a measure of fame across the Pacific. Radio Tokyo called him Japan's number one enemy and said he would be the first American hanged when the Japanese fleet steamed into San Francisco Bay.

When enlistments were finally permitted, Mike Masaoka was the first of all the Nisei to volunteer for the 442nd Regimental Combat Team. Four of his brothers also joined up, while their mother remained in the Manzanar Relocation Center.

Ben Frank Masaoka was killed in October 1944, in the fight to rescue the Lost Texas Battalion. Sergeant Akira Ike Masaoka was so gravely wounded that he is still 100 percent disabled. Mike Masaoka, Private Henry Masaoka, and Private Tadashi T. Masaoka all were wounded.

Among them, the Masaoka boys collected more than thirty medals for bravery in action.

Allan R. Bosworth, from *America's Concentration Camps*

NISEI SOLDIERS

The 442nd Regimental Combat Team, composed of Nisei recruited from the evacuation centers, became the most highly decorated unit in World War II. Its record at the end of the war showed:

7 major campaigns in Europe
7 Presidential Unit Citations
9,486 casualties
18,143 individual decorations, including:
   1 Congressional Medal of Honor
   52 Distinguished Service Crosses
   1 Distinguished Service Medal
   560 Silver Stars, with 28 Oak Leaf Clusters in lieu of second
      Silver Star awards
   22 Legion of Merit Medals
   Approximately 4,000 Bronze Star awards, with about 1,200
      Oak Leaf Clusters representing second Bronze Stars
   15 Soldier's Medals
   12 French Croix de Guerre, with two palms representing
      second awards
   2 Italian Crosses for Military Merit
   2 Italian Medals for Military Valor

Allan R. Bosworth, from *America's Concentration Camps*

IN THE GARDEN GRASS

In the garden grass
A morning dewdrop
Twinkles on a single leaf,
   Just so must I,
   A newly naturalized citizen.

Yachiyo Kido,
from *Sounds From the Unknown*

PART FOUR

Ghettos
of the Mind

Let us see, is this real,
This life I am living?

Pawnee Song

> If you put a chain around the neck of a slave, the other end
> fastens itself around your own.

Ralph Waldo Emerson, from Compensation

TOO YOUNG
TO UNDERSTAND

A little white girl was found in the colored section of our town, living with a Negro family in a broken-down shack. This family had moved in a few weeks before and little was known of them. One of the ladies in my mother's club, while driving over to her washerwoman's, saw the child swinging on a gate. The shack, as she said, was hardly more than a pigsty and this white child was living with dirty and sick-looking colored folks. "They must have kidnapped her," she told her friends. Genuinely shocked, the clubwomen busied themselves in an attempt to do something, for the child was very white indeed. The strange Negroes were subjected to a grueling questioning and finally grew evasive and refused to talk at all. This only increased the suspicion of the white group. The next day the clubwomen, escorted by the town marshal, took the child from her adopted family despite their tears.

She was brought to our home. I do not know why my mother consented to this plan. Perhaps because she loved children and always showed concern for them. It was easy for one more to fit into our ample household and Janie was soon at home there. She roomed with me, sat next to me at the table; I found Bible verses for her to say at breakfast; she wore my clothes, played with my dolls, and followed me around from morning to night. She was dazed by her new comforts and by the interesting activities of this big lively family; and I was as happily dazed, for her adoration was a new thing to me; and as time passed a quick, childish, and deeply felt bond grew up between us.

But a day came when a telephone message was received from a colored orphanage. There was a meeting at our home. Many whispers. All afternoon the ladies went in and out of our house talking to mother in tones too low for children to hear. As they passed us at play, they looked at Janie and quickly looked away again, though a few stopped and stared at her as if they could not tear their eyes from her face. When my father came home mother closed her doors against our young ears and talked a long time with him. I heard him laugh, heard mother say, "But papa, this is no laughing matter!" And then they were back in the living room with us and my mother was pale and my father was saying, "Well, work it out, Mame, as best you can. After all, now that you know, it is pretty simple."

In a little while my mother called my sister and me into her bedroom and told us that in the morning Janie would return to colored town. She said Janie was to have the dresses the ladies had given her and a few of my own, and the toys we had shared with her. She asked me if I would like to give Janie one of my dolls. She seemed hurried, though Janie was not to leave until next day. She said, "Why not select it now?" And in dreamlike stiffness I brought in my dolls and chose one for Janie. And then I found it possible to say, "Why is she leaving? She likes us, she hardly knows them. She told me she had been with them only a month."

"Because," mother said gently, "Janie is a little colored girl."

"But she's white!"

"We were mistaken. She is colored."

"But she looks—"

"She is colored. Please don't argue!"

"What does it mean?" I whispered.

"It means," mother said slowly, "that she has to live in Colored Town with colored people."

"But why? She lived here three weeks and she doesn't belong to them, she told me so."

"She is a little colored girl."

"But you said yourself she has nice manners. You said that," I persisted.

"Yes, she is a nice child. But a colored child cannot live in our home."

"Why?"

"You know, dear! You have always known that white and colored people do not live together."

"Can she come to play?"

"No."

"I don't understand."

"I don't either," my young sister quavered.

"You're too young to understand. And don't ask me again, ever again, about this!" Mother's voice was sharp but her face was sad and there was no certainty left there. She hurried out and busied herself in the kitchen and I wandered through that room where I had been born, touching the old familiar things in it, looking at them, trying to find the answer to a question that moaned like a hurt thing. . . .

And then I went out to Janie, who was waiting, knowing things were happening that concerned her but waiting until they were spoken aloud.

I do not know quite how the words were said but I told her she was to return in the morning to the little place where she had lived because she was colored and colored children could not live with white children.

"Are you white?" she said.

"I'm white," I replied, "and my sister is white. And you're colored. And white and colored can't live together because my mother says so."

"Why?" Janie whispered.

"Because they can't," I said. But I knew, though I said it firmly, that something was wrong. I knew my father and mother whom I passionately admired had betrayed something that they held dear. And they could not help doing it. And I was shamed by their failure and frightened, for I felt they were no longer as powerful as I had thought. There was something Out There that was stronger than they, and I could not bear to believe it. I could not confess that my father, who always solved the family dilemmas easily and with laughter, could not solve this. I knew that my mother who was so good to children did not believe in her heart that she was being good to this child. There was not a word in my mind that said it but my body knew and my glands, and I was filled with anxiety.

But I felt compelled to believe they were right. It was the only way my world could be held together. And, slowly, it began to seep through me: *I was white. She was colored. We must not be together. It was bad to be together. Though you ate with your nurse when you were little, it was bad to eat with any colored person after that. It was bad just as other things were bad that your mother had told you. It was bad that she was to sleep in the room with me that night. It was bad. . . .*

I was overcome with guilt. For three weeks I had done things that white children were not supposed to do. And now I knew these things had been wrong.

I went to the piano and began to play, as I had always done when I was in trouble. I tried to play my next lesson, and as I stumbled through it, the little girl came over and sat on the bench with me. Feeling lost in the deep currents sweeping through our house that night, she crept closer and put her arms around me and I shrank away as if my body had been uncovered. I had not said a word, I did not say one, but she knew, and tears slowly rolled down her little white face. . . .

And then I forgot it. For more than thirty years the experience was wiped out of my memory. But that night, and the weeks it was tied to, worked its way like a splinter, bit by bit, down to the hurt places in my memory and festered there. And as I grew older, as more experiences collected around that faithless time, as memories of earlier, more profound hurts crept closer, drawn to that night as if to a magnet, I began to know that people who talked of love and children did not mean it. That is a hard thing for a child to learn. I still admired my parents, there was so much that was strong and vital and sane and good about them and I never forgot this; I stubbornly believed in their sincerity, as I do to this day, and I loved them. Yet in my heart they were under suspicion. Something was wrong.

Something was wrong with a world that tells you that love is good and people are important and then forces you to deny love and to humiliate people. I knew, though I would not for years confess it aloud, that in trying to shut the Negro race away from us, we have shut ourselves away from so many good, creative, honest, deeply human things in life. I began to understand slowly at first but more clearly as the years passed, that the warped, distorted frame we have put around every Negro child from birth is around every white child also. Each is on a different side of the frame but each is pinioned there. And I knew that what cruelly shapes and cripples the personality of one is as cruelly shaping and crippling the personality of the other. I began to see that though we may, as we acquire new knowledge, live through new experiences, examine old memories, gain the strength to tear the frame from us, yet we are stunted and warped and in our lifetime cannot grow straight again any more than can a tree, put in a steellike twisting frame when young, grow tall and straight when the frame is torn away at maturity.

Lillian Smith,
from *Killers of the Dream*

LEGACY OF FEAR

One Negro mother put rather well the feelings I have heard many others express: "I guess we all don't like white people too much deep inside. You could hardly expect us to, after what's happened all these years. It's in our bones to be afraid of them, and bones have a way of staying around even when everything else is gone. But if something is inside of you, it doesn't mean it's there alone. We have to live with one another, black with white I mean. I keep on telling that to the children, and if they don't seem to learn it, like everything else I have to punish them to make sure they do. So I'm not surprised they don't tell me more than you, because they have to obey me; and if I have to obey you and they have to obey me, it's all the same. Just the other day my Laura started getting sassy about white children on the television. My husband told her to hold her tongue and do it fast. It's like with cars and knives, you have to teach your children to know what's dangerous and how to stay away from it, or else they sure won't live long. White people are a real danger to us until we learn how to live with them. So if you want your kids to live long, they have to grow up scared of whites; and the way they get scared is through us; and that's why I don't let my kids get fresh about the white man even in their own house. If I do there's liable to be trouble to pay. They'll forget, and they'll say something outside, and that'll be it for them, and us too. So I make them store it in the bones, way inside, and then no one sees it. Maybe in a joke we'll have once in a while, or something like that, you can see what we feel inside, but mostly it's buried. But to answer your question, I don't think it's only from you it gets buried. The colored man, I think he has to hide what he really feels even from himself. Otherwise there would be too much pain—too much."

The task, then, is one of making sure the child is afraid: of whites, and of the punishment his parents fearfully inflict upon him whenever he fails to follow their suit. The child's bravado or outrage must be curbed. In my experience even two- and three-year-old Negro children have already learned the indirection, the guile needed for survival. They have also learned their relative weakness, their need to be ready to run fast, to be alert and watchful. They have learned that white children, as well as adults, are big, strong, and powerful; and that such power is specifically related to the colored man's defenselessness.

Robert Coles, from *Children of Crisis*

SHE NEVER TALKED ABOUT IT NO MORE

One day, five months after our father died, I was washing, and mama ironing, in the kitchen. It was August, and the weight of the sky made my whole body open up and go flabby. I couldn't keep the sweat from dripping into the suds no matter how much I wiped my forehead, and the prickly heat was up inside my legs right into the crotch, and it was killing me. I had to stop once every so often and rest there, leaning over the sink and biting my lip not to scratch.

"Cille, you quit, che," mama said. "You sit down a while."

"I ain't tired," I told her, and I wasn't. It was just the heat.

But when mama said to do something, she wanted to see it done. "You go on over there and sit and breathe a while. Breathing is a very important thing for a person, and breathing is something you never did too much of. That's why you get winded so easy. Now go on over there and breathe some. Go on, do like I say."

I would of liked to finish the washing and get out, only

there wasn't no use in taking up that kind of a point with mama. So I went and sat in front of the screen door. It was just the same there as anywhere else, with the sun on the gallery and no air outside. But I slid forward in the chair and opened my legs wide, and the burning-itching eased off a little.

Dan was sitting on a chunk of the curb, playing with a stray she-cat that used to hang around the house. I could see him fine from the door. He had four or five acorns strung on an old wire, and when he rolled it between his fingers, the acorns danced. The minou wasn't much interested, but she would bat at it from time to time. Dan was used to being alone, and when he had to he could play like that for hours, stuff that would bore any other kid wild.

This open car came around the corner, skidding and splattering a little in the dry gravel and the dust. It was going pretty fast, and the man who was driving had to swing hard to the left to make up for the skid. There was a lady next to him in the front seat, and a young bald man in the back trying to keep his legs up. They was all white. I don't know what they was doing in the colored section, except maybe to fun up a dull day. Anyhow, they was laughing and not paying much mind to where they went.

They didn't mean to do it, and it wasn't all their fault, because the minou got panicky. Only instead of taking to a tree or something, she ran out right under the wheels and got squashed. Dan yelled, but too late, and it probably wouldn't of worked anyway: the man stopped the car and got out, and still wasn't exactly sure what might of took place. The cat was mashed across the middle, practically broke into different pieces. By the time the man went around to see, Dan was there trying to pick her up.

"Leave it where it is, kid," the man said, "ain't nothing you can do."

But Dan went right on trying to peel her out of the street.

"Oh, Mildred," said the man, "give me a quarter to give to this little nigger boy."

The lady in the car was all yellow and curly, and she had on a dress the same color as her mouth. She fished in her purse. "Is it a pussycat?" she said, "or what-all is it?"

The bald man behind her had one shoe off, scratching his foot. "Sure," he said, "you can always tell when it's a cat. A dog just makes one bump, but a cat hits twice. Sticks to the wheel."

"Don't talk revolting," the woman said. "I ain't got a quarter. How about a couple dimes?"

The bald man said, "Anyhow, what kind of a nigger is that? Looks like he been dipped in lye."

Dan let the cat alone and sat back down in the street. He wasn't crying. He asked, "She's dead, ain't she? Is she dead?"

The bald man leaned across over the fender and looked down. "If she ain't," he said, "you got two now."

"Shut up, Willard," the driver said. "Here, boy. Here's twenty cents. You can buy a cartful of strawberry snowballs and more cats too."

Dan didn't even look up.

"Come on, now," said the man, "take the money."

"He's holding out for the quarter," said the bald man. "They all do. Niggers get taught to do that before they can walk. Even pasty niggers."

"No, he ain't," said the driver. "Come on, kid. Take the money, I told you." He held the dimes over Dan's open hand, but it was kind of bloody so he just dropped them in it from high up.

Dan got on his feet and shuffled over to the curb. He was crying now. He looked at the bald man in the back seat. "You big shit," he said.

The man stuck one leg in the air and bust out laughing.

"Oh, come on," said the lady, "I want to go home. I really am *pained* by the whole *episode.*"

"You killed her," Dan said, "you big shit." He didn't shout it, he said it kind of low. But he meant it.

The bald man went right on laughing. "Little kid's got balls," he said. "Funny color balls, but balls."

"Get in Edward," said the lady. "I *told* you not to drive through the nigger district." She asked the bald man, "Are you going to sit there and let him call you that?"

Dan reached back and threw the dimes at the bald man's face. They missed him, and tinkered down against the side of the car. The man stopped laughing. "Hey, nigger," he said, "watch what you doing."

"Leave him alone," said the driver, getting in. "He don't know no better. Kid's upset."

The lady lifted one eyebrow way high, only nobody was watching her. She said, "What are *you*, a *altruist?*"

The car rolled away. Dan went over and kissed the cat, once on each half. Then he saw two other kids coming down the street, and he started to pick up the dimes, for mama.

"Look at him," the man in the back seat shouted, "what did I tell you?" And he said something else, but by that time, the car was too far away for me to hear. I could see the lady laughing again when they turned the corner.

I would of gone out to Dan from the first, only mama had been standing in back of me with her fingers digging into my shoulder since she heard the car skid. I looked at her afterward. She was so scared, her mouth was fixed open, and she couldn't move. She still had a half-ironed slip in her right hand, hanging loose on the floor.

I tried to signal to Dan, but it wasn't easy with mama right where she was, and he didn't see me. He came up the steps, sniffling, and he had his bloody hand stuck straight out with the two dimes in it, bringing them in to give to mama. He opened the screen door himself, and before he even saw her standing there, mama came to life.

She grabbed him by his shirt collar and she lifted him clean off the ground over where I was sitting. Dan's shirt ripped down, leaving powdery white specks all through the ray of sun that came in the window. One of the dimes fell in my lap; the other banged against the wall, and slipped down behind the stove. Mama was so angry, she couldn't talk or hit Dan.

She held him for almost a minute, and she kept looking around the room, as if that could help her.

Then she saw the gunnysack standing in the corner. She jerked Dan over and knocked it down, so the potatoes rolled out on the floor. They bounced around and got under everything. There was just potatoes all over the floor. She put Dan between her knees, and took the empty sack and slipped it over his head. Then she picked it up from the bottom, and shook him in upside down, like she was casing a pillow. Dan never opened his mouth.

Mama reached and got a cord out of the kitchen table, and tied the mouth of the sack. She took a knife, and cut two holes below the cord, next to Dan's feet. After she finished, she put the knife down, and hiked him up, and carried him outside. Around the side of the gallery, right under where one of the clotheslines attached, was where she left him. I watched her from the side window. First she tried to pin him on the line, but Dan was too heavy, so she put him on the ground, in a shady place. When she came back she was panting, and her jaw was set.

She picked up the slip from under the chair where she had dropped it. It was all dirty on one end. She held it out. "Wash it again," she said.

I said: "But, mama . . ."

"*Wash it,*" she said.

So I took and put it in the sink and washed it again. I couldn't see Dan from there, but I kept thinking of him out in that heat in the gunnysack, and I started to cry. Only, I was sweating so hard, mama didn't catch me.

She left him there two whole hours. Once I thought she was looking a little sorry, and I dried off my hands and headed out to him, but she said, "*Lucille.*" And I had to come back.

When she got ready, she went out alone and brought him in. The knot was so tight she had to cut the sack open. Dan had been sick at his stomach inside, and he was unconscious. It was hard getting him out, but she wouldn't let me help her.

She cleaned him off and put him in bed. He was sick for two days, and she tended him. She didn't even let me in there except for the bathroom, and to go to bed at night, after Dan was asleep.

When he was well enough, Dan came and sat at the table with us. Mama still hadn't said a word to him about the accident. She served Clarence first. Then me. Supper was red beans and rice; Dan liked red beans. She took an extra big scoop and put it on his plate. Then she dipped in again and gave him the whole cut of fatback. She stood by him a few seconds. "If I ever catch you saying them words or talking sassy to white people again," she said, "I will kill you, and it will be a kindness."

Then she sat down to eat, and never talked about it no more. I don't think she forgot it, though. And I don't think Dan did either. But he ate the red beans and the fatback too.

Peter S. Feibleman,
from *A Place Without Twilight*

COMIC-STRIP VIEW

For the rest, the fiesta was given over to hilarity, though a historical pageant with figures from the reconquest was played in a serious tone, and modern Santa Feans of Spanish blood rode in the parade dressed in velvet and armor. Their accouterments looked like imitations of the real thing; they themselves did not look like imitations, even though with touching enthusiasm they subscribed to the commercial good cheer of their Anglo-American fellow citizens. The artist writer group of the city helped with decorations, firework concerts, and the creation of a great effigy symbolic of gloom and care, which was burned on the opening night of the festivities. People danced in the streets. Indian and Spanish costumes were loyally undertaken by almost everyone. The Santa Fe High School band in a sort of frantically sassy style gave virtuoso performances of Latin tunes. The hotels were overrun. In the season of late summer, the skies were bright as white gold by day and immensely and closely starred by night.

The Indian was not neglected. His dances were offered by selected groups from various pueblos; and in the fiesta parade, his teachers at the United States Indian School sponsored floats on which young Indians rode, smiling and full of pep, wearing varsity sweaters, and sanctioning in innocent good manners the slogans printed on large placards above them. One, showing a vocational machine shop worked by Indian youths with a white man posed as their teacher, read this way: Papoose Want Um Be Big Chief Machinist. Another, showing a young Indian astride a stuffed bucking horse, read: Me Um Enjoy Riding Mustang. In the young Indian's acceptance of his conqueror's comic-strip view of him, the conquest was complete.

Paul Horgan, from *The Centuries of Santa Fe*

THE NEGRO
AS COMEDIAN

This generally accepted literary ideal of the American Negro constitutes what is really an obstacle in the way of the thoughtful and progressive element of the race. His character has been established as a happy-go-lucky, laughing, shuffling, banjo-picking being, and the reading public has not yet been prevailed upon to take him seriously. His efforts to elevate himself socially are looked upon as a sort of absurd caricature of "white civilization." A novel dealing with colored people who lived in respectable homes and amid a fair degree of culture and who naturally acted "just like white folks" would be taken in a comic-opera sense. In this respect the Negro is much in the position of a great comedian who gives up the lighter roles to play tragedy. No matter how well he may portray the deeper passions, the public is loath to give him up in his old character; they even conspire to make him a failure in serious work, in order to force him back into comedy. In the same respect, the public is not too much to be blamed, for great comedians are far more scarce than mediocre tragedians; every amateur actor is a tragedian.

James Weldon Johnson, from
Autobiography of an Ex-colored Man

DOUBTS
AND DUBIETIES

The good humor of the American Negro is largely founded on cynicism. He is seldom deceived by the white folks who profess to love him, and his view of the race leaders who prey upon him—for example, the clergy—is full of doubts and dubieties. I often wonder how many pious blackamoors really believe that they will turn into white angels postmortem— probably no more than a few imbecile old women. The Negro spirituals, taking one with another, are anything but confident in tone, and after singing the most hopeful of them the congregation often turns to

> I went down to the rock to hide my face;
> The rock cried out, "No hiding place,
> No hiding place down here."

H. L. Mencken, from *Minority Report*

MINSTREL MAN

Because my mouth
Is wide with laughter
And my throat
Is deep with song;
You do not think
I suffer after
I have held my pain
So long?
Because my mouth
Is wide with laughter,
You do not hear
My inner cry?
Because my feet
Are gay with dancing,
You do not know
I die?

Langston Hughes,
from *The Dream Keeper*

WHITEWASHED

By indirection, the caste sanctions also appear within the
Negro family and school in the form of distinctions between
children upon the basis of their color, hair form, and type of
facial contour. It must be remembered that the differentiating
marks of the white caste are physical. The Negro *class* sanc-

tions, moreover, are in part organized around differences in color, hair form, and features. It is also true that white people make some distinction in the punishment and patronage of individual Negroes upon the basis of the Negro's approximation to the white physical type. A colored child who is light skinned with wavy or straight hair therefore has an arbitrary and fortuitous advantage over more Negroid children, both in his own class participation and in his relations with whites.

In socially withdrawn, light-skinned groups of colored people such as the colored Creoles in New Orleans and the remnants of the "blue vein" cliques in Old City, however, parents make no effort to conceal their preference for light-skinned children, and their desire to obtain equally light mates for them. Until very recently in Old City, a dark child born to a "blue vein" family was sent away to live with dark relatives in another community. The head of the leading family in this group in 1934 said that only a few years before, "if a child turned out black or dark, it was just too bad for him." His own father had used a shotgun to drive off a brown-skinned suitor of his daughter. Even today in New Orleans, some of the light-skinned Creole families who work as white send any dark baby away to a dark branch of the family. The grandparents and parents maintain close surveillance, furthermore, upon the courting of the children to prevent the choice of a dark mate. Because these colored Creoles now attend the churches, schools, and dances as the rest of the Negroes and increasingly intermarry with them, however, such color distinctions are becoming less rigid.

The importance that color and hair form have for the Negro parent may be most clearly understood from the discussions of colored women or parents concerning a prospective or newborn child. The female interviewers heard several discussions of this kind among upper-class and upper-middle-class Negroes in Old City and in New Orleans. Parents and grandparents were extremely concerned about the color and hair form of the baby, condoling each other if the child was darker or had "worse" hair than had been expected, and felicitating each other if he was lighter or had "better" hair than had been expected. Even before the birth of a child, some upper-class and upper-middle-class parents surveyed in minute detail all the possibilities with regard to the child's color and hair form by recalling these traits in each of their parents and grandparents. It is probably safe to assume that such concern is felt by most upper-class and middle-class Negro parents, even when not verbalized. It is a justifiable point of anxiety, certainly, because it is a vital factor in the child's class and caste opportunities.

Allison Davis and John Dollard,
from *Children of Bondage*

FROM "NIGHTMARE"

My father was also belligerent toward all of the children, except me. The older ones he would beat almost savagely if they broke any of his rules—and he had so many rules it was hard to know them all. Nearly all my whippings came from my mother. I've thought a lot about why. I actually believe that as antiwhite as my father was, he was subconsciously so afflicted with the white man's brainwashing of Negroes that he inclined to favor the light ones, and I was his lightest child. Most Negro parents in those days would almost instinctively treat any lighter children better than they did the darker ones. It came directly from the slavery tradition that the "mulatto," because he was visibly nearer to white, was therefore "better."

Malcolm X and Alex Haley,
from *The Autobiography of Malcolm X*

FROM "HOMEBOY"

Shorty soon decided that my hair was finally long enough to be conked. He had promised to school me in how to beat the barbershops' three- and four-dollar price by making up congolene, and then conking ourselves.

I took the little list of ingredients he had printed out for me, and went to a grocery store, where I got a can of Red Devil lye, two eggs, and two medium-sized white potatoes. Then at a drugstore near the poolroom, I asked for a large jar of Vaseline, a large bar of soap, a large-toothed comb and a fine-toothed comb, one of those rubber hoses with a metal spray head, a rubber apron and a pair of gloves.

"Going to lay on that first conk?" the drugstore man asked me. I proudly told him, grinning, "Right!"

Shorty paid six dollars a week for a room in his cousin's shabby apartment. His cousin wasn't at home. "It's like the pad's mine, he spends so much time with his woman," Shorty said. "Now, you watch me—"

He peeled the potatoes and thin-sliced them into a quart-sized Mason fruit jar, then started stirring them with a wooden spoon as he gradually poured in a little over half the can of lye. "Never use a metal spoon; the lye will turn it black," he told me.

A jellylike, starchy-looking glop resulted from the lye and potatoes, and Shorty broke in the two eggs, stirring real fast —his own conk and dark face bent down close. The congolene turned pale-yellowish. "Feel the jar," Shorty said. I cupped my hand against the outside, and snatched it away. "Damn right, it's hot, that's the lye," he said. "So you know it's going to burn when I comb it in—it burns *bad*. But the longer you can stand it, the straighter the hair."

He made me sit down, and he tied the string of the new

rubber apron tightly around my neck, and combed up my bush of hair. Then, from the big Vaseline jar, he took a handful and massaged it hard all through my hair and into the scalp. He also thickly Vaselined my neck, ears, and forehead. "When I get to washing out your head, be sure to tell me anywhere you feel any little stinging," Shorty warned me, washing his hands, then pulling on the rubber gloves, and tying on his own rubber apron. "You always got to remember that any congolene left in burns a sore into your head."

The congolene just felt warm when Shorty started combing it in. But then my head caught fire.

I gritted my teeth and tried to pull the sides of the kitchen table together. The comb felt as if it was raking my skin off.

My eyes watered, my nose was running. I couldn't stand it any longer; I bolted to the washbasin. I was cursing Shorty with every name I could think of when he got the spray going and started soap-lathering my head.

He lathered and spray-rinsed, lathered and spray-rinsed, maybe ten or twelve times, each time gradually closing the hot water faucet, until the rinse was cold, and that helped some.

"You feel any stinging spots?"

"No," I managed to say. My knees were trembling.

"Sit back down, then. I think we got it all out OK."

The flame came back as Shorty, with a thick towel, started drying my head, rubbing hard. "*Easy*, man, *easy!*" I kept shouting.

"The first time's always worst. You get used to it better before long. You took it real good, homeboy. You got a good conk."

When Shorty let me stand up and see in the mirror, my hair hung down in limp, damp strings. My scalp still flamed, but not as badly; I could bear it. He draped the towel around my shoulders, over my rubber apron, and began again Vaselining my hair. I could feel him combing, straight back, first the big comb, then the fine-toothed one.

Then, he was using a razor, very delicately, on the back of my neck. Then, finally, shaping the sideburns.

My first view in the mirror blotted out the hurting. I'd seen some pretty conks, but when it's the first time, on your *own* head, the transformation, after the lifetime of kinks, is staggering.

The mirror reflected Shorty behind me. We both were grinning and sweating. And on top of my head was this thick, smooth sheen of shining red hair—real red—as straight as any white man's.

How ridiculous I was! Stupid enough to stand there simply lost in admiration of my hair now looking "white," reflected in the mirror in Shorty's room. I vowed that I'd never again be without a conk, and I never was for many years.

This was my first really big step toward self-degradation: when I endured all of that pain, literally burning my flesh with lye, in order to cook my natural hair until it was limp, to have it look like a white man's hair. I had joined that multitude of Negro men and women in America who are brainwashed into believing that the black people are "inferior"—and white people "superior"—that they will even violate and mutilate their God-created bodies to try to look "pretty" by white standards.

Look around today, in every small town and big city, from two-bit catfish and soda-pop joints into the "integrated" lobby of the Waldorf-Astoria and you'll see conks on black men. And you'll see black women wearing these green and pink and purple and red and platinum blond wigs. They're all more ridiculous than a slapstick comedy. It makes you wonder if the Negro has completely lost his sense of identity, lost touch with himself.

You'll see the conk worn by many, many so-called upper-class Negroes, and, as much as I hate to say it about them, on all too many Negro entertainers. One of the reasons that I've especially admired some of them, such as Lionel Hampton and Sidney Poitier, among others, is that they have kept their natural hair and fought to the top. I admire any Negro man who has never had himself conked, or who has had the sense to get rid of it—as I finally did.

I don't know which kind of self-defacing conk is the greater shame—the one you'll see on the heads of the black so-called middle class and upper class, who ought to know better, or the one you'll see on the heads of the poorest, most down-trodden, ignorant black men. I mean the legal-minimum-wage ghetto-dwelling kind of Negro, as I was when I got my first one. It's generally among these poor fools that you'll see a black kerchief over the man's head, like Aunt Jemima; he's trying to make his conk last longer, between trips to the bar-bershop. Only for special occasions is this kerchief-protected conk exposed—to show off how "sharp" and "hip" its owner is. The ironic thing is that I have never heard any woman, white or black, express any admiration for a conk. Of course, any white woman with a black man isn't thinking about his hair. But I don't see how on earth a black woman with any race pride could walk down the street with any black man wearing a conk—the emblem of his shame that he is black.

To my own shame, when I say all of this I'm talking first of all about myself—because you can't show me any Negro who ever conked more faithfully than I did. I'm speaking from personal experience when I say of any black man who conks today, or any white-wigged black woman, that if they gave the brains in their heads just half as much attention as they do their hair, they would be a thousand times better off.

Malcolm X and Alex Haley,
from *The Autobiography of Malcolm X*

MARIA

María has had to live her own life—make her own life—by herself, for her husband left her with three small children to support. She has done it without any help from the state or the family, and in doing it moved much further in spirit, if not in distance, from the world of her parents. They live in East Harlem too, just a few blocks away from María, but they speak only Spanish and do not altogether approve of María's friends who speak only English, or—like María—speak both Spanish and English and often choose to speak English. But María has always been something of a family outsider—she was born that way. This, she says, is what it is like:

"I'm the darkest one in my family. I was always being 'explained away.' I don't mind that anymore, but what I can't take is the way my parents won't face the facts. They never would really admit my color, even to me. My mother told me we were Puerto Ricans, and Puerto Ricans were white. I remember I came home from school one day and I told my mother a boy in my class was as black as my shoes, and he spoke Spanish. She told me no, if that boy spoke Spanish, he was white."

The darkest-skinned member of a Puerto Rican family often complains that he is the "lowest" in the family, and has to do all the work around home and gets little reward. The Reverend Norman Eddy, who has worked for more than five years with narcotics addicts in the neighborhood, has observed that in almost every case the Puerto Rican addict is the darkest-skinned member of his family. "He may actually have very light skin, but if you meet his family you almost always see that his skin is darker than the others in the family."

Dan Wakefield, from *Island in the City*

BROTHERS
UNDER THE SKIN

My daydreaming was splintered by my brother José kicking at the door in sheer panic. "Hey, who's in there?" he yelled.

"Me, man, me," I yelled back. "Whatta ya want?"

"Let me in. I gotta take a piss so bad I can taste it."

"Taste good?" I asked softly.

"Dammit, open up!"

I laughed, and reached out a dripping hand and flipped the latch. José rushed in like his behind was on fire. His face had a pained look on it. "Chri-sus sake," he said, "you made me piss all over my pants."

"It'll dry, man, it'll dry."

"Aggh," he said as he relieved himself. "That feels good." I looked at my brother. *Even his peter's white*, I thought, *just like James's. Only ones got black peters is poppa and me, and poppa acts like his is white, too.*

"Poppa's home."

"Yeah. Hand me the towel, simple."

"Damn, Piri, you made me piss all over my pants," José said again. He pulled back the towel he was offering me and began to wipe his pants with it.

"Man, turkey, what you doin'?" I said. "You drying that piss and I gotta wipe my face with that towel."

"It'll dry, man, it'll dry."

I yanked the towel outta his hand and carefully wiped with what seemed to be the part he hadn't used. "You know somethin', José?" I said.

"What? Jesus, I hope this piss don't stink when it dries."

"I'm goin' down South."

"Where?"

"Down South."

"What for?"

"Don't know all the way," I said, "except I'm tryin' to find somethin' out."

"*Down South!*" He said it like I was nuts.

"*Sí.* I want to see what a *moyeto*'s worth and the paddy's weight on him," I said.

"Whatta ya talking about? You sound like a *moto* who's high on that *yerba* shit. And anyway, what's the spade gotta do with you?"

"I'm a Negro."

"You ain't no nigger," José said.

"I ain't?"

"No. You're a Puerto Rican."

"I am, huh?" I looked at José and said, "Course, you gotta say that. 'Cause if I'm a Negro, then you and James is one too. And that ain't leavin' out sis and poppa. Only momma's an exception. She don't care what she is."

José didn't look at me. He decided that looking at the toilet bowl was better. "So whatta you got to find out, eh?" he said. "You're crazy, stone loco. We're Puerto Ricans, and that's different from being *moyetos.*" His voice came back very softly and his hand absentmindedly kept brushing the drying wet patch on his pants.

"That's what I've been wanting to believe all along, José," I said. "I've been hanging on to that idea even when I knew it wasn't so. But only pure white Puerto Ricans are white, and you wouldn't even believe that if you ever dug what the paddy said."

"I don't give a good shit what you say, Piri. We're Puerto Ricans, and that makes us different from black people."

I kept drying myself even though there was nothin' to dry. I was trying not to get mad. I said, "José, that's what the white man's been telling the Negro all along, that 'cause he's white he's different from the Negro; that he's better'n the Negro or anyone that's not white. That's what I've been telling myself and what I tried to tell Brew."

"Brew's that colored guy, ain't he?" José said.

"Yeah—an' like I'm saying, sure there's stone-white Puerto Ricans, like from pure Spanish way back—but it ain't us. Poppa's a Negro and, even if Momma's *blanca*, poppa's blood carries more weight with Mr. Charlie," I said.

"Mr. Charlie, Mr. Charlie. Who the fuck is he?"

"That's the name Brew calls the paddies. Ask any true *corazón* white motherfucker what the score is," I said.

"I'm not black, no matter what you say, Piri."

I got out of the shower and sat on the edge of the tub. "Maybe not outside, José," I said. "But you're sure that way inside."

"I ain't black, damn you! Look at my hair. It's almost blond. My eyes are blue, my nose is straight. My motherfuckin' lips are not like a baboon's ass. My skin is white. White, goddammit! White! Maybe poppa's a little dark, but that's the Indian blood in him. He's got white blood in him and—"

"So what the fuck am I? Something poppa an' momma picked out the garbage dump?" I was jumping stink inside and I answered him like I felt it. "Look, man, better believe it, I'm one of 'you-all.' Am I your brother or ain't I?"

"Yeah, you're my brother, and James an' sis, and we all come out of momma an' poppa—but we ain't Negroes. We're Puerto Ricans, an' we're white."

"Boy, you, poppa, and James sure are sold on that white kick. Poppa thinks that marrying a white woman made him white. He's wrong. It's just another nigger marrying a white woman and making her as black as him. That's the way the paddy looks at it. The Negro just stays black. Period. Dig it?"

José's face got whiter and his voice angrier at my attempt to take away his white status. He screamed out strong, "I ain't no nigger! You can be if you want to be. You can go down South and grow cotton, or pick it, or whatever the fuck they do. You can eat the cornbread or whatever shit they eat. You can bow and kiss ass and clean shit bowls. But—I—am—*white!* And you can go to hell!"

"And James is *blanco*, too?" I asked quietly.

"You're damn right."

"And poppa?"

José flushed the toilet chain so hard it sounded as if some-body's neck had broken. "Poppa's the same as you," he said, avoiding my eyes, "Indian."

"What kinda Indian?" I said bitterly. "Caribe? Or maybe Borinquén? Say, José, didn't you know the Negro made the scene in Puerto Rico way back? And when the Spanish spics ran outta Indian coolies, they brought them big blacks from you know where. Poppa's got *moyeto* blood. I got it. Sis got it. James got it. And, mah deah brudder, you-all got it! Dig it! It's with us till game time. Like I said, man, that shit-ass poison I've been living with is on its way out. It's a played-out lie about me—us—being white. There ain't nobody in this fucking house can lay claim to bein' paddy exceptin' momma, and she's never made it a mountain of fever like we have. You and James are like houses—painted white outside, and blacker'n a mother inside. An' I'm close to being like poppa—trying to be white on both sides."

José eased by me and put his hand on the doorknob.

"Where you going?" I said. "I ain't finished talking yet."

José looked at me like there was no way out. "Like I said, man, you can be a nigger if you want to," he said, as though he were talking with a ten-ton rock on his chest. "I don't know how you come to be my brother, but I love you like one. I've busted my ass, both me and James, trying to explain to people how come you so dark and how come your hair is so curly an'—"

I couldn't help thinking, *Oh, Crutch, you were so right. We shouldn't have moved to Long Island.* I said, "You and James hadda make excuses for *me*? Like for me being *un Negrito?*" I looked at the paddy in front of me. "Who to?" I said. "Pad-dies?"

Lights began to jump into my head and tears blurred out

that this was my brother before me. The burning came up out of me and I felt the shock run up my arm as my fists went up the side of his head. I felt one fist hit his mouth. I wondered if I had broken any of his nice white teeth.

José fell away and bounced back with his white hands curled into fists. I felt the hate in them as his fists became a red light of exploding pain on my tender, flat nose. *Oh, God!* I tried to make the lights go away. I made myself creep up a long sinking shit-hole agony and threw myself at José. The bathroom door flew open and me, naked and wet with angry sweat, and José, his mouth bleedin', crashed out of the bathroom and rolled into the living room. I heard all kinds of screaming and chairs turning over and falling lamps. I found myself on top of José. In the blurred confusion I saw his white, blood-smeared face and I heard myself screaming, "You bastard! Dig it, you bastard. You're bleeding, and the blood is like anybody else's—red!" I saw an unknown face spitting blood at me. I hated it. I wanted to stay on top of this unknown what-was-it and beat him and beat him and beat him and beat him and *beat beat beat beat beat*—and feel skin smash under me and—and—and—

I felt an arm grab me. It wasn't fair; it wasn't a *chevere* thing to do. In a fair rumble, nobody is supposed to jump in. "Goddammit, are you crazy?" a voice screamed. "Goddamn you for beating your brother like that. My God!—"

I twisted my head and saw poppa. And somewhere, far off, I heard a voice that sounded like momma crying, "What's it all about? What's it all about? Why do brothers do this to each other?"

I wanted to scream it out, but that man's arm was cutting my air from sound. I twisted and forced out, "Lemme go, poppa. *Coño*, let me go!" And the arm was gone. I stayed on bended knees. My fists were tired and my knuckles hurt at this Cain and Abel scene. As the hurting began to leave me, I slowly became a part of my naked body. I felt weak with inside pain. I wondered why.

"José, José," momma screamed, and I wondered why she didn't scream for me, too. Didn't she know I had gotten hurt the worst?

"Why in God's name?" poppa was saying.

Fuck God! I thought.

"Why in God's name?"

I looked at poppa. " 'Cause, poppa," I said, "him, you, and James think you're white, and I'm the only one that's found out I'm not. I tried hard not to find out. But I did, and I'm almost out from under that kick you all are still copping out to." I got up from my knees. "Poppa," I added, "what's wrong with not being white? What's so wrong with being *tregeño?* Momma must think it's great, she got married to you, eh? We gotta have pride and dignity, poppa; we gotta walk big and bad. I'm me and I dig myself in the mirror and it's me. I shower and dig my peter and it's me. I'm black, and it don't make no difference whether I say good-bye or *adiós*—it means the same."

Nobody said anything; everyone just stood there. I said, "I'm proud to be a Puerto Rican, but being Puerto Rican don't make the color." Still there was silence. "I'm going," I said.

"Where?" Poppa asked.

"I don't know . . ."

"He's going down South," said José, sitting on the floor with his head in his hands and the almost-blond hair, the good, straight hair that could fall down over his forehead.

"*Where?*" poppa asked.

I looked at José and felt sorry for me. I looked at the wall and said, "Down South. I joined the merchant marine and me and Brew's going, and—"

"Who? Brew? That's that colored boy, ain't it?" poppa said.

"—and I wanna find out what's happening, and . . ." I wondered why everything I was saying didn't sound like it was so important to anybody, including me. I wondered why James wasn't there. I wondered why sis wasn't there . . .

I walked away. Momma put her hand on me and she asked, "Why does it hurt you so to be *un Negrito?*"

I shook my head and kept walking. I wished she could see inside me. I wished she could see it didn't hurt—so much.

Piri Thomas, from Down These Mean Streets

CROSS

My old man's a white old man
And my old mother's black.
If ever I cursed my white old man
I take my curses back.

If ever I cursed my black old mother
And wished she were in hell,
I'm sorry for that evil wish
And now I wish her well.

My old man died in a fine big house.
My ma died in a shack.
I wonder where I'm gonna die,
Being neither white nor black?

Langston Hughes, from The Weary Blues

LOSING PERSPECTIVE

"In the relocation centers," writes Franklyn Sugiyama, "the people are like fish dynamited—they are helplessly stunned, floating belly up on the stream of life." "The most terrible factor concerning camp life," writes Frank Watanabe, "is the havoc this uneasy, restricted, and enclosed life is working upon the young people's character and personality. Many of the youngsters are growing up in this environment knowing very little about the outside. Consequently, their ideas, their outlook upon life have changed greatly. Many are bitter toward the outside society while others are just indifferent. It's just not an ordinary healthy environment. Parent-child relationships are broken down in many cases. Discipline is neglected because the parents in many cases have lost faith in themselves as well as in this country. Initiative, individual assurance, and the will to succeed have been lost in the desert sands just as water evaporates in its intense heat. Even educated men and women in a few cases have gotten this devil-may-care attitude and it sure hasn't helped matters very much." Those who have remained in the centers are becoming overcautious, more timid, highly race conscious. Their world tends to grow smaller, not larger; and it was a small airless world to begin with. They lose perspective; they become Rip Van Winkles, out of touch with the world, with the nation, with the people."

"The shock that we sustained," writes Hanna Kozasa, "and the bitterness that overwhelmed us was most trying. The barbed wire fences, the armed sentries, the observation towers, increased our sense of frustration to the point that many have not been able to regain a proper perspective. The most alarming aspect of life in the centers is the demoralization it is working in the people. It is sapping their initiative in a frightening manner. The forced labor, with its low pay, indecent housing, inadequate food, the insecurity of their position in a postwar America, have contributed to a deterioration of family life that is beginning to show in a sharply increased juvenile delinquency—this among a people that had the lowest crime rate of any group in the United States." "Evacuation," writes Howard Imazeki, "distorted the life philosophy of the Japanese Americans and their parents. It completely warped the perspective of the majority of the Nisei in its earlier stage.

Carey McWilliams, from *Prejudice*

"BOY" STATUS

Consider the following. Once last year as I was leaving my office in Jackson, Mississippi, with my Negro secretary, a white policeman yelled, "Hey, boy! Come here!" Somewhat bothered, I retorted, "I'm no boy!" He then rushed at me, inflamed, and stood towering over me, snorting, "What d'ja say, boy?" Quickly he frisked me and demanded, "What's your name, boy?" Frightened, I replied, "Dr. Poussaint. I'm a physician." He angrily chuckled and hissed, "What's your first name, boy?" When I hesitated, he assumed a threatening stance and clenched his fists. As my heart palpitated, I muttered in profound humiliation, "Alvin."

He continued his psychological brutality, bellowing, "Alvin, the next time I call you, you come right away, you hear? You hear?" I hesitated. "You hear me, boy?" My voice trembling with helplessness, but following my instincts of self-preservation, I murmured, "Yes, sir." Now fully satisfied that I had performed and acquiesced to my "boy" status, he dismissed me with, "Now, boy, go on and get out of here or next time we'll take you for a little ride down to the station house!"

No amount of self-love could have salvaged my pride or preserved my integrity. In fact, the slightest show of self-respect or resistance might have cost me my life. For the moment my manhood had been ripped from me—and in the presence of a Negro woman for whom I, a man, was supposed to be the protector. In addition, this had occurred in a public street for all the local black people to witness, reminding them that *no* black man was as good as *any* white man. All of us—doctor, lawyer, postman, field hand, and shoe-shine boy—had been psychologically "put in our place."

The self-hate that I felt at that time was generated by the fact that I and my people were completely helpless and powerless to destroy that white bigot and all that he represented. Suppose I had decided, as a man should, to be forceful? What crippling price would I have paid for a few moments of assertive manhood? What was I to do with my rage?

And if I, a physician in middle-class dress, was vulnerable to this treatment, imagine the brutality to which "ordinary" black people are subjected—not only in the South but also in the North, where the brutality is likely to be more psychological than physical.

Alvin F. Poussaint,
from *A Negro Psychiatrist
Explains the Negro Psyche*

SOLVING
THE DILEMMA

Mister Starks
hailed from Onward, Mississippi—
via Paris, Texas, *via* Broken Bow, Oklahoma.
How he got his *Christian* name is a legend
that tickles the inwards of the Zulu Club Wits.
When he was four years old,
his black mother took him to
the Big House on an *ante-bellum* estate;
and the Lady wanted to know the baby's name
and the proud mother said "Mister."
Since every Negro male in Dixie was
either a *boy* or an *uncle*,
the mistress turned blue and hot
like an arc-welder's torch.
"A pickaninny named *Mister?*" the old doll hissed;
and the maid, slamming the mop bucket down,

screamed: "Miss Leta,
it's *my* baby and I can name it
any damn thing I please!"

Melvin B. Tolson, from *Harlem Gallery*

THE BITTER CROP

Hemphill P. Pride II, a Columbia
lawyer who said last week he had been
retained by the Chaney family, said:
"Chaney is a mental problem, and it all
grew out of the killing of his brother."

New York Times,
24 May 1970

The short life of Ben Chaney, Jr., is bounded by two night-
mares. When he was eleven, his brother James, twenty, was
murdered by the Ku Klux Klan. James and two other civil
rights workers, Andrew Goodman and Michael Schwerner,
were lynched on 21 June 1964 in Philadelphia, Mississippi.
Their bodies were found under an earthen dam forty-four
days later. At the funeral for the three, Ben cried out for his
brother, "Come back, James, come back, come back . . ."

Last week Ben, now seventeen, was locked in a death row
cell at the state penitentiary in Columbia, South Carolina,
charged with murder and armed robbery. Police allege that he
and two other black teen-agers went on a three-week homi-
cidal rampage through the South, killing four white persons
and wounding two others whom they left for dead. Young
Chaney, whose only previous brushes with the police were
as a civil rights demonstrator, denies killing anyone, but admits

that he was a member of the trio. After his arrest he was permitted to call his mother, who lives in a Manhattan low-cost housing project. "He told me, 'Don't get upset and don't get worried,' " Mrs. Chaney said later. " 'They got me in jail here for murder. But you know I ain't killed nobody. I was driving the car. You *know* I ain't killed nobody.' "

Mrs. Chaney and Ben's three older sisters find it impossible to believe that the baby of the family, whom they called Junior, is a mass murderer. "He's the only son I've got now," said Mrs. Chaney. "He is a good boy, and when he was little he was always saying he wanted to be a lawyer or maybe a politician."

As a boy, Ben was familiar to civil rights workers because he followed his older brother around like a proud shadow. When James died, they tried to comfort him by suggesting that one day he would carry on James's work. "So many people said, 'You've got to live up to James,' " a sister recalled. "Maybe too much was put on him." Mrs. Chaney herself echoed the puzzlement of all who knew Ben by adding, "This whole thing is unbelievable. I can't imagine what really happened." After the murder of James, she recalled, irate whites in their native Meridian, Mississippi, took potshots at the house. These night riders forced Mrs. Chaney to consider moving north. She was aided in the move by the Walden School, a private school in Manhattan from which Andrew Goodman had been graduated. Ben received the first Andrew Goodman memorial scholarship. With the help of private tutoring, he developed into a fair student with an aptitude for mathematics and drawing. Nathan Levine, director of the school, said the boy soon made an adequate adjustment. Ben also took an active interest in soccer and basketball. But in October 1969, he dropped out of the Walden School. One of his sisters said he just seemed to lose interest. He busied himself during this period with various civil rights groups, including the Black High School Coalition, which shared offices wth the Harlem Committee for Self-Defense. He also participated in demonstrations at City College and the Harlem

YMCA. He no longer lived at home, but stayed alternately at the apartments of his three married sisters. He studied Pan-Africanism, and for a while called himself Kwame.

On 24 April of this year, Ben Chaney told his family he was going to Detroit. Instead, police say, he and two friends, Martin Rutrell, fifteen, and Lindsay Lee Thompson, nineteen, barreled south in a stolen 1970 Buick. They drove all night, and the following afternoon were in Durham, North Carolina. At dusk, two white youths were robbed, shot, and left for dead by two black hitchhikers they had picked up. The victims survived and eventually identified their assailants as Thompson and Rutrell. The victims also said they had seen Chaney near the scene in the stolen blue Buick. Several days later in Fort Lauderdale, Florida, an insurance collector was accosted by two blacks in a car who robbed him of about $100 and then shot him to death. Police said a second suspicious car was in the neighborhood of the killing. On 14 May in Boca Raton, Florida, two co-eds in a red 1969 Chevrolet Camaro were ordered at gunpoint to drive to a lover's lane where they were shot in the head and killed.

The next day, and four hundred miles to the north, two blacks walked into a fireworks stand in Hardeeville, South Carolina. A third waited outside in a red 1969 Chevrolet Camaro. According to police, Thompson shot the proprietor dead. Seconds later Thompson was killed by a sixteen-year-old employee, who, though wounded in the hand, drew a weapon from under the counter and fired. Several miles away, Rutrell and Chaney were arrested without resistance at a roadblock. Police said they were riding in the co-eds' red car. Inside the automobile, detectives found a pistol, three rifles, a sawed-off shotgun and two bayonets.

Questioned separately, each of the teen-agers said Thompson alone had done all the killing. Chaney told police that Thompson was "a guy just back from Vietnam who liked to kill for the pleasure of it." Ben Chaney insisted to police, as he did to his mother, that he had only driven the car. He had telephoned her periodically during the killing spree, and reported unfailingly that he was having "a fine time." Both Rutrell and Chaney were asked by police why they didn't leave Thompson when the bloodshed started. They were quoted as replying: "Don't we wish we could have."

A visitor to the maximum security wing of the prison last week who had also attended the funeral of James Chaney suddenly wondered how much a boy is the father of the man: The eyes of the boy who watched his brother being buried were exactly the same as those of the youth now in death row: black, liquid, absolutely haunted.

Michael Mok, from "Ben Chaney
at Eleven and Seventeen," *Life,* 19 June 1970

American Indians share with other racially visible ethnic-minority groups of low economic status the discrimination, poverty, poor housing, lack of education, and other conditions that are associated with delinquent behavior and high rates of crime. Under the weight of these deprivations, it is not surprising that American Indians have sought relief in alcohol. Alcoholic beverages have been the easiest and quickest way to deaden the senses and to forget the feeling of inadequacy. Under the influence of liquor the real world becomes substituted by an unreal one where the Indian sees himself as an equal to others, and with the physical and psychological support provided by drinking companions, the world appears less hostile and even tolerable.

Edward P. Dozier, *Problem Drinking
Among American Indians*

CHEYENNE MEMORIES

Butchering was just about the only trouble in the old days. It was not like today, with so many fights and car wrecks, and people stealing each other's property and deserting their wives and children. The police have a hard time today, trying to keep order. And whiskey or wine seems to cause a lot of the trouble.

But it always made trouble when Indians got it. They were not used to it and it made them half-crazy. The Cheyennes traded for it even back in the early days. I remember the first time I saw them after they had been drinking. I was so small I was still riding a travois. We used to go on hunting trips in the fall when the deer were fat, all the way south of Buffalo, Wyoming. A white man had a saloon down there at Crazy Woman, fifteen or twenty miles from Buffalo. His name was Harris and he had a Cheyenne wife, so the Cheyennes used to stop there. I saw some men after they came back, staggering and walking crooked and some throwing up, and when I asked grandmother what was wrong she said they had been drinking the white man's water.

The old people tried to keep the young ones away from whiskey because they always came home and made trouble, but they could not stop them and it has been that way ever since. The reservation is dry. The tribe has voted against allowing it, but it doesn't make much difference. Up to the last few years Indians had to get it from bootleggers. Now it is easier. They can go off the reservation to any little town and come home drunk or even bring it with them—though the police take it away if they catch them. A lot of them now are in the condition that they can't help it.

Except for the scouts at Fort Keogh the old Indians had a hard time getting it. My uncle Crazy Mule told how he was in

Sheridan one time when a soldier came along with a quart bottle and said he would sell it for ten dollars. He and Wolf Chief and Crooked Nose had eight dollars between them, so the soldier took that and he left kind of hurrying. They said, "Let's just us three go up on the hill and sit down and drink until we are finished." So they went through the fence and up where the water tank is on the east side of town, and sat down in the shade.

The cork would not come out so they pushed it down inside, and Crooked Nose took a big drink. He smacked his lips but he looked kind of funny. Then Wolf Chief took a drink and gave it to Crazy Mule. But it did not smell like whiskey. It smelled like coffee. And it was. The soldier had sold them a bottle of coffee for eight dollars.

Another way they got it in the early years was from old man Curly, a blacksmith at the agency. He used to come out from town and stop with my grandfather. One time I remember he announced he had whiskey and he would trade for horses. And some young men showed up with four real good ones, that he got for a quart apiece.

Sometimes the old Indians would fix a person who made trouble drinking, but they don't do it anymore. It happened once in Miles City when they had a big stampede on the Fourth of July, around 1925. Red Water, one of the first educated Indians—the one who had seen the Sioux ghost dance—was the troublemaker. He had gone to school at Haskell and was a top football player, and he got a fine place when he came back to the reservation. But he neglected it and lost it, and never used his education, and whenever he started drinking he wanted to fight. This time in Miles City he had been chasing everybody out of their camps and they got mad at him. Finally Wooden Leg threw him down and hog-tied him. He was a strong man, but it took some others to help him. They tied Red Water's hands and hung him up by the feet over the limb of a tree. His head almost touched the ground. He was there for several hours. At last somebody cut him loose. His face was all swelled up but he was all right, and he did not make any more trouble for a while. But he was always bad when he got drunk. I think he was an alcoholic. He died in the hospital.

John-Stands-in-Timber and Margot
Liberty, from Cheyenne Memories

IRA HAYES

Many Americans will have heard of Ira Hayes, the Pima Indian who with his five mates in the Marine Corps raised the United States flag on Mount Suribachi on the island of Iwo Jima. He was in the photograph, now world famous, taken by Joe Rosenthal. But Ira Hayes died of acute alcoholism in a cotton field on the Pima reservation on a night in January 1955. He lay all night on the cold ground, and death was attributed to "exposure." What had happened in the ten years intervening since the dramatic moment on Mount Suribachi?

On 12 November 1953, the *Arizona Republic*, the Phoenix morning newspaper, reported that Hayes spent the previous night in jail on a drunk-and-disorderly charge. The reporter did some digging in the files, and found that this was the forty-second occasion that Hayes had been arrested on such a charge. There would be still other arrests between November 1953 and January 1955.

He had served throughout the South Pacific, fighting at Vella Lavella and Bougainville before coming up to Iwo Jima, where he served for thirty-six days and came out unwounded. After the flag-raising incident he and two of his buddies were brought back to the United States to travel extensively in support of the seventh war loan. One of these buddies repeated that Hayes refused to be leader of a platoon because, as he explained, "I'd have to tell other men to go and get killed, and I'd rather do it myself." He was reluctant to return home, but was given no choice. That started a round of speaking engagements, parades, ticker tape—and people offering hospitality. The hospitality, unfortunately, invariably included free liquor, and Ira drank greedily. It was the quickest way to blur the painful, heedless publicity to which he was subjected.

After his discharge he went home to Arizona, in the district called Bapchule. After the excitement of the war and the hectic round of living that he had just experienced, Hayes's Indian home was not a place in which he could settle down at once. His was no longer a self-sufficient family, such as Hayes might have known in his own childhood, which certainly his ancestors had known before him. Without adequate water to grow crops, with landholdings reduced beyond any hope of economic livelihood even if there had been water, it was not a place for a returning warrior to rest and mend. Too many other mouths depended on the food he would eat.

With the help of the relocation program of the Bureau of Indian Affairs, he went to Chicago and found employment with the International Harvester Company. For a while things went well with him, then he began drinking again. He was picked up on Skid Row in Chicago, dirty and shoeless, and sent to jail. The *Chicago Sun-Times* discovered who he was, got him out of jail, and raised a fund for his rehabilitation. A job was secured for him in Los Angeles, where it was hoped that he might make a fresh start. Many organizations, including church groups, helped out.

Hayes thanked everybody gratefully, and said, "I know I'm cured of drinking now." But in less than a week he was arrested by Los Angeles police on the old charge. When he returned to Phoenix, he received no hero's welcome. He told the reporter who met him: "I guess I'm just no good. I've had a lot of chances, but just when things started looking good I get that craving for whiskey and foul up. I'm going back home for a while. Maybe after I'm around my family, I'll be able to figure things out."

But the family home still did not have the answer. Across

the road and across the fence that marks the Pima reservation, water runs in irrigation ditches. The desert is green with cotton, barley, wheat, alfalfa, and citrus fruit, pasturage for sheep and cattle. But the water and the green fields are on the white man's side of the reservation fence.

He tried once, in 1950, to plead the case of his people before government officials in Washington. He asked "for freedom for the Pima Indians. They want to manage their own affairs, and cease being wards of the federal government."

But what he was asking had become infinitely complicated. It involved acts of Congress, court decrees, a landowners' agreement, operation and maintenance requirements. So complicated had it become that the lawyers and the engineers and the administrators hired by the government had succeeded only in reducing by half the acreage that the Pima Indians, in their simple way, had cultivated, on which they had grown surpluses of grain to sell to hungry white men.

Ira Hayes, coming home, looked at the mud-and-wattle house, the ramada standing to one side, a few poor outbuildings, and knew that he would not find the answer there. He found it on the cold ground in a cotton field.

Harold E. Fey and D'Arcy McNickle,
from *Indians and Other Americans*

HOOKED

And when you're poor,
you grow up fast.

Billie Holiday

I was just born black, poor, and uneducated. And you only need three strikes all over the world to be out, and I have nothing to live for but this shot of dope.

I have nothing to shoot at. All I have to look forward to is a thrill and it's in a bag, and they run me up on the roof to get that. I don't have any place to turn, but I imagine you have. I'm poor and all I can look forward to is what I can get out of this bag. That's the only thrill in life for me, you know. I've never had anything, no opportunity, you know, to get any money, no nothing. All I can look forward to is what I can get out of this bag, and that's nothing really.

When I started I was fourteen years old, and that's twelve years ago. Drugs were much different then. For a dollar a cap poor people got rich. I started back where a man could shoot dope—hey, cook that up for me, Eddie. Can you cook? OK, hit me, man. I started back when I was fourteen years old in 1951, you understand, and I've been using dope ever since, except for the time I spent in the penitentiary. I figure if Whitey gives me half a chance, you know, when I came through school, I could have done something more than this, you know. I know it. But I didn't have the chance because, like I say, I had those three strikes against me.

I'm not really blaming him, you know, the younger ones, but all Whiteys are associated with their race, and I blame them all because there isn't anything else I can do, you know, but shoot dope.

Well, I don't think anything can be done to correct it. Me, because I'm too far gone on it, you know. But, I mean, for my brothers and sisters, you know, people that are coming up younger than I, you know, they can do something. Give them a better education and better job opportunities.

Because I've been in this so long, this is part of my life. I'm sick now. I'm supposed to be in a hospital. They tried to admit me into the hospital three days ago, but knowing that it will be detrimental for me to stay out here, I stayed anyway because I'd rather have this shot of dope than go into anyone's hospital.

Like I say, it's only natural. It's part of my life after twelve years. I never come out of jail and try to do something else but go to this cooker. So, like I say, this is all that's left to me. Look, I started when I was fourteen, I'm not going to say that I never tried to get a job. I tried to get a job, but what references can I give? When I go to State Employment Agency, and they ask where have you been working for the last—since 1952, and I tell them, well, I've been in jail—that's no reference. They won't give me a job. Or, if I get a job you tell them I've been in jail, they turn me loose anyway, you know.

There's nothing I can do, you know. What the hell else can I do? I can't get a legitimate job, but anything else I do they say is against the law. And as long as I stay in this, I'm going to stay in dope, because everyone that's doing something against the law is in dope.

Your environment, I read somewhere, is just a mirror of yourself, you know. So what can I do?

I mean, I have to get my thrills from life someway. I can't lay back. I think I can enjoy working, and raising a family, like the next man, but this is all they left me. I can't work, so I must steal. And mostly the women who will accept me are thieves, or in the trade. And I mean, they're not thinking about raising a family. I mean, they think about what would be good for them, you know. The relief won't take them, so if I had a woman she would have to go out and turn tricks. I have to go out and steal to support my habit. So what can we do but shoot dope for enjoyment? They have left us nothing else.

Work, work, some kind of work program setup where a man can work and get ahead and support himself. Then he can go to some type of school at night, you know, to learn some type of trade, because in jail you can't learn a trade. You know, they tell you that you can, but you can't. If you go there, it's just a house of brutality, you know, that's all I've ever found. A bunch of people—I don't know how the administration thinks, but I know the guards that are head over you—all the fellows are interested in are confining you there, working you, making sure you obey, not the administration's orders, but their orders, you know.

So you can't learn anything in jail, you know. All you can do there is learn to hate more. You can't learn a trade or anything. All you learn there is how to stay out of the police's way as much as possible, even if it means ducking work. You duck work—you stay away from the law, because you know the more that you stay around them, the more they see you, the more they want to whip you. I know that, because I started going to jail when I was a kid.

I don't think I could be rehabilitated, you know, not now, in this society. Maybe if I see something better offered. But I hope that in the future they offer kids, or my sister's kids, or someone's kids, a better opportunity than they offered me, because they didn't offer me anything. I either accepted a porter job for the rest of my life regardless of how much education I had, or went to jail. In fact, I think jails were built for black men. You understand? If you look at the population up there, the black man is more popular in jail than the white man. The black man makes parole less frequently than the white man; the black man gets more time than the white man; and the black man goes to the chair more often than the white man. Whitey gets all the breaks in this world.

quoted by Kenneth B. Clark,
from *Dark Ghetto*

PSALM

A young man who lives on 100th Street wrote this psalm for himself:

Heroin is my shepherd; I shall always want.
It maketh me to lie down in gutters;
It leadeth me beside still madness.

It destroyeth my soul,

It leadeth me in the paths of hell for its name's sake.

Yea, though I walk through the valley of the shadow of
    death,

I will fear no evil; for Heroin art with me;

My syringe and spike will comfort me.

Thou puttest me to shame in the presence of mine enemies.

Thou annointest my head with madness; my cup runneth
    over with sorrow.

Surely hate and evil shall follow me all the days of my life,

And I will dwell in the house of misery and disgrace
    forever.

quoted by Dan Wakefield,
from *Island in the City*

PART FIVE

Behind
These Walls

No es el infierno, es la calle.
This is not hell, but a street.

Federico García Lorca,
Poet in New York

WALLS

Without consideration, without pity, without shame
they have built big and high walls around me.

And now I sit here despairing.
I think of nothing else: this fate gnaws at my mind;

for I had many things to do outside.
Ah why didn't I observe them when they were building
the walls?

But I never heard the noise or the sound of the builders.
Imperceptibly they shut me out of the world.

C. P. Cavafy, from *The Complete
Poems of Cavafy*

THERE IS NO FOOD

*(from an English primer
for Navajo schools)*

There is no food.

There is no flour nor cornmeal
to make into bread.
There is no coffee
that my mother could boil
for us to drink.

There is no food.

The corn my father planted
in his field
is gone.

When it is time to eat,
we talk of other things,
but not of hunger.
This thing called hunger
is a pain
that sits inside me.

At first it was little,
but now
it grows bigger
and bigger.

It hurts me
to be hungry.

Ann Clark, from *Little Herder
in Winter and Autumn*

QUESTIONS
AND ANSWERS

There were times when I came home tired, late at night, on
100th Street, and climbed the stairs and opened the door of
my room and turned the light on and watched the sudden
scurry of the cockroaches that moved on the paint-chipped
kitchen wall like the scattered filings of a magnet controlled
by some invisible force. I would close the door and take a

deep breath of the stale, heavy air, and then suddenly I would remember that after all, this wasn't my real home—I would later move on to some clean, well-lighted place like the ones I had lived in before. But then I would close my eyes and concentrate and try to imagine that this was my home and would always be my home and that the clean, well-lighted places of the world were forever closed to me. Most of the time I could not believe it; I could feel nothing. Sometimes, though, for the briefest instant, I could catch a flicker of the nightmare that was only the reality for every other human being beneath that roof. I could feel the enclosure of the flaking walls and see through the window the blackened reflection of the tenement across the street that blocked out the world beyond. But it was only a glimpse.

In the short time that I was a part of this community I sometimes had to take trips outside of it, and in those trips I was often asked about the world I was living in. Once, when I had lived for several months on 100th Street, the head of a Madison Avenue business firm told me he wanted to talk to me because he was very interested in the Puerto Ricans. This was a happy surprise, and I began to talk about the neighborhood when the gentleman interrupted me. "What I want to know is," he said, "what are we going to do about the Puerto Ricans?" I asked him exactly what he had in mind, and he said, "I mean isn't there some way we can get them back to Puerto Rico? They're costing us millions of dollars in taxpayers' money."

The question was also an answer, in the same way the question of people in the neighborhood who asked if I were a detective was an answer—both are indications of the vast separation of our lives. If the head of that business firm had ever lived in East Harlem his question would have been, "I wonder what we are costing the Puerto Ricans?" In my trips outside the community that is one question I never was asked. It is the question that was answered for me every day when I lived there.

Dan Wakefield, from *Island in the City*

SOUTHERN IDYLL,
1838

You will, perhaps, be curious to know how it fares with our house servants in this respect. Precisely in the same manner, as far as regards allowance, with the exception of what is left from our table, but, if possible, with even less comfort, in one respect, inasmuch as no time whatever is set apart for their meals, which they snatch at any hour, and in any way that they can—generally, however, standing, or squatting on their hams around the kitchen fire. They have no sleeping rooms in the house, but when their work is over, retire, like the rest, to their hovels, the discomfort of which has to them all the addition of comparison with our mode of living. Now, in all establishments whatever, of course some disparity exists between the comforts of the drawing room and best bedrooms, and the servants' hall and attics, but here it is no longer a matter of degree. The young woman who performs the office of lady's maid, and the lads who wait upon us at table, have neither table to feed at nor chair to sit down upon themselves. The boys sleep at night on the hearth by the kitchen fire, and the woman upon a rough board bedstead, strewed with a little tree moss. All this shows how very torpid the sense of justice is apt to lie in the breasts of those who have it not awakened by the peremptory demands of others. In the North we could not hope to keep the worst and poorest servant for a single day in the wretched discomfort in which our Negro servants are forced habitually to live.

Frances Anne Kemble, from *Journal
of a Residence on a Georgia Plantation*

SOUTHERN IDYLL,
1968

JIMTOWN, Ky., Oct. 24 (AP)—Men and women, boys and girls prayed, sang, danced in the street and giggled with delight. There was cause for celebration. It was the day they turned on the water in Jimtown.

The small Negro community nestled on the edge of Fayette County, home of the billion-dollar thoroughbred horse-breeding business, had been without running water since its founding about a century ago.

"My shoulders are round and my feet hurt from packing water for fifty years," Jesse Edwards, one of the 125 residents said.

"Like all of you, I've carried it in cans, tubs, bottles, or anything I could find. Now I just thank the Lord, it's over," he said, minutes before a workman sent a spray showering from the new pipeline.

Jim Davis, chairman of the Jimtown Community Action Committee, held a tin cup out for one of the first drinks of water.

His olive-colored suit was soaked to the elbow, but he ignored it.

"I don't care. It's such a fine day that I just don't care about the suit," he said, beaming.

Jimtown's origin is a lost page in history, but it may have begun after the slaves were freed and moved to the outer fringes of farms so they could be close to their work.

However long it has been here, its residents carry in all drinking water, sometimes from nearby farms, sometimes from Lexington, about twelve miles away.

"Whenever somebody was going to town, they'd check with their neighbors to see who needed water," Jesse Scott, seventy-two years old, said. "And sometimes we'd borrow it from each other."

But no more. After a long series of legal, political, and business wranglings, Jimtown finally was made a part of the Russell Cave Water District.

To make it possible, the community scraped up $2,800 to go with the $6,000 put up by the water district and $10,000 from an Office of Economic Opportunity grant.

The official opening was Wednesday.

Pearlie Mae Warfield, five, watched workmen installing water meters and plastic pipelines to carry water to the homes along the dusty streets. Like her elders, she was wide-eyed.

"I'm gonna take a bath. I'm gonna take a bath," she chanted.

Her grandfather, William Warfield, seventy-one, was the first Jimtown resident to complete his personal preparation for running water. He had a sturdy faucet installed just outside his back door.

New York Times, 27 October 1968

THE MIGRANT CHILD

The birth of the migrant child will most likely be in a migrant shack or, at best, in the emergency room of a county hospital. His nursery is the field, and his toys the things that grow there. A few camps have day-care centers. There are only twenty-four registered centers in the United States. They have a total capacity of less than a thousand children.

The migrant child may never develop any idea of home. His family is never in any place long enough, and home to him is wherever he happens to be.

He seldom sees a doctor. It is almost certain that he will have pinworms and diarrhea. These diseases are so common that the migrant parents think this is just the way children are.

Other untreated common ailments are: contagious skin infections, acute febrile tonsillitis, lymphadenopathy, asthma, iron-deficiency anemia, and disabling physical handicaps.

A doctor visiting a labor camp discovered in one family the fruits of neglect. Their five-year-old daughter had not been to a doctor in three years. She was totally deaf and had learned to speak only three words. She was about to start going to the camp school.

Her six-year-old brother had a wringer injury of his arm that had developed serious complications. The one-year-old baby had had diarrhea for over two weeks. The mother had to carry it two miles to the hospital. The father had stomach ulcers, which were not being treated.

A poor diet condemns the child from the start. A report on a camp in Mathis, Texas, showed that 96 percent of the children had not drunk milk in six months. Their diet consisted mainly of cornmeal and rice. A doctor commenting on the report said there was evidence of "ordinary starvation."

The migrant child is prone to scurvy, rickets, kwashiorkor —a severe protein deficiency. Some reports have put the incidence of dental abnormalities at 95 percent, and others said that bad teeth were "universal."

Epidemics, like the one in the San Joaquin Valley a few years ago, take a heavy toll. Shigellosis, a form of dysentery, had been rampant in the valley for years. The infant mortality rate was extremely high. Within a short time, twenty-eight babies died of "dehydration and malnutrition." Contributing factors to the epidemic were primitive outhouses and crowded one-room cabins where as many as five children slept in a single bed.

The migrant child is also prey to a host of diseases now rare in the nonmigrant world: smallpox, diphtheria, and whooping cough. A medical survey in California showed that two thirds of the children under three years of age were never immunized against diphtheria, whooping cough, lockjaw, or smallpox. And two thirds of the children under eighteen had not received poliomyelitis immunization. Once a contagious disease has been discovered, it is difficult to check its spread. (There was a case of diphtheria in a migrant camp in western North Carolina last year. Health officials tried to track down all the people who were exposed to the sick child. Some were two states away before they were found.)

Truman Moore, from *The Slaves We Rent*

THE BARRIO, LOS ANGELES

My family lives in a house where the rent is cheap but the house is bad. Never a bathtub and the family lived there fifteen years. My father fixed the house so at least we could receive some company. Before that we never invited any friends. Cockroaches came from the walls, bedbugs crawled on the beds. We had to sleep on the floor and breathed on each other. This is not very sanitary. It makes you tired to go to school in the morning. And if you have no bathroom in the house, it's hard to take a bath . . . and with no toilet how can you be comfortable?

All our lives we wanted a bathroom. Then some people tore down the apartment house near us and my brothers one night brought a bathtub from that place. They scrubbed it clean, then built a little house for it. Punched a hole in the wall on the floor and made a path for the water to run into a neighbor's sewer. It took a lot of courage to take a bath in the little house of the bathtub on a cold night. The air comes in the cracks, and it's cold and dark with only the candle. The goats and chickens make little night noises—but we have our bathtub.

When we live in Aliso Village we will have clean bathtubs,

gas, lights, and water inside the house. We will have friends to play with in the playgrounds and not on the corners. The rent will be cheap. We can read books and study our lessons because there will be lots of electric lights. And the house will be big enough for some to go to bed and some to stay awake. The food will be fresh in the refrigerator. And friends can come to our house because a good home is the pride of everyone. We will be cheerful and proud.

Beatrice Griffith, from *American Me*

THE BARRIO, NEW YORK

Not long ago on 114th Street just east of Lexington Avenue, I was walking past an old apartment building when a large rat scuttled across the sidewalk and braced itself against an overloaded trash can. "Watch out, *señor*," said a small, dark-skinned boy. "He'll bite you." When the rat had disappeared, the boy showed me two mean scars on his forearm and told me they were rat bites. "When I lie down at night," he said, "I try to keep the rats away by waving my arm around, but I finally fall asleep, and then sometimes they bite me."

The horrifying thing about his remark was that he was not complaining but merely stating an everyday fact. He seldom leaves El Barrio and simply assumes that all ten-year-old boys have a constant problem with rats.

Enrique Hank Lopez, from "Spanish Harlem," *Life,* 22 September 1967

THE GATES
OF POSTON [26]

In May the physical shell of Poston began to fill with its human occupants. First came the volunteers and then a swelling stream of evacuees until the city of barracks had become alive. Many different kinds of persons were in the crowds and they were received and directed by many different kinds of administrators.

"I was the first Jap to knock on the gates of Poston," said one of eleven volunteers from Imperial Valley, California, who arrived in Poston on the warm and windy afternoon of 8 May. They had come to offer their services to the government in preparing the camp. The fact that they found the administration unaware of their approach introduced them at once to the confusions and difficulties of communication that characterized the relocation program.

These first volunteers were soon followed by others until a total of 251 turned to in the growing heat and cleaned up the barracks for the 7,450 evacuees who arrived during the succeeding three weeks. The volunteers worked at the receiving stations interviewing, registering, housing, and explaining to the travel-weary newcomers what they must do and where they must go. The volunteers became clerks, stenographers, and receptionists in the administrative offices, filled necessary positions in the small emergency hospital, laid the foundation of a kind of municipal civil service composed of block managers, set up the community store, and entered the agriculture department. On the whole they proved to be diligent workers, were prepared for hardships, seemed cheerful, and were

[26] One of the Japanese relocation centers.

among those who had reacted to the evacuation situation by a determination to make the best of it. They were receptive to the administration's new ideas for building a model community.

The new arrivals, coming in a steady stream, were poured into empty blocks one after another, as into a series of bottles. The reception procedure became known as "intake" and it left a lasting impression on all who witnessed or took part in it.

Picture the brightness of morning and a sun that heats the earth and beats down on rubbish piles and row after row of even, black tar-papered barracks. There is the sound of hammers and the hum of motors in trucks, cars, bulldozers, tractors, pumps, and graders. In the single wooden building that houses the administrative offices, desks are jammed together and the members of the departments of law, housing, supply, and transportation bump into each other as they go about their business and try to shout above each other's noise.

Everywhere is the question, When will they come? It was said yesterday that the day's quota of five hundred evacuees would arrive at eight in the morning, and everything has been in readiness since seven. Later it is learned that they will not arrive until ten. This is again changed to three and finally at five it is said that the train is in Parker and the buses have gone to get the people. Clerks, stenographers, interviewers, guides, and baggage carriers collect at the mess hall that will serve as the scene of "intake" and a crowd gathers to watch.

It is almost six when someone shouts that the first bus is coming, and it can be seen plowing through the dust, like a ship on a choppy sea. People are saying to each other that it is a good thing that they are arriving late because the worst heat of the day is over.

When the bus stops, its forty occupants quietly peer out to see what Poston is like. A friend is recognized and hands wave. The bus is large and comfortable, but the people look tired and wilted, with perspiration running off their noses. They have been on the train for twenty-four hours and have been hot since they crossed the Sierras, with long waits at desert stations. Nevertheless, there are remnants of daintiness among the woman, and all are smiling.

One of the volunteers gets into the bus and makes a short speech in Japanese and then in English. He tells them that everyone understands that they have just had a long hot train ride, that the administration, therefore, will try to send them through the necessary routine in the shortest possible fashion and that as soon as it is over, food will be served. In the allotment of apartments, they are told, if there are less than five in a family, they must be prepared to have others living with them.

They begin to file out of the bus, clutching tightly to children and bundles. Military police escorts anxiously help and guides direct them in English and Japanese.

They are sent into the mess halls where girls hand them ice water, salt tablets, and wet towels. In the back are cots where those who faint can be stretched out, and the cots are usually occupied. At long tables sit interviewers suggesting enlistment in the War Relocation Work Corps. Overhead is a placard stating briefly in Japanese the main points of the enlistment application.

Men and women, still sweating, holding on to children and bundles try to think.

A whirlwind comes and throws clouds of dust into the mess hall, into the water, and into the faces of the people while papers fly in all directions.

Order is restored again.

The new arrivals are constantly urged to be quick.

The contents of the enlistment form may be summarized as follows:

I swear loyalty to the United States and enlist in the War Relocation Work Corps for the duration of the war and fourteen days thereafter in order to contribute to the needs of the nation and in order to earn a livelihood for myself and my dependents. I will accept whatever pay, unspecified at the present time, the War Relocation Authority determines, and I will observe all rules and regulations.

In doing this I understand that I shall not be entitled to any cash or allowances beyond the wages due me at the time of discharge from the work corps; that I may be transferred from one relocation center to another by the War Relocation Authority; that medical care will be provided, but that I cannot make a claim against the United States for any injury or disease acquired by me while in the work corps; that I shall be subject to special assessments for educational, medical and other community service as may be provided for in the support of any dependents who reside in a relocation center; that I shall be financially responsible for the full value of any government property that I use while in the work corps; and that the infractions of any regulations of the War Relocation Authority will render me liable to trial and suitable punishment. So help me God.

Most people, including even lawyers, sign without reading the form, a few read it carefully, and a very few refuse to sign.

Interviewers ask some questions about former occupations so that cooks and other types of workers much needed in the camp can be quickly secured. Finally, fingerprints are made and the evacuees troop out across an open space and into another hall for housing allotment, registration, and a cursory physical examination. With them go guides, while outside there are men who periodically shout in English and Japanese, "Stay with your guide! Don't lose your guide!"

In the end, the evacuees are loaded on to trucks along with their hand baggage and driven to their new quarters; there each group who will live together is left to survey a room twenty by twenty-five feet with bare boards, knotholes through the floor and into the next apartment, heaps of dust, and for each person an army cot, a blanket and a sack that can be filled with straw to make a mattress. There is nothing else. No shelves, closets, chairs, tables or screens. In this space five to seven people, and in a few cases eight, men, women, and their children, are to live indefinitely.

"Intake" was a focus of interest and solicitude on the part of the administrative staff. The project director said it was one of the things he would remember longest out of the whole experience at Poston. He thought the people looked lost, not knowing what to do or what to think. He once found a woman standing, holding her four-day-old baby, and sent her to rest in his room. The associate project director said that one of the pictures that would always stay in his mind was one he saw in an "apartment" where people had just arrived. An elderly mother, who had been in a hospital some years, sat propped on her baggage gasping and being fanned by two daughters, while her son went around trying to get a bed set up for her. The old lady later died.

Alexander Leighton, from *The Governing of Men*

DIARY OF A RENT STRIKER

Wednesday, 5 February: I got up at 6:45 A.M. The first thing to do was light the oven. The boiler was broke so not getting the heat. All the tenants together bought the oil. We give $7.50 for each tenant. But the boiler old and many things we don't know about the pipes, so one of the men next door who used to be superintendent is trying to fix. I make the breakfast for the three children who go to school. I give them orange juice, oatmeal, scrambled eggs, and Ovaltine. They have lunch in school and sometimes they don't like the food and won't eat, so I say you have a good breakfast. Miss Christine Washington stick her head in at seven thirty and say she go to work. I used to live on ground floor and she was all the time trying to get me move to third floor next door to her because this place vacant and the junkies use it and she scared the junkies break the wall to get into her place and steal everything because she live alone and go to work.

I'm glad I come up here to live because the rats so big downstairs. We all say the "rats is big as cats." I had a baseball bat for the rats. It's lucky me and the children never got bit. The children go to school and I clean the house and empty the pan in the bathroom that catches the water dripping from pipe in the big hole in the ceiling. You have to carry umbrella to the bathroom sometimes. I go to the laundry place this afternoon and I wash again on Saturday because I change my kids clothes every day because I don't want them dirty to attract the rats.

At twelve fifteen I am fixing lunch for myself and the little one, Tom. I make for him two soft boiled eggs and fried potatoes. He likes catsup and he has one slice of Spam and a cup of milk. I have some Spam for myself and salad because I only drink a cup of coffee at breakfast because I'm getting too fat. I used to work in the shipping department of bathing suits and the boss used to tell me to model for the buyers. I was a model, but now I'm too fat.

After I go out to a rent strike meeting at night, I come home and the women tell me that five policemen came and broke down the door of the vacant apartment of the ground floor where we have meetings for the tenants in our building. They come looking for something—maybe junkies, but we got nothing in there only paper and some chairs and tables. They knocked them all over. The women heard the policemen laughing. When I come up to my place, the children already in bed and I bathe myself and then I go to bed and read the newspaper until eleven thirty.

Thursday, 6 February: I wake up at six o'clock and I went to the kitchen to heat a bottle for my baby. When I put the light on the kitchen, I yelled so loud that I don't know if I disturbed the neighbors. There was a big rat coming out from the garbage pail. He looks like a cat. I ran to my room, I called my daughter Carmen to go to the kitchen to see if the coast was clear. She's not scared of the rats. So I could go back to the kitchen to heat the bottle for my baby. Then I left the baby with a friend and went downtown.

Friday, 7 February: This morning I woke up a little early. The baby woke up at five o'clock. I went to the kitchen but this time I didn't see the rat.

After the girls left for school, I started washing the dishes and cleaning the kitchen. I am thinking about their school. Today they ain't teaching enough. My oldest girl is 5.9 in reading. This is low level in reading. I go to school and English teacher tell me they ain't got enough books to read and that's why my daughter behind. I doesn't care about integration like that. It doesn't bother me. I agree with boycott for some reasons. To get better education and better teachers and better materials in school. I don't like putting them in buses and sending them away. I like to stay here and change the system. Some teachers has to be changed. My girl take Spanish in junior high school, and I said to her, "Tell your teacher I'm going to be in school one day to teach him Spanish because I don't know where he learns to teach Spanish but it ain't Spanish."

I'm pretty good woman. I don't bother anyone. But I got my rights. I fight for them. I don't care about jail. Jail don't scare me. If have to go to jail, I go. I didn't steal. I didn't kill nobody. There's no record for me. But if I have to go, I go.

Saturday, 8 February: A tenant called me and asked me what was new in the building because she works daytimes. She wanted to know about the junkies. Have they been on the top floor where the vacant apartments is? That's why I have leaking from the ceiling. The junkies on the top floor break the pipes and take the fixtures and the sink and sell them and that's where the water comes. . . . I'm not ascared of the junkies. I open the door and I see the junkies I tell them to go or I call the police. Many people scared of them, but they scared of my face. I got a baseball bat for the rats and for the junkies. I sometimes see a junkie in the hallway taking the junk and I give him a broom and say, "Sweep the hall." And he does what I tell him and hand me back the broom after he sweep the hall. I'm not scared of no junkies. I know my rights and I know my self-respect. After supper I played cards (casino) and two hours with the girls and later I got dressed and I went to a party for the rent strike. This party was to get funds to the cause. I had a good time. Mr. Gray was there dancing. He was so happy.

Sunday, 9 February: I dressed up in a hurry to go to church. When I go to church, I pray for to have better house and have a decent living. I hope He's hearing. But I don't get discouraged on Him. I have faith. I don't care how cold I am I never lose my faith. When I come out of church I was feeling so good.

Monday, 10 February: At nine thirty a man came to fix the ratholes. He charged me only $3. Then one of the tenants came to tell me that we only had oil for today and every tenant have to give $7.50 to send for more oil. I went to see some tenants to tell them there is no more oil. We all have to cooperate with money for the oil. It's very hard to collect because some are willing to give but others start fussing. I don't know why because is for the benefit of all, especially those with children. We have to be our own landlord and supers. We had to be looking for the building and I tell you we doing better than if there is an owner. Later I went down in the basement with another tenant to see about the boiler, but we found it missing water in the inside and she didn't light it up and anyway there was not too much oil in it. I hope nothing bad happens, because we too had given $5 each tenant to buy some material to repair the boiler. If something happens is going to be pretty hard to make another collection.

Tuesday, 11 February: This morning was too cold in the house that I had to light the oven and heat hot water. We had no steam, the boiler is not running good. I feel miserable. You know when the house is cold you can't do nothing. When the girls left for school I went back to bed. I just got up at eleven thirty and this house is so cold. Living in a cold apartment is terrible. I wish I could have one of those kerosine stoves to heat myself.

My living room and my room is Alaska. I'm going to heat some pea soup and make coffee. I sat down in the kitchen by the stove to read some papers and keep warm. This is terrible situation. Living the way I live in this slum house is miserable. I don't wish nobody to live the way I live. Inside a house in this condition, no steam, no hot water, ceiling falling on you, running water from the ceiling, to go to the bathroom you have to use an umbrella, rats everywhere. I suggest that landlords having human being living this way instead of sending them to jail they must make them live at least a month in this same conditions, so they know the way they pile up money in the bank.

Wednesday, 12 February: I wake up around five o'clock and the first thing I did was light the oven and the heater so when the girls wake up is a little warm. I didn't call them to eleven because they didn't have to go to school. It still so cold they trembling. You feel like crying looking your children in this way.

I think if I stay a little longer in this kind of living I'm going to be dead duck. I know that to get a project you have to have somebody prominent to back you up. Many people get to the projects and they don't even need them. I had been feeling [filling] applications I don't know since when. This year I feel another one. My only weapon is my vote. This year I *don't vote* for nobody. Maybe my vote don't count, but don't forget if you have fourteen cent you need another penny so you take the bus or the subway. At least I can clean my house and you could eat on the floor. The rest of the day I didn't do nothing. I was so mad all day long. I cooked a big pot of soup. I leave it to God to help me. I have faith in Him.

Thursday, 13 February: I couldn't get up this morning. The house was so cold that I came out of bed at seven fifteen. I heated some water I leave the oven light up all night because the heater gave up. I fixed some oatmeal, eggs, and some Ovaltine for the girls. I had some coffee. I clean the house. The baby was sleeping. Later on, the inspector came. They were suppose to come to every apartment and look all violations. They knock at the door and asked if anything had been fixed. I think even the inspectors are afraid of this slum conditions that's why they didn't dare to come inside. I don't blame them. They don't want to take a rat or any bug to their houses, or get dirty in this filthy houses. My little girl come from school with valentine she made for me. Very pretty. At eight thirty I went downstairs to a meeting we had. We discuss about why there is no heat. We agreed to give $10 to fix the boiler for the oil. A man is coming to fix it. I hope everybody give the $10 so we have some heat soon.

Friday, 14 February: I didn't write this about Friday in my book until this Saturday morning, because Friday night I sick and so cold I go to bed and could not write in the book. But this about Friday. I got up at five to light the oven and put some water to heat. At seven I called the two oldest girls for school. I didn't send the little one, because she was coughing too much and with a running nose. I gave some baby aspirin and I put some Vick in her nose and chest and I gave some hot tea. I leaved her in bed.

It was so cold in here that I didn't want to do nothing in the house. I fixed some soup for lunch and read for a while in the kitchen and after a while I went out and clean the hallway. I didn't mop because there was no hot water, but at least the hallway looked a little clean.

Later on I fixed dinner I was not feeling good. I had a

headache and my throat hurt. I hope I do not catch a cold. I hope someday God will help me and all this experience I had be restore with a very living and happiness. It is really hard to believe that this happens here in New York and richest city in the world. But such is Harlem and hope. Is this the way to live. I rather go to moon in the next trip.

Francis Sugrue, from *Diary*
of a Rent Striker

The city's lack and mine are much the same. What, oh what can
A vagrant hope to find to take the place of what was once
Our expectation of the Human City, in which each man might
Morning and evening, everyday, lead his own life, and Man's?

David Gascoyne, from *A Vagrant*

PART SIX

Resisting

Sal si puedes.

"Get out if you can."

"DISLOYAL"

Joseph Yoshisuke Kurihara, a Hawaiian-born Nisei, was almost fifty years old at the time of evacuation. He had achieved a high measure of success in business and commercial activities in southern California. He had enlisted in the American army during World War I and served with an occupation unit in Germany. His political behavior and attitudes prior to evacuation are a matter of record, and all informants agree that he had no interest in and no connection with Japan. He had in fact never even visited the country. Although extremely sensitive to racial discrimination and slights to the minority group to which he belonged, he was known to be a firm advocate of democratic principles. He was a contributor to a vernacular newspaper with a pronounced flag-waving policy, and his contributions conformed to this policy. Following the outbreak of war between Japan and America, he made strenuous but unsuccessful efforts to participate actively in this country's war program. When evacuation came, Kurihara gave vehement expression to the embitterment he felt at his "betrayal" by America and, correspondingly, began to voice pro-Japan sentiments. He was a leader in the Manzanar [27] riot. He was arrested and incarcerated. He applied for expatriation to Japan in 1943. In Tule Lake,[28] to which he was transferred in December 1943, he was among the first to renounce American citizenship, and he successfully pressed immigration officials to be in the first contingent of voluntary deportees to Japan.

[27] Japanese relocation center.
[28] Japanese relocation center.

Kurihara agreed to prepare his life history for this study. Excerpts from this document, which are revealing of the emotional stress under which he made his decisions, will follow a brief, more formal account of his career.

Biographical Notes

Born in 1895 on Kauai Island, Hawaii. Single; no relatives in the United States. Short, stout, and balding; square face, large jaw, resonant voice. Warm and friendly in manner, but self-assertive. Proud of his honesty and integrity and regarded by others as a man of his word. A devout Catholic.

Family moved to Honolulu when Kurihara was two years old. There he completed elementary school and graduated from a Catholic high school. Concurrently attended Japanese language schools for ten years. Hoped to become a doctor, and worked for a time in a road construction crew to earn money to attend college.

Came to California in 1915; worked as fruit picker in Sacramento Valley prior to entrance in Saint Ignatius College in San Francisco. Discouraged by evidence of racial discrimination on West Coast; migrated to Middle West in early 1917.

Enlisted in U.S. Army while in Michigan in 1917. Served abroad. Honorably discharged in San Francisco in 1919. Visited Hawaii for brief period. Returned to California; entered a commercial college in Los Angeles and later Southwestern University from which he graduated in accounting in 1924.

Opened an accounting firm, serving Japanese community in Los Angeles, in 1924. In 1925, became partner in a wholesale produce firm and, at same time, operated retail fruit and vegetable store in Hollywood, which he sold at profit in 1927. Auditor and manager of Japanese-owned seafood packing company 1929–1931, earning on the average $500 a month. Opened retail fruit and vegetable store in Berkeley in an attempt to carry over to northern California a form of merchandising successful in Los Angeles area. Failed in this venture.

Studied navigation and television in Los Angeles. From 1934 to onset of war, employed as navigator of tuna fishing boat. Arrived in San Diego from fishing expedition 29 December 1941. Remained there through January in effort to get clearance to navigate, which was denied. Went to San Pedro in attempt to enter merchant marine. Unsuccessful. Sought employment in two shipbuilding firms and was refused because of ancestry.

Witnessed expulsion of Japanese from Terminal Island on orders of Eleventh Naval District in February 1942. Entered Manzanar with second volunteer contingent on 23 March 1942. Soon became active in antiadministration and anti-JACL [Japanese American Citizens League] movements. Arrested on 7 December 1942, during Manzanar riot. Sent to Moab and later to Leupp isolation camps. Transferred to Tule Lake in December 1943 as segregant; inactive politically in Tule Lake, although had personal following. Renounced his citizenship; sailed for Japan in February 1946.

Excerpts from Kurihara's Manuscripts

His appraisal of his own personality:
I go from one extreme to the other. I sympathize, cry, and give my last penny to save a person in a worthy cause, but I can be mean and devilish when aroused.

Memories of Hawaii:
We, the boys of conglomerated races, were brought up under the careful guidance of American teachers, strictly following the principle of American democracy. Let it be white, black, brown, or yellow, we were all treated alike. This glorious paradise of the Pacific was the true melting pot of human races.

Early experiences of racial discrimination in California (around 1915):

My early experiences in Sacramento were of appalling nature. While walking on K Street from the depot toward the Japanese district, suddenly a fairly well-dressed person came and kicked me in the stomach for no reason whatever. Luckily it glanced as I instinctively avoided it.

I watched his next move, maneuvering into position to fight it out the best I could. A crowd started to gather, but no sooner than it did, another person coming out of a saloon in front of which we were about to tackle, stopped this public show. I went my way feeling terribly hurt.

In this same city of Sacramento, as my friend and I were walking in the residential district, a short distance away from the Japanese center, something came whizzing by, and then another and another. We noticed they were rocks being thrown at us by a number of youngsters. As we went toward them, the boys ran and hid. Feeling perplexed, I asked my friend, "Why do they attack us in such a manner?" He answered, "It's discrimination." No such thing ever happened where I came from. It was disgusting. I felt homesick for my good old native land, Hawaii.

Enlistment in and experiences in American Army of Occupation (1917–1919):

While in Michigan I was seized with an intense desire to join the army. I felt rather ashamed of myself in civilian attire. I had purchased $500 worth of Liberty Bonds to send to my five nieces and nephews in Hawaii, but still not feeling satisfied, I finally went and enlisted. During the training period, I was befriended by many Caucasians. I made several visits to their homes. I felt very happy. Knowing that they were going out of their way to make me happy, I solemnly vowed to fight and die for the U.S. and these good people, whose genuine kindness touched the very bottom of my heart. In California my animosities against the Californians were growing with ever-increasing intensity, but in Michigan my liking for the American people was getting the best of me.

In the summer of 1918 I was sent to France with a medical corps. After the armistice, I was assigned to Koblenz, Germany, with a medical corps of the army of occupation. During my stay in Koblenz, I found out that the German people were just as human as any other race. I learned to like these people because they were kind and sincere. At every meal time, the little German girls and boys would line the walk to the garbage can for whatever scraps the boys were throwing away. I could not bear to see these little ones suffer, so I always made it my duty to ask for as much as my plate would hold and gave it to them. O Lord, my God, so this is the price of war. Why should these innocent children be made to suffer the hardships of war?

Experiences and attitudes immediately following Pearl Harbor:

After a fishing expedition off Mexico, we entered San Diego Bay immediately at daybreak on 29 December. In the bay, the boat was stopped and several officers in naval uniform came aboard. They scrutinized the papers, and finding them satisfactory they left, but they took three of us (two Portuguese and myself) along.

We were taken to the naval wharf and waited for orders but none came. Around nine thirty, we again were asked to board the official launch and this time were taken back to our own ship. No sooner had I boarded the ship than a plainclothesman yelled, "Hey! you Jap, I want some information. You better tell me everything, or I'll kick you in the _____." My blood boiled. I felt like clubbing his head off. It was just a hat rack and nothing more.

Another gentleman came aboard, and seeing that I was an Oriental, he said, "I want you to come with me to the immigration office."

At the office, I was told to take a seat in plain view of several officers. Noon came, so they went for lunch while I sat there waiting. Three o'clock came, I was feeling hungry and irritated. Finally I asked one of the officers why they apprehended me and why they were keeping me waiting without lunch. He said the instruction was to bring all Japanese nationals in for questioning.

One of the officers obligingly took out some papers, called me to his side, and started to ask the following questions:

"What do you think of the war?"

"Terrible."

"Who do you think will win this war?"

"Who knows? God only knows."

"Do you think Japan has the materials she needs to wage this war?"

"I never was there; so your guess is just as good as mine."

"Are you a navigator?"

"Yes, I navigated boats for the last eight years."

"Are you good at it?"

"Never missed my mark."

"Do you know all the bays along the coast?"

"Yes, nearly all the bays and coves along the entire coast from Seattle to Ecuador, South America."

"Have you been a good American citizen?"

"I was and I am."

"Will you fight for this country?"

"If I am needed, I am ready."

"Were you a soldier of any country?"

"Yes, I am Veteran of the Foreign Wars, U.S. Army."

I was released that evening.

Attempts to participate in the war effort:

I went to see the port master in San Diego to get a permit to sail the sea. Seeing that I was a Japanese, he said, "No permit for any Jap." We argued awhile. Losing his temper he said, "Get out or I'll throw you out." So I told him, "Say officer I wore that uniform when you were still unborn. I served in the U.S. Army and fought for democracy. I may be a Jap in feature but I am an American. Understand!" I saw fire in his eyes, but he had no further words to say.

In San Pedro, when I applied at one shipbuilding company, I was told it would be better for me to try elsewhere because I will not enjoy working here. They said the fellow workmen were very antagonistic. They said they had two Japanese boys working as welders, but they did not think they would be here very long because of discrimination of the fellow workers.

The Terminal Island evacuation:

It was really cruel and harsh. To pack and evacuate in forty-eight hours was an impossibility. Seeing mothers completely bewildered with children crying from want and peddlers taking advantage and offering prices next to robbery made me feel like murdering those responsible without the slightest compunction in my heart.

The parents may be aliens but the children are all American citizens. Did the government of the United States intend to ignore their rights regardless of their citizenship? Those beautiful furnitures which the parents bought to please their sons and daughters, costing hundreds of dollars were robbed of them at the single command, "Evacuate!" Here my first doubt of American democracy crept into the far corners of my heart with the sting that I could not forget. Having had absolute confidence in democracy, I could not believe my very eyes what I had seen that day. America, the standard-bearer of democracy, had committed the most heinous crime in its history.

The beginnings of his hatred of JACL leaders and other collaborators in the evacuation procedure:

Truly it was my intention to fight this evacuation. On the night of my return to Los Angeles from San Diego was the second meeting which the Citizens Federation of Southern California [sponsored by JACL] held to discuss evacuation.

I attended it with a firm determination to join the committee representing the Nisei and carry the fight to the bitter end. I found the goose was already cooked. The field secretary of the JACL instead of reporting what actually transpired at a meeting they had had with General DeWitt just tried to intimidate the Nisei to comply with evacuation by stories of threats he claimed to have received from various parts of the state.

I felt sick at the result. They'd accomplished not a thing. All they did was to meet General DeWitt and be told what to do. These boys claiming to be the leaders of the Nisei were a bunch of spineless Americans. Here I decided to fight them and crush them in whatever camp I happened to find them. I vowed that they would never again be permitted to disgrace the name of the Nisei as long as I was about.

Initial experiences in and reactions to Manzanar:
The desert was bad enough. The mushroom barracks made it worse. The constant cyclonic storms loaded with sand and dust made it worse. After living in well-furnished homes with every modern convenience and suddenly forced to live the life of a dog is something which one can not so readily forget. Down in our hearts we cried and cursed this government every time when we were showered with sand. We slept in the dust; we breathed the dust; and we ate the dust. Such abominable existence one could not forget, no matter how much we tried to be patient, understand the situation, and take it bravely. Why did not the government permit us to remain where we were? Was it because the government was unable to give us the protection? I have my doubt. The government could have easily declared martial law to protect us. It was not the question of protection. It was because we were Japs! Yes, Japs!

After corralling us like a bunch of sheep in a hellish country, did the government treat us like citizens? No! We were treated like aliens regardless of our rights. Did the government think we were so without pride to work for $16 a month when people outside were paid $40 to $50 a week in the defense plants? Responsible government officials further told us to be loyal and that to enjoy our rights as American citizens we must be ready to die for the country. We must show our loyalty. If such is the case, why are the veterans corralled like the rest of us in the camps? Have they not proven their loyalty already? This matter of proving one's loyalty to enjoy the rights of an American citizen was nothing but hocus-pocus.

Decision to renounce citizenship:

My American friends . . . no doubt must have wondered why I renounced my citizenship. This decision was not that of today or yesterday. It dates back to the day when General DeWitt ordered evacuation. It was confirmed when he flatly refused to listen even to the voices of the former World War veterans and it was doubly confirmed when I entered Manzanar. We who already had proven our loyalty by serving in the last World War should have been spared. The veterans asked for special consideration but their requests were denied. They too had to evacuate like the rest of the Japanese people, as if they were aliens.

I did not expect this of the army. When the Western Defense Command assumed the responsibilities of the West Coast, I expected that at least the Nisei would be allowed to remain. But to General DeWitt, we were all alike. "A Jap's a Jap. Once a Jap, always a Jap." . . . I swore to become a Jap 100 percent, and never to do another day's work to help this country fight this war. My decision to renounce my citizenship there and then was absolute.

Just before he left for Japan, Kurihara wrote:

It is my sincere desire to get over there as soon as possible to help rebuild Japan politically and economically. The American democracy with which I was infused in my childhood is still unshaken. My life is dedicated to Japan with democracy my goal.

Opinions of Administrators

In connection with Kurihara's own account of the development of his attitudes, it is of interest to quote the opinions of administrators from our own field notes, recorded by Togo Tanaka in Manzanar during the fall of 1942:

WRA [War Relocation Authority] administrators familiar with Kurihara's case were, in general, sympathetic with him. In August 1942, after Kurihara had made several public speeches that some listeners considered "subversive" and "anti-American," one project administrative officer said he had a talk with Kurihara. "I find Joe Kurihara very bitter about the entire situation, but he is bitter and sore in quite an American way," was his observation. The assistant project director, in a conversation with a group at which Kurihara was not present, remarked: "If I were Joe Kurihara, I'd be mad too. He was a veteran of the World War, was discharged from the United States Army honorably, had done his part as a citizen. It's just as if I had saved one of you guys from getting stabbed or killed in a street brawl, and you rewarded me by kicking me into the gutter. Hell, sure I'd be bitter."

Dorothy Swaine Thomas and Richard S. Nishimoto, from *The Spoilage*

JESSE GRAY: THE WAR AGAINST THE LANDLORDS

A freezing wind whipped through Harlem, stirring the trash in the gutters, tugging at rattling windows, blowing down long, dark hallways left open to the street. It was warmer inside the well-lighted gymnasium on West 118th Street, but the men and women packed into six hundred chairs on the basketball court kept their overcoats on. This was not the kind of audience that checked its coats. These people were slum tenants, inhabitants of the wasteland of crumbling buildings and decaying garbage heaps that covers the northern end of Manhattan Island. Most of them had gone for months with no heat in their icy radiators and no hot water in their sinks and bathtubs. Gray rats as big as squirrels prowled through their kitchens and scurried under their beds. Now, encouraged to believe that if they acted together, "the Man" could not put all of them "on the street," they had stopped paying rent. All together, on that bleak mid-January day, three thousand Harlem families were holding back rents worth over $100,000 a month.

Jesse Gray, who had persuaded these people to strike, climbed up on a platform at one end of the room and began to speak. Gray has a large moustache and widely spaced buckteeth and, because he was once a tailor, his suits fit well. His voice, however, is far more aggressive than his appearance. That day it shook with belligerence and outrage.

"In Harlem the landlords have been on strike for a long time," Jesse shouted. "Now *we're* going on strike."

"That's right," chorused the crowd.

"We've got to clear all the rats out of this town," Jesse said, pointing to two large placards in front of the platform. One portrayed the head of the Democratic donkey joined to the body of a rat. The other depicted the Republican elephant similarly transformed.

"Harlem," said Jesse, "has got to let Mayor Wagner know that there'll be no votes for him this year. That he shouldn't come looking for 'em. When we vote, we'll write in our votes for rats. At least they live with us up here in Harlem."

"That's right," they shouted.

"We're going to say to the mayor and to the governor and to the president of the United States that in all the ghettos of this country, it's time to stop paying rent to keep rats alive and landlords fat. They can't evict twenty million Negroes from this country!" The crowd roared.

Jesse Gray's rent strike is not important only to New York. If this tactic is successful in Harlem, it will spread to all the other American cities where Negroes are cooped in grimy ghettos. For the strike—along with New York's recent school boycott in which 360,000 students walked out in protest against racial imbalance in the city schools—is dramatic evidence of the Negro's new militancy in the North. Said Bayard Rustin, the fifty-three-year-old Negro who organized last summer's march on Washington and led the one-day school strike, "The boycott and the rent strike are fair warning that the civil rights revolution has reached out of the South and is now knocking at our own doors."

As an indication of the effect this is having, a number of city and state politicians, union leaders, and civil rights chieftains, types ranging from U.S. Congressman William Fitts Ryan to novelist James Baldwin, had chosen to sit on the platform that afternoon with Jesse Gray. As one endorsement followed another ("It is always hopeful for democracy when the people turn out to air their grievances"), one veteran New York newspaperman watched in amazement.

"For ten years Jesse Gray's been complaining about living conditions in Harlem, but nobody would listen to him. Now all of a sudden he's holding press conferences, he's on the front page, and all the pols are scrambling to sit on a platform with him. You know why? The slums haven't changed. But this year everybody suddenly realizes that the people living in those slums are Negroes."

In these days of the Negro revolution a man does not need a downtown office, letterhead stationery and frequent invitations to dine at the White House in order to become a civil rights leader. All he needs is a following. Jesse Gray, born thirty-nine years ago in Louisiana, a merchant seaman during the war, and after that a tailor in Harlem, has a following. To the people of Harlem it doesn't matter that the articulate leaders of the NAACP, CORE, and the Urban League deplore splinter movements and independent leaders such as Jesse Gray. Nor do they care that Jesse Gray has been accused by anonymous postcards of being a Communist. (Gray supported the right of American Communist Benjamin Davis to run for the New York state senate in 1958, and he took the fifth amendment when asked to name other Communists he knew. In heated arguments he makes statements such as, "If private property means that rats can eat my children, I don't care about private property." But he has denied under oath any Communist Party affiliation, and no contrary evidence ever has been produced.) The only thing that matters in Harlem is that Jesse Gray has been demanding for ten years that something be done about living conditions in Harlem's slums. Now, in its awakening sense of power, Harlem itself has begun to make this demand. And on this issue at least, it has made Jesse Gray its angry voice.

To understand why Jesse Gray and Harlem are protesting, it is necessary to walk through the blighted streets north of Central Park. Dirty sidewalks are lined with five-story houses, each divided into fifteen apartments. Windows are patched with cardboard, doors wobble loose on their hinges, hallways smell of age and dirt and poverty. In such a house Mrs. Joyce Borden, a tall, serious woman of thirty-one, lives in conditions that are appalling even by Harlem's miserable standards.

In the basement of her building at 105 West 114th Street, a flashlight beam picks out the remains of a dismantled boiler. The boiler was destroyed a year ago, and Joyce Borden has been without heat and hot water ever since. There is a broken pipe in the apartment above Mrs. Borden's, and for six weeks a steady downpour of cold water has drenched her bathroom.

Worse, since the week before Christmas Joyce Borden's apartment has been without electricity. She cannot even get light from outside; her window shades are drawn to preserve a few extra degrees of the thin heat that filters from her kitchen oven. Ten-year-old Samuel Borden does his homework in the afternoon by the light of a kerosene lamp. After supper, when his mother goes off to clean an empty, well-heated office in midtown New York, Samuel Borden gets into bed and tries to keep warm.

To call on Joyce Borden, a visitor must walk in from the sunlit street, grope down a damp, dark hallway and up a set of creaking stairs. Standing in her doorway in a bathrobe and hair curlers, Joyce Borden shows a surprisingly even temper toward her misfortunes.

"I've lived here for eight years, and I've always paid about fifty dollars a month rent. Now the landlord says he can't afford to fix the boiler and give us heat. Con Edison says they can't give us electricity because that's the landlord's responsibility. We've called all kinds of city inspectors, but they just come and make notes and go away. Since it didn't seem to be anybody else's responsibility, I decided to make it mine. I went to Jesse Gray, and he helped me organize this building. Now we're on strike."

Joyce Borden knows the name of her landlord. City records list him as Walter Giles, 152–23 116th Avenue, Jamaica, New York. Mr. Giles has moved, however, to New City, a small town up the Hudson River from New York. He admits owning the house in which Joyce Borden lives but has declined to discuss it with a reporter.

Many landlords cannot be found at all. They hide behind the façade of quickly erected corporations, or place titles in the names of their wives, their secretaries, their lawyers. Some landlords choose to live outside New York state; some are across the river in the suburbs of New Jersey, others live in Florida or Puerto Rico.

There is at least one house in Harlem, at 11 West 107th Street, which nobody owns. A buildings department investigation revealed seventeen different names listed as owners, co-owners, and mortgagees, but all of these people disclaim ownership and responsibility. Presumably the last owner, unable to face the massive costs of repairing the house, simply gave up and disappeared. The pipes have been ripped out of the basement, and the building has neither heat nor running water. The tenants remain, paying no rent, hoping that the city will take over the building under receivership law.

One of these tenants is Mrs. Eunice Bates, a short, round-faced grandmother who talks with a heavy wheeze. Mrs. Bates gets water from a house in the basement next door and carries it up to her apartment in buckets and wastebaskets. She does not seem to have much hope that conditions will improve.

"You reporters come, the city inspectors come, but nothing ever gets better. I had to send my two boys to Connecticut this winter to live with my sister. One of them has asthma, and he can't keep alive in this cold. I don't know what we're going to do."

In the apartment directly above Mrs. Bates, Shirley Williams, an attractive young woman in her twenties, has not yet given up. This is because James Williams, Shirley's husband, is a head shipping clerk at a Seventh Avenue dress house, and his weekly income, $75, is enough to qualify him for one of the city's low-income housing projects. There is a long waiting list, but the Williamses have been promised an apartment fairly soon. Meanwhile, Shirley Williams carries water from next door and keeps it in pails until it is time to cook, clean, flush a toilet, or wash the diapers of her ten-month-old daughter.

"We've been here five years, and we've tried to make this a nice place," she says, gesturing toward the new couches in her living room and the new encyclopedia on her shelves. "We want to pay rent, but nobody comes to collect it. Instead, we pay $70 a month for gas to keep the oven going for heat. We worry about it causing a fire, we worry about the rats getting into my baby's crib. My son has had double pneumonia, and my daughter has had meningitis. My husband works hard, because we want something better for our kids. But we just can't go on like this." Her eyes, which had been flashing with indignation, began to fill with tears. Spreading her arms and shaking her head slowly, Shirley Williams said, "Nobody would believe how we're living here. Nobody would believe it."

There are many people in Harlem who would believe Shirley Williams; for one, there is Mrs. Annabelle Alexander of 2174 Lexington Avenue. On 2 January her five-year-old son John was bitten on the lower lip by a rat, and rushed to a hospital for the first of a series of fourteen antirabies shots. Annabelle Alexander easily recognized the creature that bit her son; he had lived with the family for months.

Richard Moore, a twenty-two-year-old stock clerk, would also agree with Shirley Williams. On 11 January, in his apartment at 1787 Madison Avenue, he found a large rat in the crib with his baby son. Moore chased the rat before it could bite, and killed it by his usual method. "They don't run too fast. I just take a box and mash 'em against the wall."

At night the temperature inside Moore's unheated apartment sometimes drops to 18°. But he is tired of moving. "I moved into this place four months ago from a place that was worse," he says wearily. But he has stopped paying his monthly rent of $65, he has organized his own building, and helped Jesse Gray organize nine others.

There probably would not have been a rent strike in Harlem if the city of New York had been able to enforce the minimum housing standards required by law. But one million people still live in forty-three thousand buildings erected before 1901. To replace these buildings would cost an estimated $17 billion.

Landlords complain that New York's rent-control law holds rents so low that they cannot afford to make repairs. So far, however, no city administration has dared risk voter displeasure by removing these controls. On 23 January, with controls due to expire on 1 February, the City Council held hearings to listen to both sides. A group of small property owners showed up and one of them began shouting that the continuance of rent controls would be "compromising with communism and fascism." Outside, Jesse Gray and a group of strikers picketed the hearings, then burst inside to demand that "all tenants leave this slumlords meeting." Disorders broke out and a number of the more vehement landlords were ejected. Gray led his followers outside and relative calm returned. On 28 January, the council extended rent controls another two years, leaving matters about where they were in the beginning.

But while both sides argue, buildings continue to decay. Even when violations are found and landlords are convicted, penalties remain low.

Fines for housing violations may be as low as $5; the average fine is $30. Says Mayor Wagner, "The slumlord will say —if you can find him—'I would rather pay that low fine than all the money it would take to make these places proper.' " For several years Wagner has asked the legislature to set minimum housing-violation fines at $100, but he has been unsuccessful. In 1962 Wagner did persuade the legislature to enact a receivership law, empowering the city to take over buildings in violation, collect the rents, and use the money to make repairs. By mid-January of this year the city had taken over twelve buildings.

Delay is compounded by confusion and overlapping authority. If Joyce Borden has no heat, she must call the health department to complain. If she has no hot water, she must call the buildings department. If she has no water at all, she must call the department of water supply, gas and electricity. If Shirley Williams has a rathole, she is supposed to ask a buildings department inspector to call. If a rat emerges from the hole, she must ask for a health inspector. Leaky pipes are buildings' responsibility, big leaks belong to water supply, overflow from the apartment above is a police matter. Sometimes inspectors may call simultaneously from three separate departments. Each writes on his clipboard and goes away. More often, tenants are shunted from one telephone switchboard to another and simply give up.

Until now Harlem has always accepted delay and despair. But in 1963, with fellow Negroes braving fire hoses and police dogs in southern cities, a new mood began to sweep through Harlem's tenements. In October Jesse Gray's Community Council on Housing persuaded the tenants of Numbers 15, 16, and 18 East 117th Street to stop paying rent. By Christmas fifty-eight buildings in Harlem were on strike. In Shirley Williams's building a gas leak was discovered on Christmas Day, and the gas had to be turned off. For Christmas dinner she served her family spiced-ham sandwiches.

The rent strike got a crucial lift on 30 December. On that day thirteen of the striking families living at 16 and 18 East 117th Street were to be haled into court by their landlord. The tenants were prepared to list the 157 uncorrected violations in the two buildings, but Jesse Gray had an additional dramatic idea. "Bring a rat to court," he told the strikers.

On the morning of 30 December Gray and his followers carried eight dead rats down to the City Courthouse at 111 Centre Street. Court bailiffs found three of the rats and forced their owners to check the rodents in a cloakroom. But five rats, concealed under clothing and in women's pocketbooks, made it into the courtroom. Judge Guy Gilbert Ribaudo ruled that the thirteen tenants thereafter should turn over their accruing rents to his court. The landlord could get the rent from the court once he had repaired the violations. Gray dangled the rats before a mob of photographers and TV cameramen, tossed them into a wastebasket, and went home happy.

The strike gathered additional legal support from a decision handed down in Brooklyn by Judge Fred G. Moritt. Judge Moritt ruled that tenants in substandard dwellings were not required to deposit rent with anybody until repairs were made.

"My decision means that the landlord in extreme cases is not entitled to any rent until the conditions are remedied," he declared. "Some of the buildings aren't fit for pigs. . . . If it takes the landlord two years to make the repairs, he gets no rent for two years. I am merely applying the ancient and elementary law that you don't owe for what you don't get."

Many New York lawyers doubt that the law is quite so elementary as Judge Moritt believes. "Judge Moritt decided that case on purely emotional grounds. His decision will be thrown out by the appellate courts," said one Manhattan lawyer. Mrs. Hortense W. Gabel, the city's rent and rehabilitation administrator, also doubts that Judge Moritt's decision will be upheld by the higher courts. Therefore, said Mrs. Gabel, "it would be most unfortunate if tenants were not required to pay their rents to the courts." Privately Mrs. Gabel explained that she feared landlord reprisals against tenants if the ruling is overturned. But Jesse Gray interpreted her statement as an attack on the rent strike. "Hortense Gabel helps landlords, and Hortense Gabel has to go," he tells his rallies. Hearing this, Mrs. Gabel shrugs and smiles. "If government is supposed to be the art of managing crises," she says, "I think we could have managed this one a little better."

Jesse Gray himself does not worry about the legality of the rent strike. "Once you've got fifteen thousand people not paying rents, it's not a legal problem. It's a political problem," he says. "Now it's up to the mayor and the governor."

New York Governor Nelson Rockefeller does not accept Gray's placement of responsibility. Gray's response was to call for a Rats to Rockefeller campaign and to order three thousand black rubber rats from a toy manufacturer, which his followers could mail to the governor. This bit of showmanship finally provoked Rockefeller to reply. Climbing out of a plane from New Hampshire, he accused New York City of failing to enforce housing and sanitation laws. "The rent strikers know where the problem is. It's right in City Hall," said the governor. He added that if he found any rats in his mail, he would "readdress" them to Mayor Wagner. In rebuttal to Rockefeller's attack, city officials point to the omission from Governor Rockefeller's annual message to the legislature of any proposals for new low-rent public housing. Instead, Rockefeller's message promised a commission report on the "feasibility of providing low-rent housing with private capital."

Mayor Wagner, during his ten years in office, has periodically announced "a massive attack" or a "new and more effective attack" on slumlords. These battle cries come in cycles, as do elections. This year's slogan is "a pocketbook attack on the slumlords." Immediately after Judge Ribaudo's decision, when the number of buildings on strike had jumped to nearly two hundred, the mayor announced a new program. It included ending duplication and overlap among city agencies with housing responsibilities, stiffer fines and jail sentences for slumlords, a speedup in the processing of complaints and, most important, a legalizing of rent withholding if the department of health certified a building as a menace to health. A week later the mayor announced that the city would spend one million dollars to kill rats beginning in March.

"Wagner has talked about helping us for ten years," says Jesse Gray, as he sits in his tiny, windowless office at 6 East 117th Street, "but conditions are worse now than they ever have been. The mayor has authority under the receivership law to take over these substandard buildings."

The more he talks, the madder Jesse Gray gets. "Wagner won't act unless the pressure's on him. We're going to keep it on. I don't care what Wagner does, or Rockefeller, or even LBJ. It would be the simplest thing in the world for LBJ to put up half a billion dollars to tear down these slums and give our people decent housing. Rockefeller? Ha! He owns a whole lot of raggedy property all over this town. He's just like any other landlord. The landlords are fat, fat, fat!" The hand pounds the battered desk.

Despite the attacks, most Harlem landlords have stayed undercover. A few have written to newspapers, stating that their tenants "urinated in the halls, threw garbage in the backyard," and "lived it up on welfare money at the corner gin mills." Two landlords, Arnold Schildhaus and Lee Sterling, appeared on a local television program with Jesse Gray and counterattacked directly. Sterling, who owns a building at 100th Street and First Avenue, said, "I went in last summer and tried to put the building in shape. We plastered and painted, but two weeks later the holes were all back again. Some tenants went up on the roof and tore down the chimney and threw the bricks at the police cars in the street."

Schildhaus went even further. "The truth is that in Harlem today the average family is very destructive," he said. Both landlords claimed that rent controls prevented them from making repairs. "We are losing thousands of dollars," said Schildhaus, "but we can't get rid of these buildings. The law won't even permit us to give them away."

According to several city officials, Schildhaus's statement is not completely accurate. "The owner has an absolute right to withdraw from the rental market if he can prove that the cost of repairing violations is greater than the assessed valuation of the building," said one top city official. "Under the law, when you don't pay taxes for four years, the city may foreclose on a building," added Milton Mollen, Mayor Wagner's chief housing adviser. "But the great majority of landlords, and the slumlords particularly, continue to pay taxes because they are making money."

But while the argument goes on, the rent strike tactic continues to gather momentum. By mid-February there were three hundred buildings and forty-five hundred families on strike in Harlem. The Congress of Racial Equality already has conducted limited rent strikes in other parts of New York City and in Cleveland, and is planning them for other northern cities. But CORE's rent strikes have never been as successful as Jesse Gray's and CORE's Executive Director James Farmer is not pleased with this situation.

"Rent strikes are a CORE project," says Farmer. "I announced last spring that they would be one of our tactics. We are very glad to see others join us. But I would not wish to comment on Mr. Gray." In ten days of trying, NAACP Executive Secretary Roy Wilkins could not be reached for comment.

Fighting slums in a huge metropolis is discouraging work. In 1957 Mayor Wagner told New York *World-Telegram* housing reporter Woody Klein, "There's nothing you can do about slums, you know that. They're always going to be that way." But living in slums is discouraging too. Especially when the people who live there realize that their society could build new buildings if it really wanted to.

Less than five miles from the teeming Harlem streets where

Jesse Gray lives and works, where people shiver and guard their children against rats, new buildings worth almost one billion dollars have been erected within the past eighteen months. They are the gleaming, well-heated halls and palaces scattered through the Flushing Meadow site of the 1964 New York World's Fair. But these soaring buildings, erected to celebrate the imaginative genius of New York and America, are for people to visit, not to live in.

Robert K. Massie, "Harlem Goes To War
Against the Slumlords," *Saturday
Evening Post,* 29 February 1964

Some good friends of the cause we represent fear agitation. They say: "Do not agitate—do not make a noise; work." They add: "Agitation is destructive or at best negative—what is wanted is positive constructive work."

Such honest critics mistake the function of agitation. A toothache is agitation. Is a toothache a good thing? No. It is supremely useful, for it tells the body of decay and death. Without it the body would suffer unknowingly. It would think: All is well, when lo! danger lurks.

W. E. B. Du Bois, from *The Crisis* 1910

DINNER AT STONER'S

Three CORE members were refused lunch at Stoner's, a white-tablecloth restaurant in the heart of Chicago's Loop in October 1942. Mr. Stoner met the three as they came through the swinging doors and said he could not give them a seat—

he did not serve colored. He seemed annoyed when the three asked him why he had this policy. When he stated that he could do as he liked in his own restaurant, they sat down on a sofa near the door to await service.

They waited for forty-five minutes in vain.

They asked for seats at tables on several occasions. Mr. Stoner refused to make an appointment to discuss the question with CORE committees. Attempts were made by letter and phone. Finally CORE decided to send committees to see him without appointment. Two white women ate lunch there one noon, and had a brief talk with Mr. Stoner. He claimed he would lose all his white trade if colored people came to his restaurant. He said that 90% of his trade came from women and they would not want to eat beside Negroes. He said that if members of the two races ate in the same restaurant, it would lead to interracial marriage and he was opposed to this.

Another interracial CORE committee visited Mr. Stoner in his office one morning before the restaurant opened for business. This committee talked with him for fully half an hour, but without satisfaction. He claimed that other restaurants of his class did not serve Negroes.

Following these attempts to negotiate, small interracial groups visited the restaurant on many occasions to try to get service. At first Mr. Stoner refused to allow the hostesses even to seat the groups at the tables.

As time passed, some of the small test groups would be seated after a considerable wait, only to be served meat with egg shells scattered on it, or a plate of food salted so heavily that it could not be eaten, or a sandwich composed of tomato and lettuce cores picked out of the garbage in the kitchen (so the group was told by Negro bus girls who witnessed the making of the sandwiches).

For one entire week in December 1942, CORE passed out leaflets to the patrons of Stoner's both at noon and in the evening, calling their attention to the policy of discrimination and asking them to protest as they paid their bills.

The facts of the case were publicized among many groups in Chicago and again and again the question was asked of CORE, "Why pick on Mr. Stoner? Don't other restaurants discriminate as well?" As a result of this prodding CORE investigated the policies of all eating places within an area of sixteen square blocks of the Loop. In not a single case was outright discrimination practiced. A leaflet entitled "*50 Loop Restaurants Which Do Not Discriminate*" was published by CORE as a result of this investigation, and it received wide circulation among both Negro and white groups.

Following the survey, CORE felt entirely justified in taking action against Stoner's, for no other place was known to be so flagrant in its violation of the civil rights law of Illinois. Mr. Stoner was informed of the results of the survey. When a few further attempts were made to receive service in Stoner's without success, it was decided that a sit-in should be tried. CORE realized that it would be difficult to stage a successful sit-in at Stoner's, for this restaurant could seat at least 200 persons. Nevertheless, the sit-in was planned and executed in June 1943.

Approximately sixty-five persons participated—sixteen of whom were Negroes. All participants were pledged to non-violence. The whites had agreed to remain in their seats (all night if necessary) until the Negroes were seated and given good service. The action took place in late afternoon and early evening of a Saturday. Between 4:30 and 5:10 most of the white participants went by twos, threes and fours into the restaurant. They were, of course, seated without difficulty by the hostesses. At 5:15 the first of two interracial groups consisting of six Negroes and two whites walked through the revolving doors of the restaurant. This group was ignored when the spokesman asked for seats. So the group stood quietly at the front of the restaurant, waiting to be seated and watching while others who had come in after them were seated by the hostesses. Finally, after a wait of only half an hour, one of the hostesses approached the group and asked them to follow her. A special table, large enough for them all, had been set in a prominent place. Immediate service was given these persons. The only regrettable event marking the seating of this first interracial group was that Mr. Stoner without provocation kicked one of the white persons in the leg.

The seating of the first group was the signal for the second group to enter. Nine Negroes and one white made up this unit. They were not seated by the hostesses, but rather were threatened by Mr. Stoner. For an hour and a half this group of ten persons stood at the front of the restaurant. During that time the police were called on three occasions. The police were, however, quite friendly to the CORE members. They wanted to know what was going on and were told—there was nothing they could do for the interracial group was far from causing a disturbance. The third time the police were called, they told Mr. Stoner not to call them again or they would arrest him.

The attention of everyone in the restaurant was, of course, attracted to the interracial group. CORE members who were seated explained the situation to other patrons. Much sympathy was aroused. Even some of the white employees expressed sympathy, including one of the hostesses who whispered into the ear of a sitdowner: "Keep it up—we're all with you." The Negro bus girls were excited about the non-violent action. They said to several CORE members that they planned to quit their jobs immediately if the interracial group were not served.

Only two persons (a middle-aged couple) were observed walking out of the restaurant without eating. It was evident that most of the patrons supported the action.

It began to look as though the second group might have to stand all night. But unexpectedly the deadlock was broken. An elderly woman, not connected with CORE, walked up to one of the Negro girls who was standing and asked if she would sit down at the table with her. Of course the CORE member accepted. Then several of the seated white CORE members followed the lead of this woman. In a very few minutes only two of the ten persons in the second interracial group were still standing. One of the hostesses advanced toward them and asked them to follow her. She seated them at a table for two near the center of the restaurant. Then a very unexpected spontaneous demonstration took place—a wild applause broke out. Practically everyone in the restaurant took part in this sustained acclamation. It was a fitting climax to a well-executed non-violent demonstration for racial justice.

Although good food was served to all the persons who participated in this action, Stoner's was not yet entirely clear of discrimination. On two occasions, Negroes received service, but only after carrying on a conversation with Mr. Stoner, explaining why they wanted to eat there. On another occasion two girls, one white and one colored, were seated but were not served for the hour in which they remained in their seats. But finally the policy of the restaurant changed completely, according to all reports. Over three years after the sit-ins, in the fall of 1946, interracial groups visiting the restaurant indicated that they had no trouble. . . .

George Houser, from *Negro Protest Thought in the Twentieth Century*

STANDING UP
TO THE WEEDS

I must relate a story I heard from a Negro woman in Louisiana. She had faced mobs and risked death enough times to smile quietly about it all as she talked. Her daughter was one of the little Negro girls who pioneered school desegregation in that state. She was telling me about the *privilege* all that suffering had been: "I never had the chances my children are getting. I just grew up and picked cotton, and so are my brothers' children doing that right now, today. But we came to the city, so we got into all this. Well, as I see it, you have to think like you're growing flowers. We always grew flowers near our house after we came home from the fields. My momma said that the flowers were ours, no one else's, and prettier than cotton. Well, I told my girl she's going to be a beautiful flower, and so she has to fight off all the weeds—the people who don't care but for their own selves. And I told her not to be a timid plant, because they die; and it's no good, to want to be something and then fail and die." I asked her whether she thought the mob we had seen that day were weeds. No, she knew exactly what she wanted to say: "The weeds are just there. I think those mob people are like a tornado or a flood. They aren't part of the ground at all. The weeds, they'll be around always, no matter how much you cultivate; but some plants are timid and some aren't. That's what I mean: you have to stand up to the weeds—and the tornadoes, and anything."

Robert Coles, from *Children of Crisis*

THE IDEA
OF BLACK POWER

Byron had never lived in or visited the South and therefore had never seen a Jim Crow car in his life, but the moving car, in which he was presently standing, must be very much like one, he thought. The procession had crowded into it, together with the other cars that made up the train, although all the seats had already been preempted by black workers who had entered at stations farther up the line. There were, to be sure, a few white faces, faces of men and women who had come from the upper reaches of the island, but most of the skins were black or brown or mulatto. We should be known as the rainbow race, Byron assured himself.

He marveled as he reflected that he was bound to a destination similar to that which was the goal of all these others, and yet he was not acquainted with a single person in the car. Perhaps even, he mused, their whole thinking processes, their very ideas, are different. I am no more like them than they are like me, than I am like any of my friends, he assured himself. In temperament and opinions we all disagree. Each of us has his own standard of thought and behavior and yet we are forced by this prodigious power of prejudice to line up together. To the white world we are a mass. . . .

What would happen to this mass? Might it not be possible that prejudice was gradually creating, automatically and unconsciously, a force that would eventually solidify, in outward opinion at least, a mass that might even assume an aggressive attitude? Or would this mass, under this pressure of prejudice, be dissipated and swept apart?

Carl Van Vechten, from *Nigger Heaven*

FINDING
AN IDENTITY

Since Stokely Carmichael of the Student Nonviolent Coordinating Committee first shouted the words there has been almost constant debate about the meaning of Black Power.

Many believe the slogan means only that Negroes should take pride in their race and organize themselves for political and economic action. Others view it as an antiwhite rallying cry. Still others see it as a sort of paramilitary slogan that leads to riots and rebellion. And a few look upon it as a chant that will ultimately lead the Negro out of the United States and to his own "homeland."

No one is likely to resolve the debate anytime soon, and some of the most outspoken Black Power advocates are glad. They have recognized from the outset that the very ambiguity of the phrase is its major strength as a rallying cry for Negroes.

This was illustrated at week's end at Newark when more than seven hundred Negroes showed up from all over the nation for a national Black Power conference that was scheduled weeks before violence erupted in the city.

It was probably the most diverse group of Negroes ever to assemble in this country, and they were able to come together under the same roof because each interpreted Black Power in his own way.

There was Ron Karenga, leader of a black nationalist organization called US, who showed up with an orange robe, a Charlie Chan-style moustache, and with his head freshly shaved. Karenga would not be opposed to armed revolution if necessary, but thinks his race—by and large—is wasting its time in rioting.

Then there was H. Rap Brown, chairman of the Student Nonviolent Coordinating Committee, who—contrary to his organization's name—believes rioting has its value and may help the Negro find his identity. Brown has found his in a "natural-style" African hairdo, a drooping moustache, and tight-fitting pants.

At the other end of the spectrum and wearing conservative business suits were such men as Owen Brooks, director of the Delta Ministry (the civil rights arm of the National Council of Churches), and Horace Sheffield, who is on the staff of the United Automobile Workers. They believe in nonviolent political action and look upon Black Power as a way of achieving political unity.

There was Floyd B. McKissick, national chairman of the Congress of Racial Equality, who thinks Negroes should spend less time trying to break out of the ghetto and more time working en masse for political and economic power. And there was Jesse Jackson of the Southern Christian Leadership Conference, who marched all over Chicago last summer in an effort to get Negroes into white neighborhoods.

And though such prominent civil rights leaders as Roy Wilkins, executive director of the National Association for the Advancement of Colored People; Whitney Young, Jr., executive director of the National Urban League; and the Reverend Martin Luther King, Jr., head of the Southern Christian Leadership Conference, stayed away from the conference, their organizations were represented by other, generally younger, men.

You could find pamphlets and newsletters denouncing all white men, and still others saying you did not have to be anti-white in order to be pro-black.

One question, of course, was whether such a loosely knit conference could lead to real unity among Negroes. And assuming that it does, would such a massive common front bring the Negro a fair share of the nation's goods and services, or would it only increase polarization among whites and deny the Negro what he had organized himself to achieve?

James Farmer, who served as national director of CORE during its era of nonviolent protest and left the organization with the coming of Black Power, showed up at the conference and thought it "extremely doubtful that there will be any consensus on tactics and methods."

"But, at least," he added, "people are talking."

Most delegates felt that little more than a consensus on goals would be reached, but some thought the conference might accomplish more than that, possibly accord on unified political action and economic boycotts.

But no matter what the conference portended for the future, it told much about the present in the nation's Negro ghettos.

For one thing, the size and diversity of the conference made it clear that the Black Power slogan contains a kind of magnetism that cannot be totally ignored by those Negroes who hope for influence in the nation's ghettos. While Black Power leaders still have to prove they can work together, they are beginning to demonstrate they can work against anyone who scoffs at the Black Power phrase.

And this alone was enough to attract some to the conference who might otherwise have preferred to remain at home.

New York Times, 23 July 1967

THE KIVA

The symbol of Pueblo resistance through the centuries is the kiva, the earth-fast sanctuary of an earth-regarding people, the secret place where they are safe from all intruders. In these kivas, which they have maintained for fifteen hundred years, each with its entrance to the spirit world of an essential chthonic religion and with its rainbow ladder for the ascent of the gods, the Pueblos have initiated fifty generations of their boys into tribal membership, handing on to them the accumulating riches of their religious lore. There, dance steps and movements, ritual observances of all kinds have been taught; the words of very many long chants and litanies have been memorized. The kiva is, in fact, the perfect focus for an underground resistance movement.

J. B. Priestly and Jacquetta Hawkes,
from *Journey Down a Rainbow*

THE PRIDE
AND THE POWER

The Pueblo Indians are unusually closemouthed, and in matters of their religion absolutely inaccessible. They make it a policy to keep their religious practices a secret, and this secret is so strictly guarded that I abandoned as hopeless any attempt at direct questioning. Never before had I run into such an atmosphere of secrecy; the religions of civilized nations today are all accessible; their sacraments have long ago ceased to be mysteries. Here, however, the air was filled with a secret known to all the communicants, but to which whites could gain no access. This strange situation gave me an inkling of Eleusis, whose secret was known to one nation and yet never betrayed. I understood what Pausanias or Herodotus felt when he wrote: "I am not permitted to name the name of that god." This was not, I felt, mystification, but a vital mystery whose betrayal might bring about the downfall of the community as well as of the individual. Preservation of the secret gives the Pueblo Indian pride and the power to resist the dominant whites. It gives him cohesion and unity; and I feel sure that the Pueblos as an individual community will continue to exist as long as their mysteries are not desecrated.

C. G. Jung, from *Memories, Dreams, Reflections*

AS THE ROPE
TIGHTENS

GBATALA, Liberia, Nov. 4—They are calm and big men, who walk across a hacked-out clearing in the heart of West

Africa with the long, easy stride of Americans. Their eyes and their mouths do not smile. If they laugh, it is when they tell the familiar stories of the restaurants in the United States that would not serve them a cup of coffee when they were soldiers and in the South.

They talk a little too, about the buses they drove in Chicago because the jobs they wanted were not the jobs they could get. At these times, in those soft, solemn voices, there is an echo of the bitterness they say they no longer feel.

They are American Negroes—two words they wish to forget. They left their apartments and television sets and big cars to lead a back-to-Africa movement—as what they call Hebrew Israelites, which, to them, is not a sect but a way of life.

The site they chose, more than a year ago, is three hundred acres in a clammy, snake-infested, ugly part of central Liberia, eleven miles from a village called Gbatala. It is more than eighty miles from Monrovia, the capital of this African country with 121 years of independence behind it. Founded by the American Colonization Society in 1820 and declared independent 26 July 1847, Liberia became after the Civil War a haven for slaves freed in the United States.

The new settlers are strange immigrants, for they are clearly city men with city ways who once earned salaries beyond the dreams of an educated African and who possessed more than many Africans ever see.

"America is a sinking ship—and the captain wants us to take our turn at the steering wheel," a twenty-nine-year-old man said. He was in a group of five men—all from Chicago's South Side—who were playing cards on a Sunday afternoon in the Camp, their name for the colony.

"My age? That's immaterial," another man said.

In the United States, the men said, talking by turn, they never starved, they made out OK, but they felt that there was no way to stay men unless they left for good. Civil rights groups, Black Power, the Black Panthers—these are words that make them shrug their shoulders. They do not speak that language.

"And if they win—what is there really to win?" a bearded man wearing a skullcap asked. "The only choice was to get out, there is no hope to change anything."

A reported total of 173 black men, women, and children arrived in the camp from the United States between July and December of 1967. No one here will deny or confirm this figure. Nor will any of the men say how many people are here now. In Monrovia, there is talk that 50 persons have returned to the United States and that about 65 remain in the camp.

"What does it matter, why does it make a difference?" one of the cardplayers asked. "What is significant are not the details, but the achievements," he said.

The achievements are obvious. They are the bush the men cleared, and keep clearing, without any power tools. They are the wells they dug, learning as they went along. They are the green peppers, the string beans, the American corn, the sweet potatoes, and the mustard greens they planted—and the houses they live in. Each man built his family's home, and now he is apt to look at it critically and with love.

They are small houses, with a slightly crooked look. Made of bamboo, they have tin roofs and cement floors. Inside there is not much furniture. The camp has its own generator so there are electric lights.

The wives, moving quietly in long African shirts, cook on kerosine stoves and wash the dishes in basins of cold water on the verandas. They do not speak much when outsiders come. The youngest child in the camp is less than two months old, the oldest is fourteen years. The children stay outdoors under the huge old trees of Africa, playing the games they played on city pavements more than four thousand miles away.

"We are not trying to impress anybody. It is not a sect here, it is a way of life that Hebrews lead for we are Hebrew Israelites and we come out of the seed of Jacob," said one man whose name is now Ahshare Ahkiba Israel.

"We are all men here and we are all free," he said. "The door is open—all we ask is that everyone observe the Sabbath."

"We do not number ourselves," another man said, "for no number can be given to Israel."

There is resentment when they are pressed for their names.

"What do you want my name to be? Jody Johnson? Jimmy Jones? How did we get our names in the United States and what do they mean? Well, this name is one that I have chosen and I am proud of it and it is the only name I have," said a tall, strapping man in a beige windbreaker, who spells his name Yishiyah Israel.

The men call one another brothers, the women are sisters. Hebrew lessons are given in the camp. The Torah is the law. When men speak of divine guidance, which they say led them to Liberia and not to Israel, they do not grin or look self-conscious.

Other Americans working in Monrovia seem horrified, or occasionally touched, by the religious commitments of the immigrants.

"They need something to believe in, to keep them going, and maybe to give them the dignity and conviction that they felt so deprived of in their own country," said one American in Monrovia, who did not wish to be identified.

Their commitment to their religion has disturbed some outsiders.

"Anyone can wish a Negro well who's willing to work hard, and break his back, in that swamp where they live, but that religious talk is more than I can listen to," said a white man in Monrovia.

But the men who have chosen the names of El Kannann ben Israel and Gavreale Kahtan Israel and Ahshare Ahkiba Israel do not try to convert others. They only try to explain themselves. They admit that it has been a struggle to make homes in Liberia, that some of them have been ill with malaria, that a few have dropped out, and that Liberia suits them better than America ever did.

"Sure, not all the people in this country can read or write, but they have common sense," said El Kannann, who is twenty-nine years old and the father of four children.

"Perhaps we are considered foreign here but we were more foreign to the people of the United States," a former Chicago bus driver said.

He did not deny that for many Liberians, especially in rural areas, blackness of skin is not a bond.

"You don't find people starving here but you do in the States," the former bus driver continued. "In the South you find areas much worse than any here. We are much more friendly with the government here than we were to the government of the United States," he added.

And, then, in one of the frequent pronouncements made by these men, he said with sincerity:

"We feel that any nation that carried a people into captivity must in turn be led into captivity and that they who kill by the sword must perish by the sword. And we prefer to be here as onlookers rather than to be there and part of it."

In the camp the men admit they need money to buy tractors and power tools.

Various projects to raise money include operating a Monrovia night club where a five-man American band plays, except on Friday nights, and a snack bar that will open soon. It is called Mr. C's Misada Tova, the Hebrew words for "good restaurant."

There are six tables, made by a former carpenter, and a soda bar in Mr. C's Misada Tova. No one will explain who Mr. C is, for, they say, what does it matter? Soul Chicken—Southern Fried—Exciting Shakes and Sundaes Plus for the First Time in Africa Slushade, reads the sign for the restaurant. Slushade is a little soft ice, one man said. The ice cream will be imported from the United States. The ice cream creations are advertised as Soul on Ice.

Some of the men predict an influx of newcomers to the camp after the elections, or early next year, when they expect the back-to-Africa movement to swell.

It is not certain what the attitude of the Liberian government would be to a huge increase in immigrants. The settlers, who have retained American citizenship, do not pretend to be certain that they will spend their lives in this country, or in Africa. They do not know their future.

The brothers in Liberia, who belong to a movement called the Liberation of Our People, have so far in Africa survived physical punishment and psychological pressure. They prefer these to the racial tensions they left behind.

"We're not opting out of anything, we're beginning to live and act as men should," a former mechanic in Chicago said. "Others will join us as the rope tightens."

Gloria Emerson, from the *New York Times*,
6 November 1968

NOSOTROS VENCEREMOS: THE STORY OF CESAR CHAVEZ

ITEM: At a dinner party in New York's Westchester County, the dessert includes grapes. The hostess notices that her fellow suburbanites fall to with gusto; the guests from Manhattan unanimously abstain.

ITEM: At St. Paul's, a fashionable New Hampshire prep school, grapes are the only part of the meal invariably left untouched.

ITEM: In San Francisco, a Safeway official observes: "We have customers who come to the store for no other reason than to buy grapes. They'll load up their car with grapes and nothing else."

ITEM: In Oakland, a conscience-ridden housewife explains apologetically to her dinner companions: "I really wanted to have this dessert, and I just decided that one little bunch of grapes wouldn't make that much difference."

ITEM: In Honolulu, the Young Americans for Freedom or-

ganizes an "emergency grape lift" by jet from the mainland, inviting "all of those starved for the sight of a California grape to come to the airport."

Why all the excitement about this smooth, sweet, and innocent fruit? The answer is that the table grape, *Vitis vinifera*, has become the symbol of the four-year-old strike of California's predominantly Mexican-American farm workers. For more than a year now, table grapes have been the object of a national boycott that has won the sympathy and support of many Americans—and the ire of many others. The strike is widely known as *la causa*, which has come to represent not only a protest against working conditions among California grape pickers but the wider aspirations of the nation's Mexican-American minority as well. *La causa's* magnetic champion and the country's most prominent Mexican-American leader is Cesar Estrada Chavez, forty-two, a onetime grape picker who combines a mystical mien with peasant earthiness. *La causa* is Chavez's whole life; for it, he has impoverished himself and endangered his health by fasting. In soft, slow speech, he urges his people—nearly five million of them in the U.S.—to rescue themselves from society's cellar. As he sees it, the first step is to win the battle of the grapes.

Magnified Movement

To enter the public consciousness, a labor conflict must ordinarily threaten the supply of essential goods and services, such as steel or transportation. Politicians and the public take notice only when there is great impact on the economy, when spectacular bloodshed occurs, or when well-recognized issues are at stake. The grape strike seems to meet none of these criteria. Americans could easily live without the table grape if they had to, and even that minor sacrifice has been unnecessary. The dispute has been relatively free of violence. Neither great numbers of men nor billions of dollars are involved. The welfare of agricultural workers has rarely captured U.S. atten-

tion in the past, but the grape strike—*la huelga*—and the boycott accompanying it have clearly engaged a large part of the
nation.

The issue has divided husband and wife, inspired countless
heated arguments at social occasions, and engendered public
controversy from coast to coast. As if on a holy crusade, the
strikers stage marches that resemble religious pilgrimages,
bearing aloft their own stylized black Aztec eagle on a red
field along with images of the Virgin of Guadalupe, patroness
of Mexicans and particularly of those who work the soil. As
the workers and their sympathizers march, supermarket chains,
middle-class consumers, and even the grape growers are choos-
ing sides. Some supermarkets are leaving the choice to the
shopper. Others sell only grapes imported from Africa or Israel, and make a point of advertising that they do not carry
the California product. On Capitol Hill, diners in the House
restaurants have not seen a grape for months, while the Senate
refectory has been using fifteen to twenty pounds a week.
When one California congressman sent large bags of grapes
to each of his colleagues, many of the recipients returned them.
Within a few hours, the corridor outside the congressman's
office was asquish with trod-upon fruit.

Governor Ronald Reagan calls the strike and boycott "im-
moral" and "attempted blackmail." Senator George Murphy,
like Reagan, an old Hollywood union-man-turned-conserva-
tive, terms the movement "dishonest." The Nixon administration has seemed ambivalent, putting forward legislation that
would ostensibly give farm workers organization rights but
would also limit their use of strikes and boycotts. The Pen-
tagon has substantially increased its grape orders for mess-hall
tables, a move that Chavez and his followers countered last
week by preparing a lawsuit to prevent such purchases on the
ground that grapes are the subject of a labor dispute. Some
auto-bumper stickers read: Nixon Eats Grapes. The growers'
answering slogan: Eat California Grapes, The Forbidden Fruit.

Edward and Ethel Kennedy, following the late Robert Kennedy's example, have embraced Cesar Chavez as a brother. The

so-called Beautiful People, from Peter, Paul and Mary to the Ford sisters, Anne Uzielli and Charlotte Niarchos, are helping to raise funds for the strikers. That support is one of the few issues that find Chicago Mayor Richard Daley, iconoclastic writer Gloria Steinem, and liberal senators Jacob Javits and George McGovern in total agreement. Ralph Abernathy lends black help to what is becoming the Brown Power movement.

The fact that it is a movement has magnified *la huelga* far beyond its economic and geographic confines. At stake are not only the interests of 384,100 agricultural workers in California but potentially those of more than four million in the U.S. Such workers have never won collective bargaining rights, partially because they have not been highly motivated to organize and partially because their often itinerant lives have made them difficult to weld into a group that would have the clout of an industrial union. By trying to organize the grape pickers, Chavez hopes to inspire militancy among all farm laborers. Because most of the grape pickers are Mexican Americans, he also believes that he is fighting a battle on behalf of the entire Mexican-American community, which as a group constitutes the nation's second biggest deprived minority.

Unlettered and Unshod

Like the blacks, Mexican Americans, who are known as *Chicanos,* are a varied and diverse people. Only recently have they emerged from a stereotype: the lazy, placid peasant lost in a centuries-long siesta under a sombrero. Unlike the blacks, who were brought to the U.S. involuntarily, the *Chicanos* have flocked to the U.S. over the past thirty years, legally and illegally, in an attempt to escape the poverty of their native Mexico and find a better life. Whatever their present condition may be, many obviously find it better than their former one, as evidenced by the fact that relatives have often followed families into the U.S. The *Chicanos* do not speak in one voice but many, follow no one leader or strategy. Their level of ambition and militance varies greatly from barrio to barrio between Texas and California.

No man, however, personifies the *Chicanos'* bleak past, restless present, and possible future in quite the manner of Cesar Chavez. He was the unshod, unlettered child of migrant workers. He attended dozens of schools but never got to the eighth grade. He was a street-corner tough who now claims as his models Emiliano Zapata, Gandhi, Nehru, and Martin Luther King. He tells his people: "We make a solemn promise: to enjoy our rightful part of the riches of this land, to throw off the yoke of being considered as agricultural implements or slaves. We are free men and we demand justice."

The dawning of Chavez's social awareness came in a seamy San Jose, California, barrio called *Sal Si Puedes*—"Get out if you can." Through Fred Ross, a tall, quiet organizer for Saul Alinsky's Community Service Organization, Cesar began to act on Alinsky's precept that concerted action is the only means through which the poor can gain political and economic power. Chavez, a Roman Catholic, has delved deeply into the papal social encyclicals, especially *Rerum Novarum* and *Quadragesimo Anno*.[29] "What Cesar wanted to reform was the way he was treated as a man," recalls his brother Richard. "We always talked about change, but how could we go about it?" Cesar Chavez went about it by working with the CSO among Mexican Americans for ten years. Then, in 1962, he left to form a farm workers' union.

The conditions under which farm laborers toil have improved somewhat since the squalid depression era so well evoked by John Steinbeck in *The Grapes of Wrath* and *In Dubious Battle*; yet field work remains one of the most unpleasant of human occupations. It demands long hours of back-

[29] *Rerum Novarum*, published by Leo XIII in 1891, contended that the rich had in effect enslaved the poor, and that every man has a right to a decent wage and reasonable comfort. Pius XI, in *Quadragesimo Anno* (1931), criticized the economic despotism that results from "limitless free competition" and reiterated the principle of a just wage.

breaking labor, often in choking dust amid insects and under a flaming sun. The harvest-time wage for grape pickers averages $1.65 an hour, plus a 25¢ bonus for each box picked, while the current federal minimum wage is $1.60.

Despite this, the seasonal and sporadic nature of the work keeps total income far below the poverty level. Average family income is less than $1,600 a year. There is no job security, and fringe benefits are few. If they are migrants, the workers must frequently live in fetid shacks without light or plumbing (though housing, bad as it is, is frequently free or very cheap). As a result, many have moved to the cities, where even unskilled labor can find work at decent wages.

Chavez was not the first to try to organize farm workers. Ineffective efforts to found agricultural unions date back to the turn of the century. But only in Hawaii, where Harry Bridges's tough longshoremen's union used its muscle to win the first farm-labor contract for sugarcane workers in 1945, did unionization take hold. Agriculture is outside the jurisdiction of the National Labor Relations Board, which has provided federal ground rules for industrial workers' unions since 1935; on a national level, there is no similar mechanism for farm workers. In May the Nixon administration proposed an independent Farm Labor Relations Board, but chances for passage of such a law this year are small. Without NLRB protection, and with farm labor normally transient and seasonal, the difficulties of organizing are enormous.

Rose Grafts and Table Grapes

Undeterred by these obstacles, Chavez took his $1,200 in savings and started the National Farm Workers' Association seven years ago, setting up its headquarters in the San Joaquin Valley agricultural town of Delano. He clocked off three hundred thousand miles in a battered 1953 Mercury station wagon, crisscrossing the San Joaquin and talking to more than fifty thousand workers in the first six months. His money was soon gone, but he found people who were willing to give him food. The NFWA had its first formal meeting in Fresno in September 1962; 287 people showed up. Chavez soon started a death-benefits plan for his members, a curious echo of the burial societies organized decades ago by Eastern European immigrants on their arrival in the U.S. He also set up a credit union with $35 in assets (it now has more than $50,000). By August 1964, he had one thousand members, each paying $3.50 a month in dues—no small sum for a farm worker's family. Soon he began publishing a union newspaper called *El Malcriado* ("The Misfit"), whose circulation is 18,000.

At last the union felt strong enough to tackle growers on a substantive issue. In 1964, the NFWA took one employer to court for paying less than the then minimum wage of $1.25 per hour, and after months of wrangling, won the case. The amounts of money gained were small but the point was made: a boss could be beaten. Then the association sued the Tulare County housing authority over the rents and conditions at two labor camps, built in the late 1930s and intended to be used for only a few years. The camps were a hideous collection of nine-foot by eleven-foot tin shacks, boiling in the summer sun and lacking both indoor plumbing and heat for the chill nights. Tulare officials subsequently built modern accommodations.

In May 1965, Chavez signed up a group of rose grafters and won a strike vote for higher wages. Everyone pledged not to go to work, but just to make sure that no one did, Chavez and Dolores Huerta, his tiny, tough assistant, made the rounds early on the strike's first morning. Mrs. Huerta saw a light in one house where four of the workers lived. She reminded them of their pledge, but they had changed their minds. Mrs. Huerta moved her truck so that it blocked their driveway and put the key in her purse. The incident illustrated the charge that Chavez and his aides sometimes coerce those who would rather work than strike. After only four days of the strike, the grower agreed to give the workers a 120 percent wage increase.

That same spring, in the Coachella Valley east of Los

Angeles, the largely Filipino grape pickers of the AFL–CIO's fledgling Agricultural Workers Organizing Committee won a brief strike for pay equal to that given field hands imported from Mexico. When the workers moved north to Delano at the end of the summer, grape growers there refused to make a similar agreement, and AWOC once more went on strike. On 16 September, which just happened to be Mexican Independence Day, Chavez's group held a tumultuous meeting and voted unanimously to join the walkout. The hall of the Roman Catholic church on Delano's west side resounded with cries of "*Viva la huelga!*" "*Viva la causa! Viva la unión!*" The NFWA and the AWOC merged two years later to form the United Farm Workers Organizing Committee, headed by Chavez.

Table-grape growers were particularly vulnerable to strikes because their product requires continual attention through much of the year. Since the appearance of the fruit affects its value—unlike the case of wine grapes—the bunches must be carefully picked by hand. Because of their vulnerability, Chavez picked the table-grape growers as his first target. In 1966, after a strike, he got his first contract when Schenley Industries capitulated because it had a nationally known name at stake. Later that year he won the right to represent workers at the mammoth Di Giorgio ranch in an election monitored by the American Arbitration Association. Both Di Giorgio and Schenley have since sold their table-grape holdings, however, and Chavez's only contracts now are with wine producers: Gallo, Christian Brothers, Masson, Almadén, Franzia Brothers, and Novitiate.

Boycott and Breakthrough

Chavez has never been able to get large numbers of laborers to join the strike. Many of those who do follow him are fanatic in their loyalty, but a large segment of the shifting, transient work force continues to be indifferent to unionism. Wages have been rising even in the absence of contracts, and few farm workers can afford to go unpaid for long. Although federal regulations theoretically prohibit the hiring of aliens, or "green-carders," as strikebreakers, the owners have nevertheless continued to use imported workers of Mexican citizenship.

Chavez decided to resort to the boycott to keep pressure on the table-grape growers. He applied it first in 1967 to the Giumarra Vineyards Corp., the largest U.S. table-grape producer. Giumarra started using the labels of other growers—in violation of Food and Drug Administration rules—to circumvent the boycott. In retaliation, the Chavez people began to appeal to stores and consumers not to buy any California table grapes at all. The boycott has been extended overseas to Britain and Scandinavia.

Chavez has now finally achieved a breakthrough: nationwide grape sales were off 12 percent in 1968, and prices for this year's first California grapes are down as much as 15 percent. Last month ten growers representing about 12 percent of the state's table-grape production announced that they would sit down with Chavez to write a contract. If negotiations with Chavez succeed, some other vineyards may also sign contracts, but a determined majority still barely acknowledge his existence and remain adamantly opposed to union recognition.

If the union does begin to win contracts with an increasing number of growers, a new difficulty could arrive: How is the consumer to tell the difference between union and nonunion grapes? Boxes can be labeled easily, but not loose bunches of grapes in a market. The union claims that existing boycott machinery can be turned around to promote the produce of those who have signed; they could be marketed through the chain stores that have refused to handle the produce of struck growers. However, any such confusing procedure is bound to dilute the boycott's effectiveness.

Most of the growers bitterly dispute Chavez's contentions. His claim to represent the workers is false, they say; only 3 percent of California's grape pickers have joined his union. Chavez has not been able to strip the fields of workers and, they argue, even if he personally preaches nonviolence, his followers do not practice it. Packing sheds have been set afire, foremen threatened, tires slashed. Chavez also has outside help. Long-haired pickets came down from Berkeley in the early days of *la huelga,* and the union gets $14,500 a month in grants from the AFL–CIO and Walter Reuther's United Automobile Workers. By insisting that all workers join his union, moreover, Chavez wants what amounts to a closed shop (which is illegal under the Taft-Hartley Act, but the act does not apply to agricultural workers). This means that, for now at least, Chavez's goal, however unpalatable, is a legal one. Chavez opposes placing farm workers under the National Labor Relations Board precisely because that would make the closed shop he seeks unlawful.

The California growers also pay the second highest agricultural wages in the U.S. (after Hawaii, where unionized workers average $3 an hour).

While they generally belittle the extent of his support, however, the growers have gone to some lengths to counter Chavez's moves. The anti-UFWOC campaign even included for a time a group called Mothers Against Chavez. The growers are using the J. Walter Thompson agency to place $400,000 worth of ads extolling the benefits of table grapes. The California public relations firm of Whitaker and Baxter has been retained to advise the growers about how to counter the boycott. Whitaker and Baxter helped to manage Richard Nixon's unsuccessful campaign for governor of California in 1962, and masterminded the American Medical Association's attempt to defeat Medicare.

On $10 a Week

One reason for the lack of comprehension between Chavez and the growers is that each has different concepts of the fundamental issue. The growers see themselves as management in a classic labor dispute, while Chavez and his followers believe that the cause of all Mexican Americans is at stake.

That is what inspires Chavez's devotion to *la causa*. For years he and his wife and eight children have lived jammed into a tiny two-bedroom house in Delano, subsisting on $10 a week from the union and on food from the communal kitchen in nearby union headquarters. Chavez has grown increasingly ascetic. He has given up casual socializing as well as liquor and cigarettes; his idea of a real treat is an eclectic meal of Chinese food, matzos, and diet soda. The fight has become his life. "The days and weeks and months run together," he told *Time* correspondent Robert Anson. "I can't think back to a time when we were not on strike." Nor does he contemplate surrender to the growers. "Either the union will be destroyed," he says, "or they will sign a contract. There's no other alternative."

The use of only peaceful means has been central to his thinking since a 1953 showdown in the San Joaquin Valley between his Mexican-American CSO pickets and a public official. Suddenly, he realized that if there were any violence or serious disorder it would be his responsibility. He began reading Gandhi, and he says now: "If the strike means the blood of one grower or one grower's son, or one worker or one worker's son, then it isn't worth it."

In February 1968, Chavez began a twenty-five-day fast "as an act of penance, recalling workers to the nonviolent roots of their movement." Although he insisted that his decision was essentially a private one, the fast took on a certain circus aura and raised suspicions that its motivation was more theatrical than theological. During the fast, Chavez had to make a court appearance in Bakersfield, on charges of improper picketing, in a case that has yet to come to trial. As he did so, two thousand farm workers knelt outside in prayer. One woman solemnly asked him if he were indeed a saint. When the fast ended, Senator Robert Kennedy knelt next to him to receive communion. Some eight thousand others joined them in Delano's Memorial Park for a bread-breaking ceremony.

The fast, and Chavez's years of twelve- to sixteen-hour

days, took their toll. Last September he suffered a muscular breakdown in his back—he had been in pain for years before that—and found his legs nearly paralyzed. After spending more than two months in traction, he has now substantially recovered, but is still bedridden much of the time. Instead of spending long hours driving around the state, he receives a constant stream of subordinates at his bedside.

Chavez's religious conviction mingles with the exigencies of the movement. He opposes birth control for his people, but only partly out of conventional Catholicism; he argues that smaller families would diminish the numerical power of the poor. A priest brings him communion daily. To correspondent Anson he explained: "God prepares those who have to suffer and take punishment. Otherwise, how could we exist? How could the black man exist? There must be something special. I really think that He looks after us."

Cesar Chavez came to his mission from a background of poverty and prejudice that is a paradigm of that of many *Chicanos*. Like most Mexican Americans, he is of mixed Spanish and Indian blood, with liquid brown eyes, deeply bronze skin, and thick, jet-black hair. He was born on an eighty-acre farm in Arizona's Gila Valley near Yuma, where his parents tried to scratch a living from the arid desert earth. Chavez met racial hostility early in daily rock fights between Anglo and *Chicano* kids at the village school.

The farm failed in the depression, and when Chavez was ten, the family packed everything it owned into a decrepit automobile and headed across the Colorado River into California. In Oxnard, Chavez's father found work threshing lima beans; when all the beans were harvested, the family took off, looking for other jobs and often turning up just a few days after a crop was in.

Anglos on the Left

That first winter back in Oxnard, with the little money earned in the fields already gone, was the family's worst time. Cesar's brother Richard remembers: "There was this nice lady there, and she had a vacant lot that she let us use. So we put up a tent. It was a very small tent—I guess about eight by ten. That's all we had. All the family stayed there. And it rained that winter. Oh, it rained. Rain, rain, rain. We had to go to school barefoot. We had no shoes. I can't forget it."

The family lived that winter on beans, tortillas, and an occasional potato. Chavez's father sometimes picked peas for 50¢ a day, half of which went to the contractor who drove the workers to the fields in the back of a flatbed truck. There was nothing else to do. By the next spring, the family had learned more of the harvest schedule, and it set off for the first of many years on the circuit familiar to every migrant worker in California. Starting in the Imperial and Coachella valleys of the south, through the state's bulging middle, the San Joaquin Valley, on up north of San Francisco and into the Napa Valley, they worked each crop in its turn: asparagus, grapes, beets, potatoes, beans, plums, apricots—anything that needed picking, hoeing, thinning, leafing, tipping, girdling, digging, or pruning.

In 1941, the family moved to Delano, where Chavez met his future wife, Helen Fabela. At the movies with her one night, he had a jarring brush with discrimination. He refused to stay on the right side of the theater, which was reserved for Mexicans, and sat instead with the Anglos on the left. "The assistant manager came," Chavez recalls. "The girl who sold popcorn came. And the girl with the tickets came. Then the manager came. They tried to pull me up, and I said, 'No, you have to break my arms before I get up.'" Chavez, then sixteen, was hustled off to the station house for a lecture from the chief of police, but he would not promise not to do the same thing again.

Like many other teen-age Mexican Americans, Chavez became a *pachuco*, affecting a zoot suit with pegged pants, a broad flat hat, and a ducktail haircut. Some sociologists now see the *pachuco* movement as the first example of militant separatism among *Chicanos*, an assertion of a distinct identity hostile to Anglo culture. The Anglos took it that way, in any case, and reacted violently: during a series of riots in the Southwest during the summer of 1943, several thousand soldiers, sailors, and marines beat up hundreds of *Chicano* youths. Police promptly arrested some of the victims.

Because of his own experience of poverty and acquaintance with prejudice, Cesar Chavez has made *la causa* more than a labor movement. He is determined to better the lot of all Mexican Americans. There is much room for improvement. There have never been Jim Crow laws against them, like those against blacks, but overt discrimination undeniably exists. *Chicanos* still find it hard to get into the barbershops and public swimming pools of south Texas. Still, though the *Chicano* is set apart by language, assimilation is often easier for him than for the Negro. For this reason, and because most of the *Chicano* population lives in relative obscurity in the barrios or rural areas, the Mexican-American community has been slow to develop aggressive leadership.

Now, because they have seen that organized black action gets results, the *Chicanos* have begun to stir with a new militancy. They have formed the Brown Berets, modeled on the Black Panthers, and set up a $2,200,000 Mexican-American Legal Defense and Educational Fund, financed by the Ford Foundation. "We are about ten years behind the Negroes, and we must catch up," says Dr. Daniel Valdes, a Denver behavioral scientist. "But I think we will do it without extreme violence." Lawyer Donald Pacheco puts the plight of the Mexican American more bluntly: "We're the 'nigger' of ten years ago."

If he is a migrant farm worker, the Mexican American has a life expectancy of about forty-eight years compared to seventy for the average U.S. citizen. The *Chicano* birth rate is double the U.S. average—but so is the rate of infant mortality. More than one-third live below the $3,000-a-year level of family income that federal statisticians define as poverty. Eighty percent of the Mexican-American population is now urban, and most live in the barrio.

Forbidden Language

The overwhelming majority work as unskilled or semi-skilled labor in factories and packing plants, or in service jobs as maids, waitresses, yard boys, and deliverymen. Particularly in Texas, Mexican Americans sometimes get less pay than others for the same work. Even the few who have some education do not escape discrimination. *Chicano* women find that jobs as public contacts at airline ticket counters are rarely open; they are welcome as switchboard operators out of the public eye. Mexican-American men who work in banks are assigned to the less fashionable branches. Promotions come slowly, responsibility hardly ever.

One major impediment to the Mexican American is his Spanish language, because it holds him back in U.S. schools. Mexican Americans average eight years of schooling, two years less than Negroes and a full four years less than whites. Often they are forced to learn English from scratch in the first grade, and the frequent result is that they become not bilingual but nearly nonlingual. In Texas, 40 percent of *Chicanos* are considered functionally illiterate. In Los Angeles, only an estimated 25 percent can speak English fluently. *Chicano* children in some rural areas are still punished for speaking Spanish in school. Only this year, *Chicano* students at Bowie High School in El Paso—in a predominantly Mexican-American section—managed to get a rule abolished that forbade the speaking of Spanish on the school grounds.

The *Chicano* is as vulnerable to mistreatment at the hands of the law as the black. Seven Mexicans were beaten by drunken policemen at a Los Angeles police station on Christmas Eve, 1952; six of the officers were eventually given jail terms. During an eighteen-month period ending last April, the American Civil Liberties Union received 174 complaints of police abuses from Los Angeles Mexican Americans. Two of the recent landmark Supreme Court decisions limiting police questioning of suspects involved Mexican Americans—

Escobeda v. *Illinois* and *Miranda* v. *Arizona*. Many Mexicans still look on the Texas Rangers and U.S. border patrols with terror.

Pluralism *v.* the Melting Pot

That Chavez has dramatized the problems of Mexican Americans in the city as well as on the farm seems beyond dispute. Father Bernardo Kenny, a Sacramento priest with a sizable Mexican-American congregation, believes that even if Chavez never wins his strike he will have made a "tremendous contribution." Says Kenny: "He focused attention on the problem of the farm workers, and he made the Mexican Americans proud to be Mexican Americans. Chavez must be given credit, I think, for really starting the Mexican-American civil rights movement." Ironically, mechanization hastened by unionization may eventually diminish Chavez's farm-labor base—but it will not slow the momentum of *la causa*.

The new Mexican-American militancy has turned up a mixed *piñata* of leaders, some of them significantly more strident than Chavez. In Los Angeles, twenty-year-old David Sanchez is prime minister of the well-disciplined Brown Berets, who help keep intramural peace in the barrio and are setting up a free medical clinic. Some of them also carry machetes and talk tough about the Anglo. Reies Lopez Tijerina, forty-five, is trying to establish a Free City State of San Joaquin for *Chicanos* on historic Spanish land grants in New Mexico; at the moment, while his appeal on an assault conviction is being adjudicated, he is in jail for burning a sign in the Carson National Forest. Denver's Rudolfo ("Corky") Gonzales, forty, an ex-prizefighter, has started a Crusade for Justice to make the city's eighty-five thousand Mexican Americans *la causa*-conscious.

As with the blacks, the question for those who lead the *Chicanos* is whether progress means separatism or assimilation. Cal State Professor Rafael Guzman, who helped carry out a four-year Ford Foundation study of Mexican Americans, warns that the barrio is potentially as explosive as the black ghetto. He argues for a new pluralism in the U.S. that means something other than forcing minorities into the established Anglo-Saxon mold; each group should be free to develop its own culture while contributing to the whole.

Yet there is no real consensus in the barrio. The forces for assimilation are powerful. A young Tucson militant, Salomon Baldenegro, contends: "Our values are just like any Manhattan executive's, but we have a ceiling on our social mobility." While federal programs for bilingual instruction in Mexican-American areas are still inadequate, that kind of approach—if made readily available to all who want it—leaves the choice between separatism and assimilation ultimately to the individual *Chicano* himself. He learns in his father's tongue, but he also learns in English well enough so that language is no longer a barrier; he retains his own culture, but he also knows enough of the majority's rules and ways to compete successfully if he chooses to.

Cesar Chavez has made the *Chicano's* cause well enough known to make that goal possible. While *la huelga* is in some respects a limited battle, it is also symbolic of the Mexican-American's quest for a full role in U.S. society. What happens to Chavez's farm workers will be an omen, for good or ill, of the Mexican-American's future. For the short term, Chavez's most tangible aspiration is to win the fight with the grape growers. If he can succeed in that difficult and uncertain battle, he will doubtless try to expand the movement beyond the vineyards into the entire Mexican-American community.

"Cesar's War," *Time,* 4 July 1969

Note: By 29 July 1970, when twenty-six grape growers signed contracts with the United Farm Workers Organizing Committee, 65 percent of the growers had become unionized. The UFW had become the first successful union in the history of agriculture.

FROM THE "CONSTITUTION OF THE NATIONAL INDIAN YOUTH COUNCIL"

Preamble to the Constitution

We, the younger generation, at this time in the history of the American Indian, find it expedient to band together on a national scale in meeting the challenges facing the Indian people. In such banding for mutual assistance, we recognize the future of the Indian people will ultimately rest in the hands of the younger people, and Indian youth need be concerned with the position of the American Indian. We further recognize the inherent strength of the American Indian heritage that will be enhanced by a National Indian Youth Council. We, the undersigned, believing in a greater Indian America, in order to form a nonprofit corporation for the purposes hereinafter enumerated, do hereby certify as follows:

Founding Resolution

Whereas, the National Indian Youth Council holds it to be in the best interest of Indian people for better understanding of conditions for all Indians to carry forward our policies to make clear the inherent sovereign rights of all Indians;

Whereas, in order to gain this end the National Indian Youth Council strongly opposes the termination of federal trusteeship over Indians, and;

Whereas, the National Indian Youth Council holds that it is morally and legally right that Indians have a voice in matters of jurisdiction directly or indirectly affecting Indians, and;

Whereas, the National Indian Youth Council recognizes the inherent rights guaranteed all people in statutes of the United States and holds Indians must exercise their rights;

Now therefore be it resolved, that the National Indian Youth Council endeavors to carry forward the policy of making their inherent sovereign rights known to all people, opposing termination of federal responsibilities at all levels, seeking full participation and consent on jurisdiction matters involving Indians, and staunchly supporting the exercise of those basic rights guaranteed American Indians by the statutes of the United States of America.

Statement of Purpose

The history of the American Indian records the suppression of a proud people and meager redresses by the federal government. Today, the suppressed are still a proud people who have made many concessions to a changing world. Through the years, individuals, agencies, and organizations have acted on behalf of the Indian people. These individuals and organizations have enjoyed a considerable extent of success; yet there remains an important role, which can only be occupied by the Indian people themselves.

This role is one of understanding and assumption of leadership responsibilities for the values and beliefs that make our Indian people worthy of honor and pride. This role has been and is being filled by dedicated Indians. However, if we are to maintain and strengthen our position as America's original inhabitants, the younger generation of Indian people must participate in fostering of our values and beliefs.

A group of young Indians who first met at the American Indian Chicago Conference and later at Gallup, New Mexico, on 10–13 August 1960, have formed the National Indian Youth Council, which considered the above stated position. This group decided after considerable preliminary correspondence and deliberations that the NIYC shall be organized to develop greater leadership responsibilities, especially when our basic values and beliefs are jeopardized.

With the belief that we can serve a realistic need, the National Indian Youth Council dedicated its activities and projects to attaining a greater future for our Indian people. We believe in a future with high principles derived from the values and beliefs of our ancestors. We further believe in a strong place in American society being held by Indian blood, and the development of greater leadership with Indian youth.

The Indian people are going to remain Indians for a long time to come. However, every ethnic group of people who are to live within a changing world of good and bad influences must possess a sense of security within their own group. Being of Indian origin should always be held in high regard but never as a disadvantage. American Indians rightfully hold an esteemed and influential position based on their past and present record. Generosity, understanding of feelings, and values based on fairness is well-known to the Indian people and their friends. The adaptability of natural talents of our people are to be revered. Notwithstanding our present and potential achievements, there is and always will be need for the Indian people themselves to protect our birthright. We should never abuse the integrity of our people.

There are many particular problems and needs facing our people, which we acknowledge. A great amount of lip service has been given to "Indian problems and solutions"; so much that we are sometimes labeled as a problem people. Of course, this is not fair! The ultimate realization of man lies in being content with his livelihood and beliefs. This goal can only be realized with individuals and leaders of strong character. It is the aim of the NIYC that we promote activities and projects for the development of upstanding leaders.

Our council does not intend to draw lines with elaborate rules nor do we intend to propose any radical movements. We consider rules based on Indian thinking as being sufficient. It is hoped that the overall purposes and goals will guide the organization to its success. We sincerely hope that all Indians will join us in establishing and maintaining a greater Indian America.

National Indian Youth Council, 10 August 1960

TEN-POINT PROGRAM OF BLACK LIBERATION

1. We want freedom. We want power to determine the destiny of our black community.

2. We want full employment for our people.

3. We want an end to the robbery by the capitalist of our black community.[30]

4. We want decent housing, fit for shelter of human beings.

5. We want education for our people that exposes the true nature of this decadent American society. We want education that teaches us our true history and our role in the present day society.

6. We want all black men to be exempt from military service.

7. We want an immediate end to police brutality and murder of black people.

8. We want freedom for all black men held in federal, state, county, and city prisons and jails.

9. We want all black people when brought to trial to be tried in court by a jury of their peer group or people from their black communities, as defined by the Constitution of the United States.

10. We want land, bread, housing, education, clothing, justice, and peace. And as our major political objective, a

---

[30] Recently changed from *white man* to *capitalist*.

United Nations-supervised plebiscite to be held throughout the black colony in which only black colonial subjects will be allowed to participate, for the purpose of determining the will of black people as to their national destiny.

Black Panthers

"I order you to be black to your very veins. Pump black blood through them. Let Africa circulate in them. Let Negroes negrify themselves."

Jean Genet, from *The Blacks*

We cannot stand still: Time is dying
We are dying: Time is farewell!

Delmore Schwartz, from *In Dreams
Begin Responsibilities*

FREE HEALTH CARE
FOR ALL!

The Young Lords party has always said that the time will come when the people take over all the institutions and machinery that control and exploit our lives. On 17 June the Young Lords party put this idea into practice. On this day, we liberated an X-ray truck from the politicians that had been using the truck only for propaganda purposes that serve their own interests and profiteering businessmen that only think about making money.

The truck was seized only after the members of the YLP had gone to the Tuberculosis Society several times asking them for the use of the truck. Each time, the request was refused. By refusing us, they made it clear that they aren't concerned with the health of our people. These trucks have been seen in our community only on a very limited part-time basis. We realized that the reason our people didn't use it was because the people running the show prior to the Lords were outsiders, who couldn't relate to our people, our language, and our customs. They never made any real attempt to get the people to use the X-ray facilities.

In the three days that we have had the truck, we have already tested 770 people. According to the technicians, the usual amount of people taken care of in the same amount of time is about 300. So, as far as the Young Lords party is concerned this truck rightfully belongs to the people!

The last point of our Thirteen-Point Program and Platform states that we want a socialist society. Under a socialist society, medical services are extended outside of the hospital by setting up clinics in all communities and by visiting people's homes. This type of medical service is called preventive medicine. Although doctors admit it is needed, preventive medicine will never be done in amerikkka as it is today: because in the capitalist society in which we live, capitalists run health services in order to make more money, not to improve health care. The sicker we are, the more money the capitalist makes. The Young Lords party believes that health care should be a right for all people, not a privilege. That is why we put the X-ray facilities in the hands of the people.

The Ramon Emeterio Betances Free X-ray truck now belongs to the people. It will be on the streets seven days a week, ten hours a day. The truck is here to service the needs of our people.

ALL POWER TO THE PEOPLE!

FREE HEALTH CARE FOR ALL!
LIBERATE PUERTO RICO NOW!

Carl Pastor, Ministry of Health
Young Lords Party

Palante, Latin Revolutionary News
Service, 3 July 1970

THIRTEEN-POINT PROGRAM AND PLATFORM OF THE YOUNG LORDS PARTY

1. We want self-determination for Puerto Ricans—liberation on the island and inside the united states.

For five hundred years, first spain and then the united states have colonized our country. Billions of dollars in profits leave our country for the united states every year. In every way we are slaves of the gringo. We want liberation and the Power in the hands of the People, not Puerto Rican exploiters.

QUE VIVA PUERTO RICO LIBRE!

2. We want self-determination for all Latinos.

Our Latin Brothers and Sisters, inside and outside the united states, are oppressed by amerikkkan business. The *Chicano* people built the Southwest, and we support their right to control their lives and their land. The people of Santo Domingo continue to fight against gringo domination and its puppet generals. The armed liberation struggles in Latin America are part of the war of Latinos against imperialism.

QUE VIVA LA RAZA!

3. We want liberation of all Third World people.

Just as Latins first slaved under spain and the yanquis, black people, Indians, and Asians slaved to build the wealth of this country. For four hundred years they have fought for freedom and dignity against racist Babylon (decadent empire). Third World people have led the fight for freedom. All the colored and oppressed people of the world are one nation under oppression.

NO PUERTO RICAN IS FREE UNTIL ALL PEOPLE ARE FREE!

4. We are revolutionary nationalists and oppose racism.

The Latin, black, Indian, and Asian people inside the u.s. are colonies fighting for liberation. We know that washington, wall street, and city hall will try to make our nationalism into racism; but Puerto Ricans are of all colors, and we resist racism. Millions of poor white people are rising up to demand freedom and we support them. These are the ones in the u.s. that are stepped on by the rulers and the government. We each organize our people, but our fights are the same against oppression and we will defeat it together.

POWER TO ALL OPPRESSED PEOPLE!

5. We want community control of our institutions and land.

We want control of our communities by our people and programs to guarantee that all institutions serve the needs of our people. People's control of police, health services, churches, schools, housing, transportation, and welfare are needed. We want an end to attacks on our land by urban removal, highway destruction, universities, and corporations.

LAND BELONGS TO ALL THE PEOPLE!

6. We want a true education of our Creole culture and Spanish language.

We must learn our history of fighting against cultural, as well as economic genocide by the yanqui. Revolutionary culture, culture of our people, is the only true teaching.

7. We oppose capitalists and alliances with traitors.

Puerto Rican rulers, or puppets of the oppressors, do not help our people. They are paid by the system to lead our people down blind alleys, just like thousands of poverty pimps who keep our communities peaceful for business, or the street workers who keep gangs divided and blowing each other away. We want a society where the people socialistically control their labor.

VENCEREMOS!

8. We oppose the amerikkkan military.

We demand immediate withdrawal of u.s. military forces and bases from Puerto Rico, Vietnam, and all oppressed communities outside the u.s. No Puerto Rican should serve in the u.s. army against his Brothers and Sisters, for the only true army of oppressed people is the people's army to fight all rulers.

U.S. OUT OF VIETNAM, FREE PUERTO RICO!

9. We want freedom for all political prisoners.

We want all Puerto Ricans freed because they have been tried by the racist courts of the colonizers, and not by their own people and peers. We want all freedom fighters released from jail.

FREE ALL POLITICAL PRISONERS!

10. We want equality for women. *Machismo* must be revolutionary . . . not oppressive.

Under capitalism, our women have been oppressed by both the society and our own men. The doctrine of *machismo* has been used by our men to take out their frustrations against their wives, sisters, mothers, and children. Our men must support their women in their fight for economic and social equality, and must recognize that our women are equals in every way within the revolutionary ranks.

FORWARD, SISTERS, IN THE STRUGGLE!

11. We fight anti-Communism with international unity.

Anyone who resists injustice is called a communist by "the man" and condemned. Our people are brainwashed by television, radio, newspapers, schools, and books to oppose people in other countries fighting for their freedom. No longer will our people believe attacks and slanders, because they have learned who the real enemy is and who their real friends are. We will defend our Brothers and Sisters around the world who fight for justice against the rich rulers of this country. VIVA CHE!

12. We believe armed self-defense and armed struggle are the only means to liberation.

We are opposed to violence—the violence of hungry children, illiterate adults, diseased old people, and the violence of poverty and profit. We have asked, petitioned, gone to courts, demonstrated peacefully, and voted for politicians full of empty promises. But we still ain't free. The time has come to defend the lives of our people against repression and for revolutionary war against the businessman, politician, and police. When a government oppresses our people, we have the right to abolish it and create a new one.

BORICUA IS AWAKE! ALL PIGS BEWARE!

13. We want a socialist society.

We want liberation, clothing, free food, education, health care, transportation, utilities, and employment for all. We want a society where the needs of our people come first, and where we give solidarity and aid to the peoples of the world, not oppression and racism.

HASTA LA VICTORIA SIEMPRE!

Young Lords party

CHALE
CON LA DRAFT!

Chale con la draft is becoming a rallying cry for *Chicanos* that are being drafted. *Chicanos* throughout the United States are realizing that they are being used and killed in unholy wars created by the system they are trying to free themselves from. In the past *Chicanos* have willingly died for their country as is evidenced by the fact that *Chicanos* won more medals for bravery during World War II than any other group. They were rewarded for their heroic deeds by being treated as "veterans of second-class citizenship" after their discharge. They were unable to secure jobs to feed their hungry families; discrimination was felt everywhere.

Chicanos have for a long time been helping to keep America free by dying for her in wars, but America in return keeps *Chicanos* enslaved in poverty and misery. *Todo para mi y nada para usted!* Up to now, this has worked but *La Raza Nueva* knows that many injustices must be rectified before we serve in any white man's war.

Rosalio Munoz, former student body president at UCLA, recently refused induction. On 16 September, Mexico's Independence Day, Uncle Samuel attempted to "liberate" Rosalio by drafting him for Vietnam duty. Rosalio responded with a liberation demonstration of his own supported by at least one hundred other *Chicanos*. Their cry was *Chale con la draft!*

El Barrio Communications Project,
from *La Raza*, December 1969

UNTIL THAT TIME . . .

I accuse the legislature of the United States of gerrymandering the Mexican people out of their proper representation in the political system.

I have my induction papers, but I will not respect them until the government and the people of the United States begin to use the *machismo* of the Mexican male and the passion and suffering of the Mexican female to the benefit of themselves and of their own heritage, deferring all *Chicano* youth who serve our people, and providing the money and support that would make such work meaningful in social, political, and economic terms.

I will not respect the papers until the United States government and people can provide the funds and the willingness to improve the educational system so that all Mexican youth, the intelligent, the mediocre, and the *tapados*, just like the white youth, the intelligent, the mediocre, and the *tapados*, have the opportunity to go to college and get deferments.

I will not respect the papers until the welfare and other community agencies of the United States foster and allow for self-respect in the Mexican-American community so that our youth can stay home and be men among our own families and friends.

I will not respect the papers until the systematic harassment of the law enforcement agencies has ended, and these agencies begin truly to protect and serve the Mexican-American community as well.

I will not respect the papers until the armed forces, the largest domestic consumer of California table grapes, recognizes the United Farm Workers' Organizing Committee. Until that time, I cannot recognize the armed forces, or any of its political uses of the American people. Until they begin to boycott the sellers and growers of California table grapes, I must boycott them.

CHALE CON LA DRAFT!

Rosalio U. Munoz, from
La Raza, 16 September 1969

El Barrio Communications Project, from *La Raza*

RECLAIMING
THE LAND

When fourteen Indian college students invaded Alcatraz on a cold, foggy morning in the first part of November—claiming ownership "by right of discovery," and citing an 1868 treaty allowing the Sioux possession of unused federal lands—they seemed in a lighthearted mood. After establishing their beachhead, they told the press that they had come there because Alcatraz already had all the necessary features of a reservation: dangerously uninhabitable buildings; no fresh water; inadequate sanitation; and the certainty of total unemployment. They said they were planning to make the five full-time caretakers wards of a Bureau of Caucasian Affairs, and offered to take this troublesome real estate off the white man's hands for $24, payment to be made in glass beads. The newspapers played it up big, calling the Indians a raiding party. When, after a nineteen-hour stay, the Indians were persuaded to leave the island, everyone agreed that it had been a good publicity stunt.

If the Indians had ever been joking about Alcatraz, however, it was with the bitter irony that fills colonial subjects' discourse with the mother country. When they returned to the mainland, they didn't fall back into the cigar-store stoicism that is supposed to be the red man's prime virtue. In fact, their first invasion ignited a series of meetings and strategy sessions; two weeks later they returned to the rock, this time with a force of nearly one hundred persons, a supply network, and the clear intention of staying. What had begun as a way of drawing attention to the position of the contemporary Indian, developed into a plan for doing something about it. And when the government, acting through the General Services Administration, gave them a deadline for leaving, the Indians replied with demands of their own: Alcatraz was theirs, they said, and it would take U.S. marshals to remove them and their families; they planned to turn the island into a major cultural center and research facility; they would negotiate only the mechanics of deeding over the land, and that only with Interior Secretary Walter Hickel during a face-to-face meeting. The secretary never showed up, but the government's deadlines were withdrawn.

Peter Collier, from "Better Red Than Dead," *Ramparts,* February 1970

CHRISTMAS DAY ON ALCATRAZ

I spent Christmas Day on Alcatraz with the native Americans because it seemed to me the most logical place to be. A friend of mine has a small motorboat, and we crossed the bay that windy morning with a cargo of propane gas. Butane and propane gas for cooking are among the great needs of the Indians there. Once the boat was moored on the wind-swept dock of Indian land, we began the steep climb up the cold north side of the island toward the sun. Jeeps and trucks stood abandoned along the way, for the Indians need mechanics, and gas, and motor oil, and batteries, to get the mechanical hearts of these stubborn vehicles to beating once again. And there was a little pile of abandoned clothing too, clothing that charitable members of the white middle class had sent over to the Indians on their bleak rock: blue-satin, spike-heeled slippers lay there, and tinsel dancing shoes, both pairs quite worn from somebody else's dancing, and a not new apron embroidered with holly sprigs and the legend: Now is the season to be jolly.

The road winds up between overhanging rock and crumbling balustrades; green moss and wild, thick vines on one side, and on the other, barges and boats below straining at their moorings. Beyond them, freighters were passing in the rough waters of the bay. We were not kings bearing gifts, nor had we followed any star. We were simply two white Americans stumbling up the narrow stairways that weave in and out of the old walls, carrying cooking gas to an almost annihilated people, our only virtue that it was not, for a change, either tear gas or napalm that we were using as currency. In this legal taking over of Alcatraz, in this stunning act of the imagination and the will, not the least of the triumphs is that the needs of the Indians are, as on the reservation, material ones. The essentials of the spirit, isolated from the mainstream of the country's life, have heroically survived.

At the top is the prison itself, and having passed the ruined buildings that once housed the guards and their families, and the storerooms and offices, you come to this monument that has stood for a long time in monstrous celebration of man's implacable fury against man. No place in these United States could be more appropriate as symbol of the Indian's imprisonment on his own soil. I walked with a young North Dakota Indian through its long hallways, mounted the spiral iron stairs, knowing this was neither federal, nor even American, but a place constructed by men of every nation, every creed, every time, for the purpose of depriving humanity itself of whatever hope there might be left. Even though the cell doors hang open now, the memory of desperation speaks hollowly from every stone. The Indians have spread newspapers on the cement floors of these cells, and they sleep there. In the isolation row of the third tier, there are no bars, but blank doors, four inches thick, that served to close each prisoner off from life and light. In one of these cells, an endless row of small even lines moves from the door around the walls, scraped by the fingernail of a man who had perhaps endured in solitude there for twenty years. "Each mark is maybe for each month or year he spent in here," I said, and the young Indian who stood beside me, touching this record with his fingertips, cried out: "Not each month or year! Each century, each century!"

In the hall far below, the Christmas tree in Indian land was a limb of driftwood, its forked branches ornamented with the tops of tin cans hung on threads. They moved in the cold air, taking the light, the names of tribes painted in color on them, and on some the single word *genocide*. In the office, where uniformed men had once sat, were stacked cartons of toys donated by the dozen by toy manufacturers. There is no heat in the prison, but the thought of the generosity of man for a moment warmed the blood. It was cold waiting in line for Santa to come, and when you held the children who got tired, they put their arms tight around your neck and looked closely, gravely, into your eyes, as if searching an unknown territory, uncertain what they might find. I remember Bill Brandon saying that the Indian child approaches the outside world prepared for a joyous embrace, and gradually the outside world makes him understand that he is out of kilter with the people he had expected so to love.

That Christmas Day, the white Santa did not arrive from the mainland; and what were the toys so lavishly donated but playthings that the outside world was not buying in such great quantities as before. There were machine guns, bazookas, and tanks with revolving turrets. "A couple of real tanks would be more useful," one young Indian father said with uncharacteristic bitterness.

Since the last week of December (provided the generators are functioning) Radio Free Alcatraz has been broadcasting at seven-fifteen every evening on the Pacifica network. The broadcasts are not appeals for assistance or for donations, but are interviews with the Indians who have come to this focal point from every state. The twenty-three-year-old Indian organizer of the program (who served four years in the navy) is John Truedell, and he speaks of the Indian civilization of wisdom that was submerged by the white man's civilization of knowledge. "It does not seem as if knowledge has done the best thing for humanity," he says. "In the time of wisdom, I respected my brother's dream and he respected mine."

The question of the ways and means of making a living on the reservation comes into the interviews. One girl described a government enterprise that had recently opened on her reservation, the manufacturing of army guns. Indian workers are paid $1.60 an hour for this work, but only one member of a family is permitted to apply. Another spoke of the Indian rodeos, where cash prizes are to be won in the competitions; but this is a seasonal source of revenue, as is the leasing out of grazing land. Another had turned down a scholarship at Brigham Young University because no courses in American Indian history or culture are available there. "We can learn more about our past and about our future right here on Alcatraz," they say. John Truedell has not at any time referred to the Mylai incident, and it was perhaps not his intention to draw a parallel when he said that the killing of Indian women and children was the customary practice of the territorial white man. "This was the best way to strike at the roots, at the reproduction, of a people they wanted to efface," he said.

If our government grants the Indians this piece of their own territory, it must be the beginning of restitution, not the end. To concede them nothing but another prison would be a tragic irony. More than once on Christmas Day, when I spoke to them of the grimness of the conditions on the Rock,

Indian women smiled and said: "It's no worse than on the reservation where we lived." And others said: "We are learning how to work together, tribe with tribe. It hasn't happened before like this. This is where our new nation will begin."

Kay Boyle, from "A Day in Alcatraz
with the Indians," *New Republic*, 17 January 1970

PART SEVEN

The Breaking Point

The nation is rapidly moving toward two increasingly separate Americas.

Report
of the National Advisory Commission
on Civil Disorders

AMERICA IS
A CIGARETTE MACHINE

You see, America ain't nothing but a cigarette machine now: you can't communicate with her. You know if you're running through the airport and put 40¢ in the cigarette machine, pull it, and you don't get cigarettes, that's a funny feeling when you can't talk to that machine. You go up to the ticket counter and you say, "Look, I just put my money in the cigarette machine," and the girl says, "Look, I work for TWA, I just write tickets, I have nothing to do with that machine." You say, "Well, look miss, somebody tell me." She says, "Well, look, go back and look at the little mirror there, you see yourself and there's a little message to tell you what to do if you blow your dough." And you go back and there it is. "Welcome to Hartford, Connecticut. In case of problems with this machine, call Giddings Jones, Kansas City, Missouri." Now you hear the last call for your flight and you stand there looking at the cigarette machine that you can't relate with and that's got your 40¢ and your flight's leaving, so you do the normal thing—you kick that machine—pow. You didn't get no money, but you see that old dent in it and you feel pretty good. You go on down there and get your plane feeling, well, you feel mellow. Let me tell you something, when you kick that machine, if that machine had kicked you back, you would have canceled your flight and taken that damn machine outside and torn it up in little pieces. Now, let's see if this is funny. America is a cigarette machine to us. We didn't put 40¢ in it to get something that was going to make us sick, we put four hundred years of our lives in that machine, baby, to get something that was going to make us well, and we din't get nothing, man, and we went to every ticket counter and they kept sending us to Kansas City, so in the form of Detroit, Watts, and Chicago we kicked that machine and in the form of the national guard and the police that machine kicked us back, and we're going to do the same thing you would. We say, cancel the flight, we're going to break this machine up in little, bitty pieces, that's what we say.

Dick Gregory, from "Let's First Make It
Right," *Yale Alumni Magazine,* February 1968

SUPERMARKET SWEEP

Most of the police in the large city ghettos are white, and they are mostly regarded as occupying troops by the black residents, and in turn their attitudes are those of colonial legionnaires overseeing the natives. This racial aspect of the urban wars is certainly significant, and yet there is also a strong purely "poverty" strain in it all that lures the poor whites in these areas to join their black neighbors in what is really "integrated looting." A Negro woman in Detroit who lived two doors from a warehouse that was looted and burned told a reporter there were whites as well as blacks in on the action, and so it was really not a race riot. "It's an all of 'em riot," she explained.

A white woman who lived across the street and watched the pillage of the warehouse confirmed that view to the press, and added that the integrated rioters got along just fine: "They were laughing, talking, having a good time. It seemed like everyone was enjoying themselves." So the riots, in Detroit at least, did what all the radical organizations had failed to do—brought the poor of both races together in a common cause, made them see that the enemy was not race but class and they should be battling together for what they needed, instead of against each other.

These people *do* share a deep bond beyond difference of color, for they are common victims of what must be one of the most frustrating positions in history; being have-nots in a society that seems to have everything, and unlike former lord-and-serf societies in which the order was taken to be in the nature of things, in this society they are taunted by not having all the best, the latest sleek car and fine mink lounging pajamas and color TVs and washing machines and all of the incredible effluvia of the cornucopia filled by the richest country in the history of the world. You see how "the other half lives"; in fact, you are taken into the very living rooms of the rich and powerful by the magic of television, and the ads you see say that the wonderful products offered, the luxury vacations in Caribbean islands, the mighty new automobiles, the sleek, jeweled women are for *you*, Mr. Viewer, not just the lords, but all of you out there in videoland.

Consider how it must feel not to have any of it; to see it and hear about it every day and not be able to touch it, and how fine an emotional thing it must be to smash the glass that separates it from your rightful possession as a citizen of this most affluent land, and to push and drag, as the poor of both races did in Detroit, the gleaming appliances up over the curbs and through peoples' yards and into your own home where it surely belongs. In discussing the passion of these things with the vice-president of the United States, I asked if he didn't think this teasing sort of lure on television added to some of the force behind the lootings, and he said, "Oh, my yes, why, did you know that they found that the things the people took from the stores were the ones that were most advertised? They took the TVs or the stoves or whatever that had been best promoted in TV and papers and magazine ads. Why, the way the people selected those things they looted was the greatest triumph of advertising the world has ever seen!"

As the bounty groans and gleams all around, it is only natural that people want to take it, and in fact that natural instinct is shown every weekday on television. There is a program called "Supermarket Sweep," in which three teams, each composed of a nice young husband and wife, are given a grocery cart and set loose for a certain limited time in a supermarket, and the team that stuffs the greatest amount of goodies, worth the most money, and returns first to the check-out counter is the winner. The studio audience squeals and cheers as the great steaks and roast and frozen delicacies and gourmet foods are stuffed into the carts as they madly careen through the aisles in a frenzy of acquisition. It is a fantasy acted out, a form of legalized looting as entertainment. Who has not entered a great supermarket and not imagined doing just that, being alone with all the carts and wheeling out everything you wanted? No wonder the program has great appeal.

There is of course one flaw for identification purposes of the whole viewing audience. In the dozen or so times I watched the show (always with fascination), there were never any Negro couples. In the subconscious of the general white public, it might seem too much like real looting if the goods were grabbed by the blacks. The NAACP might even object to having Negroes participate in such a televised pillage on the grounds that it might be bad for their image.

And think how it would look if a Negro couple won.

Dan Wakefield, from *Supernation
at Peace and War*

BILLY FURR

I met Billy Furr at the corner of Avon and Livingston when he barged into my conversation with a Black Muslim who called himself Haking X. Haking was predicting that the riot would go on "until every white man's building in Newark is burned." But Billy disagreed.

"We ain't riotin' agains' all you whites. We're riotin' agains' police brutality, like that cab driver they beat up the other night," Billy declared. "That stuff goes on all the time. When the police treat us like people 'stead of treatin' us like animals, then the riots will stop."

With that he turned away from me and went with his friends in search of cold beer, which he knew he could not buy legally because of the curfew.

Billy, who was twenty-four, had been stranded in Newark. He came to the city to pick up a $50 unemployment check and look for a job to replace the one he lost at a bakery when it went out of business. When the buses back to Montclair, where he lived with his mother and grandparents, were stopped by the riot, Billy stayed on in Newark with friends.

Photographer Bud Lee and I came on Billy again later—a block farther down Avon at Mack Liquors. He and his friends were looting the store, which already had been broken into the day before. They loaded all the beer they could carry into car trunks and handed it out to passersby. When he noticed me, Billy thrust a can in my hand.

"Have a beer on me," he said. "But if the cops show up get rid of it and run like hell."

I opened the beer and went off to view ratholes and roaches in a cruddy $85-a-month apartment, which the tenant, William Jackson, had invited me to inspect. The apartment was only half a block away, and as we stepped back out the door tires screeched and a city police car skidded to a halt directly in front of Mack Liquors. There had been no warning—it had raced in with its siren silent. This was the first sign of police authority on the block in more than an hour, except for a young Newark police trainee who had sipped beer and watched the looting with me.

In an instant the shotguns that bristled from the cruiser's windows shattered the relative calm. The sudden explosions, rather than clearing the streets, sent mothers screaming out to pull children to safety. Apartment windows that had been empty were now full of dark faces, each of them in danger of being shot.

For the looters caught in the store there was no place to run. They simply fell to the floor or froze in their tracks, hands above their heads. But Billy was standing outside with part of a six-pack in his left hand. He'd been arrested before. This time he ran.

He raced past me down Avon. I was barely thirty feet away from a yellow-helmeted officer with a shotgun pointed toward my head.

"Get down," he screamed. I fell hard to the sidewalk just as a blast from the weapon exploded over me and the officer shouted an order to halt. But apparently Billy kept running behind me. From the ground I looked up into the sweating face of the policeman as he squinted down the long barrel. I prayed he wouldn't shoot. He pulled the trigger.

Tiny pieces of the spent shell fluttered down on me as blue uniform trousers of the Newark Police Department flashed past toward Billy lying on the ground. Already people were screaming obscenities from the windows and bottles arched from a rooftop. More gunfire cleared the windows for a moment, but they were quickly filled again.

"Call an ambulance," a policeman yelled back to the car. Up the street the officer who had shot Billy stood over him, the shotgun resting in the crook of his arm. Billy's blood poured onto the dirty sidewalk. Then a girl was beside him sobbing and ignoring the order to "get the hell out of here."

"I'm his girl friend. Help him. Please do something. God, don't let him die," she pleaded.

Back at the corner of Livingston there was more shooting as a line of police reinforcements arrived with an ambulance. I ran toward the crowd being held back at gunpoint on the corner. In the center, blood streaming from his neck, lay little Joe Bass, Jr., a twelve-year-old who had been shining shoes at home with his brother an hour earlier when playmates asked him to come out.

Two pellets from the same shotgun blast that killed Billy had struck Joey in the neck and thigh. Around his form surged about fifty sobbing men and women, trying to break through the small ring of police. Nearby two other youngsters cried quietly on the curb. The people who wanted to help were clubbed away with rifle and shotgun butts. Their frantic efforts kept the police too busy to help the boy, who we all thought was dying. One Negro appeared to try to snatch the pistol from an officer's holster. He was knocked to the pavement.

I watched as Joey was put in the ambulance and rushed off to the hospital. (His wounds, I learned later, were serious but he is recovering.) I walked back toward Billy's lifeless body. The girl was still kneeling beside it. She would not believe he was dead and ambulance attendants had to pull her away before they could cover Billy Furr.

Dale Wittner, from "Caught in the
Act," Life, 28 July 1967

ROCKS ARE ONLY
A BEGINNING

The riot is certainly an awkward, even primitive, form of history-making. But if people are barred from using the sophisticated instruments of the established order for their ends, they will find another way. Rocks and bottles are only a beginning, but they get more attention than all the reports in Washington. To the people involved, the riot is far less lawless and far more representative than the system of arbitrary rules and prescribed channels that they confront every day. The riot is not a beautiful and romantic experience, but neither is the day-to-day slum life from which the riot springs. Riots will not go away if ignored, and will not be cordoned off. They will only disappear into a more decisive and effective form of history-making.

Men are now appearing in the ghettos who might turn the energy of the riot into a more organized and continuous revolutionary direction. Middle-class Negro intellectuals and Negroes of the ghetto are joining forces. They have found channels closed, the rules of the game stacked, and American democracy a system that excludes them. They understand that the institutions of the white community are unreliable in the absence of black community power. They recognize that national civil-rights leaders will not secure the kind of change that is needed. They assume that disobedience, disorder, and even violence must be risked as the only alternative to continuing slavery.

The role of organized violence is now being carefully considered. During a riot, for instance, a conscious guerrilla can participate in pulling police away from the path of people engaged in attacking stores. He can create disorder in new areas the police think are secure. He can carry the torch, if not all the people, to white neighborhoods and downtown business districts. If necessary, he can successfully shoot to kill.

It is equally important to understand that the guerrilla can employ violence during times of apparent peace. He can attack, in the suburbs or slums, with paint or bullets, symbols of racial oppression. He can get away with it. If he can force the oppressive power to be passive and defensive at the point where it is administered—by the caseworker, landlord, store owner, or policeman—he can build people's confidence in their ability to demand change. Such attacks, which need not be on human life to be effective, might disrupt the administration of the ghetto to a crisis point where a new system would have to be considered.

These tactics of disorder will be defined by the authorities as criminal anarchy. But it may be that disruption will create possibilities of meaningful change. This depends on whether the leaders of ghetto struggles can be more successful in building strong organization than they have been so far. Violence can contribute to shattering the status quo, but only politics and organization can transform it.

The ghetto still needs the power to decide its destiny on such matters as urban renewal and housing, social services, policing, and taxation. Tenants will need concrete rights against landlords in public and private housing, or a new system of tenant-controlled living conditions. Welfare clients still need the power to receive a livable income without administrative abuse, or be able to replace the welfare system with one that meets their needs. Consumers still need to control the quality of merchandise and service in the stores where they shop.

Citizens still need effective control over the behavior of those who police their community. Political structures belonging to the community are needed to bargain for, and maintain control over, funds from government or private sources. In order to build a more decent community while resisting racist power, more than violence is required. People need self-government. We are at a point where democracy—the idea and practice of people controlling their lives—is a revolutionary issue in the United States.

Tom Hayden, from "The Occupation
of Newark," *Rebellion in Newark*

Yet law-abiding scholars write;
Law is neither wrong nor right,
Law is the clothes men wear
Anytime, anywhere,
Law is Good-morning and Good-night.

W. H. Auden, from *Law, Say the Gardeners,*
Is the Sun

CHICAGO INCIDENT

It was 4:44 A.M. on the morning of 4 December. The block on Chicago's West Side was cordoned off. Police stood guard on rooftops. State's attorney's police were stationed at the front and rear of the first floor apartment, armed with a submachine gun and shotguns.

There was a knock on the front door, and then the sound of more than two hundred shots echoed through the early morning hour. When it was over, Fred Hampton, chairman of the Illinois Black Panther party, was dead in bed. Mark Clark, a Panther member from Peoria, Illinois, was dead behind the front door. Four others were critically wounded, and three were arrested unharmed. One policeman was slightly wounded.

State's Attorney Edward V. Hanrahan held a press conference later that day, displaying what he said was the arms cache recovered from the apartment (each bullet carefully placed on its end) and pronounced to the television cameras: "We wholeheartedly commend the police officers for their bravery, their remarkable restraint, and their discipline in the face of this Black Panther attack—as should every decent citizen in our community." He stressed the word *decent*.

Under normal circumstances, that would have been the end of it. Hanrahan, the key figure in Mayor Daley's 1968 election strategy, the man named to run the city's "war on gangs" last June, would ordinarily have enhanced his reputation as a tough crime fighter and as the most popular Democratic vote-getter.

But these are not normal times. The story did not end with that press conference, but grew into an international scandal. The glare of publicity that focused on every aspect of that eight-minute raid illuminated the workings of Chicago's law enforcement machinery and we glimpsed momentarily, as by a flash of lightning, the face of repression.

The story would not die, in part because of the stark imagery of the early morning raid by heavily armed police. "For those of us alive in the late thirties," said Professor Hans Mattick of the University of Chicago, "this brought back one of those nightmare images—the knock on the door at night, the Jews intimidated and dragged away."

It would not die because the Black Panther party opened up the apartment at 2337 W. Monroe Street for the world to see, and the evidence was inescapable: police had massed a heavy concentration of machine-gun and shotgun fire at one living room wall and into two bedrooms. There was little if any sign of return fire.

Christopher Chandler, from "Black Panther Killings
in Chicago," New Republic, 10 January 1970

NEWS ITEM,
7 DECEMBER 1969

The police described the encounter as a ferocious gun battle that ensued after a woman opened up on the officers with a shotgun. The Panthers said the police burst into the apartment and started shooting and no one else got a chance to.

"There must have been six or seven of them firing," Police Sergeant Daniel Groth told a news conference after the raid. "The firing must have gone on ten or twelve minutes. If two hundred shots were exchanged, that was nothing." One policeman was grazed on the left leg by a shotgun pellet; another was cut by a piece of glass.

An inspection of the five-room first floor apartment did not seem to square with the police accounts of a torrid gun battle. Most of the walls were not scarred with the bullet and shotgun marks one would expect of a shoot-out. There were no bullet marks around the two doors through which the police said they entered. There were no bullet marks in the kitchen and dining room. There were a lot of bullet marks where the Panthers were shot.

John Kifner, *New York Times*

NEWS ITEM,
7 JANUARY 1970

. . . Bobby Rush, the acting chairman of the Illinois Panthers, charged that Fred Hampton [deceased chairman of the Illinois Black Panther party] had been drugged before the raid.

The Panther leader said that an independent autopsy by Dr. Victor Levine, a former coroner's pathologist, had found a heavy dosage of Seconal, a sleep-inducing drug, in the body.

"This was such a heavy dose that Fred could not have gotten out of bed or engaged in a shoot-out," he said. "A pig agent must have given it to him because Fred never used any drugs and J. Edgar Hoover has said he has infiltrators in the Black Panther party."

John Kifner, *New York Times*

NEWS ITEM, 9 JANUARY 1970

Just before the recess, the jurors were shown the nineteen weapons and packets of ammunition the police said they seized in the raid. Among them were a carbine and a half-dozen handguns and shotguns. One of the shotguns was sawed off, and another, the police said, had been stolen from the police department.

During the afternoon session, Sergeant Daniel R. Groth, who commanded the raiding party of policemen attached to the state's attorney's office, was asked if fingerprints had been taken from the weapons.

"I don't believe anybody checked for them," he said.

John Kifner, *New York Times*

NEWS ITEM,
9 MAY 1970

All criminal charges were dropped today against the seven Black Panthers who survived a shooting incident with Chicago policemen last December.

State's Attorney Edward V. Hanrahan said there was not sufficient proof that any of the defendants had fired a weapon at the police.

Seth King, *New York Times*

PAPA RAGE: A VISIT
WITH ELDRIDGE CLEAVER

One night, just before I left New York to see Eldridge Cleaver in Algiers, a squad car eased alongside me and stopped. Two policemen jumped out. The older one carried a walkie-talkie and the younger one blocked my path and demanded some identification. I was walking briskly from my East Side apartment, late for the theater. Despite the fact that I, like many other black people, experience this type of harassment constantly, I was impatient. When I asked why I had to identify myself, the younger one warned me that he would run me in if I didn't. "I'd prefer that," I said. He copped out, assuring me that things could be worked out there on the street. Then he informed me I was in a wealthy neighborhood where there had been several robberies lately.

"Do I look like a robber to you?"

"All robbers don't go around wearing little black masks," he said.

"And all robbers don't go around wearing black faces," I countered. As I reached for my wallet to prove once again that I wasn't a criminal, his hand inched toward his gun.

"You two are pretty jumpy," I said, pulling out my card.

I have always tuned out the term *pig*. But when those two fat faces reddened at the sight of that card, I too got the image—very clearly. I turned and walked off.

"Sorry, Mr. Parks." I kept walking. "Just doing our job. Trying to protect you. Merry Christmas." I went on without answering, shocked at my thoughts of rifles with silencers, of rooftops—and pigs.

Several days later I told Cleaver about my experience. He smiled easily and spoke softly. "Things haven't changed much in Babylon since I've been on vacation." To him my incident must have seemed like absolutely nothing. His last encounter with the California police ended with seventeen-year-old Bobby Hutton shot to death, one Black Panther and two policemen injured, and Cleaver being hustled off to jail with a bullet-shattered leg.

Cleaver was now living with his wife Kathleen and their five-month-old son, Maceo, outside of Algiers in one of those yellowish-white concrete houses that line the Mediterranean coast. It was wet, windy, and unusually cold for Algiers. He was slumped in a chair, his legs stretched out, the infant slung across his shoulder. He gently massaged the boy's back. In the soft, rain-filtered light from the sea, he looked like any other father trying to burp his child. But his mind was on a tragic, more violent thing—the killing of his fellow Panthers, Fred Hampton and Mark Clark, by Chicago police. "It was cold-blooded murder," he said in a low voice.

I handed him some clippings from the American press, most of which, I felt, condemned the police action in the killings. Cleaver started to read and I watched for some type of reaction. As his eyes moved over the print his dark face was immobile. Maceo finally burped. Eldridge called Kathleen.

"Come get this Panther." As she took Maceo away, Eldridge frowned. "That little cat will give them hell one of these days." He lit a cigarette, took a healthy swallow of Scotch, and started reading again. I got up and looked about the house.

There were five rooms, counting a tiled kitchen that also faced the sea. Emory Douglas, the Panthers' minister of culture, and his wife, Judy, occupied one room. Connie Matthews, an attractive girl who represented the Panthers in Scandinavia, had the other room. Off a dark hallway was the workshop, littered with typewriters, mimeograph machines, printing materials, Emory's posters and party leaflets in several languages. The large living room–bedroom in which I had left Eldridge was the gathering point.

There was very little laughter in that house. Too many brothers were in coffins or prisons. The cold evenings were spent talking of friends, revolution, and death, thinking and planning to Otis Redding's blues, to Elaine Brown's protest songs, and to the soul-stirrings of Aretha Franklin and James Brown. It was the cluttered, temporary shelter of a black man in exile—where bags stay packed and all precious things are portable.

Cleaver had finished reading the clippings when I returned. "Well, what do you think?" I said.

"Crap. Unadulterated objective crap. So we have to be shot up and murdered in our homes before people become indignant. We have charged the police with ambush and murder over and over again. Now, after twenty-eight murders, people are taking a look. What are we supposed to do, pray for deliverance?" He asked the question in a soft, dispassionate voice, then answered it himself. "Their deaths will have to be avenged. The cops who murdered them must be punished in the same way they committed the crime."

"Right on, Papa Rage," Kathleen snapped. Her blue-green eyes were smoldering beneath a great copper-colored bushy Afro. Her face—pale, strong, and intense—revealed a fearlessness equal to her husband's. "Right on," she repeated.

Maceo began to cry. Eldridge picked him up. "He's angry. He was born angry—like a real Panther."

When Maceo quieted, I mentioned that Arthur Goldberg and Roy Wilkins were forming a committee to do some investigating of their own.

"And what are those dudes going to investigate?"

"The killing of Hampton and Clark."

Eldridge scratched his beard and smiled for the first time. "And they will wind up saying the police were justified in shooting the brothers."

"They might find just the opposite."

"It doesn't make much difference what they find. It's too late for their concern. The brothers are dead. All that is left is the problem. The Panther is the solution."

"You know about the great sympathy that has sprung up among even the black moderates since the Chicago incident?"

"Sympathy won't stop bullets. And we can't defend every black person in Babylon. Right now it's a big job just to keep ourselves alive. It's the brother's job, and right to defend his own home. And there's only one way for him to do that. When cops bust through your door, put a gun in their faces and say, 'Split, mother!' There's alternatives. Call the UN, or the civil liberty boys, or the police station, and tell them you're being shot up. Then wait."

"What do the Panthers have to offer black moderates other than violence, or a fight to death?"

"Nothing. Not even condolences, for they will bring about their own deaths through their own apathy." He got up and moved across the room. He is big, well over six feet, broad-shouldered and powerfully built. He moves with the brutal grace of a fighter. "Violence? Our people are programmed into worse violence by Uncle Sam. Tell me, why should black boys have to go fight Koreans and Vietnamese boys, instead of the Maddoxes, Reagans, and Wallaces at home? A white lunatic can attack a black man on the street. But when the cops come they first club the 'violent nigger.' Violence? We hate it. But is it violent to shoot a cop who breaks into

your home bent on killing you? If so, the Panthers are violent."

I remember that right after the murder of Martin Luther
King, Black Panthers spread through the ghettos cautioning
angry young blacks against violence and rioting. It only gives
the cops a chance to kill more of us, they warned. And I
thought it significant that after a study of violence, the Lem-
berg Center at Brandeis University reported that "of 381 racial
disorders occurring between January and August 1969, only
17 involved Black Panthers, and of those 17 only 8 were
violent confrontations between police and Black Panthers."

But the police have demanded the Panthers' heads, and the
Panthers pridefully tell the police to come and get them. As
I sat there with Cleaver, I thought that to avoid the even
greater tragedy, all of us would have to become more than
idle witnesses. The police must be urged not to provoke the
black revolution into a ferocious blindness; the Panthers must
realize that they have emerged as a vital part of our fight,
but that reason, more than tough rhetoric, is the order of those
thousands, black or white, who would support us. Surely, I
thought, somewhere in our history of hatred and death for one
another, there must be an even greater place for courage and
love.

"What is the future of the young black man in America?"
I said.

"Right now their future is in the hands of the Wallaces,
Agnews, Nixons, Reagans, McClellans, and their cops. The
black youth in Babylon won't have a future unless they have
the guts to fight for it."

So many times during his own life, I thought, Cleaver has
appeared to have had no future. He had found himself while
behind prison walls. There he wrote *Soul on Ice*, a powerful
and remarkably frank insight into himself. He had been in
and out of jail since he was sixteen, and when he left prison,
at thirty-one, he got involved in the black revolution, politics,
and the Black Panther party.

"And from then on," he said, "the parole authorities gave

me more trouble than they did when I was a robber. The cops tried to kill me one night in a planned ambush. They murdered little Bobby Hutton instead. They slammed me into Vacaville with a shot-up leg and revoked my parole without a hearing."

I was in California when Superior Court Judge Raymond J. Sherwin freed him on a writ of habeas corpus, observing that Cleaver had been a model parolee. I told Cleaver that I was surprised at this ruling—because the authorities from Reagan on down had lined up against him.

"That didn't stop them," he went on. "They trumped up some more charges and ordered me back to prison. I knew that if I went back to prison I would be killed. So I split." Now, despite suggestions that, for his own safety, he prolong his "vacation from Babylon," Cleaver told me, "I'm going back home to San Francisco. Two-seven-seven-seven Pine is my address. Nobody is going to keep me away from it."

I asked him if he couldn't do the party more good by writing from Algiers, citing as an example the tremendous sale of his books back in the States. He bristled. "You can't fight pigs with eloquence. I've got to physically commit myself."

If he comes back, and I am sure he will, I believe it is to avoid another kind of death. The death inside him in exile is as bad as the other kind of death I fear awaits him back here. Cleaver is armored with the brutal truth of Panther history, of hard streets, and tough prisons. Yet a basic naïveté makes him vulnerable at times. "Do you think Reagan and his cops really want me back?" he asked me with all seriousness. "Or do you think they would sleep better if I stayed lost?"

I didn't know. "But do you want them to sleep better?" I asked.

"I want them in a constant state of nightmare," he answered. He sat down, lit another cigarette, and crossed his legs. Then, eying me closely, he told me that the Black Panthers would like for me to join their party. "You could serve as a minister of information." I spent an uncomfortable moment thinking that one over. "A lot of young cats would be glad to follow you in."

"I'm honored," I finally said, "but—"

"We need you more than the Establishment does."

"I'm honored," I repeated, "but you must realize that as a journalist I'd lose objectivity." Objectivity, I thought, the word he hated so much. "I have things I want to report to as big an audience as possible."

"I'm more concerned about young strong cats following you into the party." He had me thinking—back to the inflexible Malcolm X. Cleaver was proving to be even more intransigent—the most uncompromising individual I ever met.

I explained that my interests go beyond those of the Black Panthers, to other minorities and factions of the black movement who want change. He eased off, suggesting that we leave it open. I wondered whether he felt my position was a creditable one. Looking back to that moment I find that I am displeased with my answer. I should have said: Both of us are caught up in the truth of the black man's ordeal. Both of us are possessed by that truth, which we define through separate experience. How we choose to act it out is the only difference. You recognize my scars and I acknowledge yours. You are thirty-five. I am fifty-seven. We meet over a deep chasm of time, the events of which forged different weapons for us. If I were twenty years old now, I would probably be a Black Panther. I remember as a kid I always took the first lick before I fought back. But a fist is not a bullet. I too would shoot a cop, or anyone else, who forced his way into my house to kill me. You are risking everything by going back to challenge a system we both dislike. I will continue to fight also, but on my terms. I prefer to change things without violence—providing violence is not thrust upon me. If this is your position too, then your weapons and mine are not as irreconcilable as you might think.

Cleaver went on: "Black people are afraid to join a militant group. They're afraid the cops will shoot them. That's just why we made the cops our political target—to prove to the brother that cops are just fat, gristle and blood."

I asked him what chances the Panthers had against the

overwhelming police power. "If we worried about the odds, we would be defeated from the start," he said.

It was dusk. Kathleen brought in a bowl of lamb stew. Cleaver reached over and spooned a mouthful, talking all the while. "We won't be alone. A lot of whites relate to the same issues that we do. They're just as uptight. The Establishment will have to deal with them as well. Enough tear gas and head-whipping will establish the common enemy."

"Do you welcome whites to the fight?"

"Of course. There has to be some interconnection. We hope through some sort of coalition to bring a change for everyone. I just don't believe that most whites will stand by and see a minority wiped out without trying to put a stop to it."

"And the Communists? There are a lot of reports that they are trying to infiltrate your party."

"Black people don't need Communists to teach them about trouble. The jails in Babylon produce more rebels and revolutionaries than the Communists could dream of producing back there. An incredible number of those rebels are black, and their numbers are growing by the hour. We are out to tear down the system not with fire, not with guns—but with solid political and scientific know-how. If it comes to guerrilla warfare, individuals will die. But individual tragedy can't block liberation for the masses."

"And what will you build in the rubble?"

"Social justice. If the blacks took power tomorrow and treated the whites like the whites have treated us for four hundred years, I'd try to crush them too. We promise to replace racism with racial solidarity. There are no better weapons. We are disciplined revolutionaries who hate violence. That's why we aim to stop it at our front and back doors. Then we won't have to worry about our children dying in blood-drenched beds."

That night I left Cleaver on a wet, wind-swept street. It was strange that his last words were about social justice, the kind that is irrespective of a man's color. I thought about other brilliant young black men like Stokely Carmichael, Malcolm X, and Martin Luther King, one self-exiled, two long since gunned down. I couldn't help but feel that Cleaver's promise, like their dreams, would go unfulfilled. Social justice, it seems, is much more difficult to come by than martyrdom.

Gordon Parks, from *Born Black*

PART EIGHT

The Left-Out Heart:
A Notebook on Prejudice

*Treat men as pawns and ninepins
and you shall suffer as well as they.
If you leave out their heart,
you shall lose your own.*

Ralph Waldo Emerson

Janet, six years of age, was trying hard to integrate her obedience to her mother with her daily social contacts. One day she came running home and asked, "Mother, what is the name of the children I am supposed to hate?"

Gordon W. Allport, from
The Nature of Prejudice

THE LESSON

Mr. Head awakened to discover that the room was full of moonlight. He sat up and stared at the floorboards—the color of silver—and then at the ticking on his pillow, which might have been brocade, and after a second, he saw half of the moon five feet away in his shaving mirror, paused as if it were waiting for his permission to enter. It rolled forward and cast a dignifying light on everything. The straight chair against the wall looked stiff and attentive as if it were awaiting an order and Mr. Head's trousers, hanging to the back of it, had an almost noble air, like the garment some great man had just flung to his servant; but the face on the moon was a grave one. It gazed across the room and out the window where it floated over the horse stall and appeared to contemplate itself with the look of a young man who sees his old age before him.

Mr. Head could have said to it that age was a choice blessing and that only with years does a man enter into that calm understanding of life that makes him a suitable guide for the young. This, at least, had been his own experience.

He sat up and grasped the iron posts at the foot of his bed and raised himself until he could see the face on the alarm clock, which sat on an overturned bucket beside the chair. The hour was two in the morning. The alarm on the clock did not work but he was not dependent on any mechanical means to awaken him. Sixty years had not dulled his responses; his physical reactions, like his moral ones, were guided by his will and strong character, and these could be seen plainly in his features. He had a long tubelike face with a long rounded open jaw and a long depressed nose. His eyes were alert but quiet, and in the miraculous moonlight they had a look of composure and of ancient wisdom as if they belonged to one of the great guides of men. He might have been Vergil summoned in the middle of the night to go to Dante, or better, Raphael, awakened by a blast of God's light to fly to the side of Tobias. The only dark spot in the room was Nelson's pallet, underneath the shadow of the window.

Nelson was hunched over on his side, his knees under his chin and his heels under his bottom. His new suit and hat were in the boxes that they had been sent in and these were on the floor at the foot of the pallet where he could get his hands on them as soon as he woke up. The slop jar, out of the shadow and made snow white in the moonlight, appeared to stand guard over him like a small personal angel. Mr. Head lay back down, feeling entirely confident that he could carry out the moral mission of the coming day. He meant to be up before Nelson and to have the breakfast cooking by the time he awakened. The boy was always irked when Mr. Head was the first up. They would have to leave the house at four to get to the railroad junction by five thirty. The train was to stop for them at five forty-five and they had to be there on time for this train was stopping merely to accommodate them.

This would be the boy's first trip to the city though he claimed it would be his second because he had been born there. Mr. Head had tried to point out to him that when he was born he didn't have the intelligence to determine his whereabouts but this had made no impression on the child at all and he continued to insist that this was to be his second trip. It would be Mr. Head's third trip. Nelson had said, "I will've already been there twict and I ain't but ten."

Mr. Head had contradicted him.

"If you ain't been there in fifteen years, how you know you'll be able to find your way about?" Nelson had asked. "How you know it hasn't changed some?"

"Have you ever," Mr. Head had asked, "seen me lost?"

Nelson certainly had not but he was a child who was never satisfied until he had given an impudent answer and he replied, "It's nowhere around here to get lost at."

"The day is going to come," Mr. Head prophesied, "when you'll find you ain't as smart as you think you are." He had been thinking about this trip for several months but it was for the most part in moral terms that he conceived it. It was to be a lesson that the boy would never forget. He was to find out from it that he had no cause for pride merely because he had been born in a city. He was to find out that the city is not a great place. Mr. Head meant him to see everything there is to see in a city so that he would be content to stay at home for the rest of his life. He fell asleep thinking how the boy would at last find out that he was not as smart as he thought he was.

He was awakened at three thirty by the smell of fatback frying and he leaped off his cot. The pallet was empty and the clothes boxes had been thrown open. He put on his trousers and ran into the other room. The boy had a corn pone on cooking and had fried the meat. He was sitting in the half-dark at the table, drinking cold coffee out of a can. He had on his new suit and his new gray hat pulled low over his eyes. It was too big for him but they had ordered it a size large because they expected his head to grow. He didn't say anything but his entire figure suggested satisfaction at having arisen before Mr. Head.

Mr. Head went to the stove and brought the meat to the table in the skillet. "It's no hurry," he said. "You'll get there soon enough and it's no guarantee you'll like it when you do neither," and he sat down across from the boy whose hat teetered back slowly to reveal a fiercely expressionless face, very much the same shape as the old man's. They were grandfather and grandson but they looked enough alike to be brothers and brothers not too far apart in age, for Mr. Head had a youthful expression by daylight, while the boy's look was ancient, as if he knew everything already and would be pleased to forget it.

Mr. Head had once had a wife and daughter and when the wife died, the daughter ran away and returned after an interval with Nelson. Then one morning, without getting out of bed, she died and left Mr. Head with sole care of the year-old child. He had made the mistake of telling Nelson that he had been born in Atlanta. If he hadn't told him that, Nelson couldn't have insisted that this was going to be his second trip.

"You may not like it a bit," Mr. Head continued. "It'll be full of niggers."

The boy made a face as if he could handle a nigger.

"All right," Mr. Head said. "You ain't ever seen a nigger."

"You wasn't up very early," Nelson said.

"You ain't ever seen a nigger," Mr. Head repeated. "There hasn't been a nigger in this county since we run that one out twelve years ago and that was before you were born." He looked at the boy as if he were daring him to say he had ever seen a Negro.

"How you know I never saw a nigger when I lived there before?" Nelson asked. "I probably saw a lot of niggers."

"If you seen one you didn't know what he was," Mr. Head said, completely exasperated. "A six-month-old child don't know a nigger from anybody else."

"I reckon I'll know a nigger if I see one," the boy said and got up and straightened his slick sharply creased gray hat and went outside to the privy.

They reached the junction some time before the train was due to arrive and stood about two feet from the first set of tracks. Mr. Head carried a paper sack with some biscuits and a can of sardines in it for their lunch. A coarse-looking orange-colored sun coming up behind the east range of mountains was making the sky a dull red behind them, but in front of them it was still gray and they faced a gray transparent moon, hardly stronger than a thumbprint and completely without light. A small tin switch box and a black fuel tank were all there was to mark the place as a junction; the tracks were double and did not converge again until they were hidden behind the bends at either end of the clearing. Trains passing appeared to emerge from a tunnel of trees and, hit for a second by the cold sky, vanish terrified into the woods again. Mr. Head had had to make special arrangements with the ticket agent to have this train stop and he was secretly afraid it would not, in which case, he knew Nelson would say, "I never thought no train was going to stop for you." Under the useless morning moon the tracks looked white and fragile. Both the old man and the child stared ahead as if they were awaiting an apparition.

Then suddenly, before Mr. Head could make up his mind to turn back, there was a deep warning bleat and the train appeared, gliding very slowly, almost silently around the bend of trees about two hundred yards down the track, with one yellow front light shining. Mr. Head was still not certain it would stop and he felt it would make an even bigger idiot of him if it went by slowly. Both he and Nelson, however, were prepared to ignore the train if it passed them.

The engine charged by, filling their noses with the smell of hot metal and then the second coach came to a stop exactly where they were standing. A conductor with the face of an ancient bloated bulldog was on the step as if he expected them, though he did not look as if it mattered one way or the other to him if they got on or not. "To the right," he said.

Their entry took only a fraction of a second and the train was already speeding on as they entered the quiet car. Most of the travelers were still sleeping, some with their heads hanging off the chair arms, some stretched across two seats, and some sprawled out with their feet in the aisle. Mr. Head saw two unoccupied seats and pushed Nelson toward them. "Get in there by the winder," he said in his normal voice, which was very loud at this hour of the morning. "Nobody cares if you sit there because it's nobody in it. Sit right there."

"I heard you," the boy muttered. "It's no use in you yelling," and he sat down and turned his head to the glass. There he saw a pale ghostlike face scowling at him beneath the brim of a pale ghostlike hat. His grandfather, looking quickly too, saw a different ghost, pale but grinning, under a black hat.

Mr. Head sat down and settled himself and took out his ticket and started reading aloud everything that was printed on it. People began to stir. Several woke up and stared at him. "Take off your hat," he said to Nelson and took off his own and put it on his knee. He had a small amount of white hair that had turned tobacco-colored over the years and this lay flat across the back of his head. The front of his head was bald and creased. Nelson took off his hat and put it on his knee and they waited for the conductor to come ask for their tickets.

The man across the aisle from them was spread out over two seats, his feet propped on the window and his head jutting into the aisle. He had on a light blue suit and a yellow shirt unbuttoned at the neck. His eyes had just opened and Mr. Head was ready to introduce himself when the conductor came up from behind and growled, "Tickets."

When the conductor had gone, Mr. Head gave Nelson the return half of his ticket and said, "Now put that in your pocket and don't lose it or you'll have to stay in the city."

"Maybe I will," Nelson said as if this were a reasonable suggestion.

Mr. Head ignored him. "First time this boy has ever been on a train," he explained to the man across the aisle, who was sitting up now on the edge of his seat with both feet on the floor.

Nelson jerked his hat on again and turned angrily to the window.

"He's never seen anything before," Mr. Head continued. "Ignorant as the day he was born, but I mean for him to get his fill once and for all."

The boy leaned forward, across his grandfather and toward the stranger. "I was born in the city," he said. "I was born there. This is my second trip." He said it in a high positive voice but the man across the aisle didn't look as if he understood. There were heavy purple circles under his eyes.

Mr. Head reached across the aisle and tapped him on the arm. "The thing to do with a boy," he said sagely, "is to show him all it is to show. Don't hold nothing back."

"Yeah," the man said. He gazed down at his swollen feet and lifted the left one about ten inches from the floor. After a minute he put it down and lifted the other. All through the car people began to get up and move about and yawn and stretch. Separate voices could be heard here and there and then a general hum. Suddenly Mr. Head's serene expression changed. His mouth almost closed and a light, fierce and cautious both, came into his eyes. He was looking down the length of the car. Without turning, he caught Nelson by the arm and pulled him forward. "Look," he said.

A huge coffee-colored man was coming slowly forward. He had on a light suit and a yellow satin tie with a ruby pin in it. One of his hands rested on his stomach, which rode majestically under his buttoned coat, and in the other he held the head of a black walking stick that he picked up and set down with a deliberate outward motion each time he took a step. He was proceeding very slowly, his large brown eyes gazing over the heads of the passengers. He had a small white moustache and white crinkly hair. Behind him were two young women, both coffee-colored, one in a yellow dress and one in a green. Their progress was kept at the rate of his and they chatted in low throaty voices as they followed him.

Mr. Head's grip was tightening insistently on Nelson's arm. As the procession passed them, the light from a sapphire ring on the brown hand that picked up the cane reflected in Mr. Head's eye, but he did not look up nor did the tremendous man look at him. The group proceeded up the rest of the aisle and out of the car. Mr. Head's grip on Nelson's arm loosened. "What was that?" he asked.

"A man," the boy said and gave him an indignant look as if he were tired of having his intelligence insulted.

"What kind of a man?" Mr. Head persisted, his voice expressionless.

"A fat man," Nelson said. He was beginning to feel that he had better be cautious.

"You don't know what kind?" Mr. Head said in a final tone.

"An old man," the boy said and had a sudden foreboding that he was not going to enjoy the day.

"That was a nigger," Mr. Head said and sat back.

Nelson jumped up on the seat and stood looking backward to the end of the car but the Negro had gone.

"I'd of thought you'd know a nigger since you seen so many when you was in the city on your first visit," Mr. Head continued. "That's his first nigger," he said to the man across the aisle.

The boy slid down into the seat. "You said they were black," he said in an angry voice. "You never said they were tan. How do you expect me to know anything when you don't tell me right?"

"You're just ignorant is all," Mr. Head said and he got up and moved over in the vacant seat by the man across the aisle.

Nelson turned backward again and looked where the Negro had disappeared. He felt that the Negro had deliberately walked down the aisle in order to make a fool of him and he hated him with a fierce raw fresh hate; and also, he understood now why his grandfather disliked them.

Flannery O'Connor, from "The Artificial Nigger,"
in *A Good Man Is Hard to Find and Other Stories*

Two points stand out above all others from anthropological work on race. First, except in remote parts of the earth very few human beings belong to a pure stock; most men are mongrels (racially speaking); hence the concept has little utility. Second, most human characteristics ascribed to race are undoubtedly due to cultural diversity and should, therefore, be regarded as ethnic, not racial.

Gordon W. Allport, from
The Nature of Prejudice

RACIAL
EXERCISE

Let us do some easy exercises in racial purity.

And let me offer myself for dissection purposes.

If I go the right way about it, I come of an old English family, but the right way is unfortunately a crooked one. It is far from easy going in the branches of my genealogical tree. I have to proceed via my father to his mother, thence to her mother, and thence to her father. If I follow this zigzag course I arrive in the satisfactory bosom of a family called Sykes, and have a clear run back through several centuries. The Sykeses go right away ever so far, right back to a certain Richard of Sykes Dyke who flourished somewhere about the year 1400. Whether inside their dyke, which lay in Cumberland, or outside it, which was Yorkshire, this family never did anything earthshaking, still they did keep going in the documentary sense, they made money and married into it, they became mayors of Pontefract or Hull, they employed Miss Anna Seward as a governess, and in the seventeenth century, one of them, a Quaker, was imprisoned on account of his opinions in York Castle, and died there. I come of an old English family, and am proud of it.

Unfortunately in other directions the prospect is less extensive. If I take a wrong turning and miss the Sykeses, darkness descends on my origins almost at once. Mrs. James is a case in point, and a very mortifying one. Mrs. James was a widow who not so very long ago married one of my great-grandfathers. I am directly descended from her, know nothing whatever about her, and should like at all events to discover her maiden name. Vain request. She disappears in the mists of antiquity, like Richard of Sykes Dyke, but much too soon. She might be anyone, she may not even have been Aryan. When her shadow crosses my mind, I do not feel to belong to an old family at all.

After that dissection, let us proceed to do our easy racial exercise.

It is this: Can you give the names of your eight great-grandparents?

The betting is eight to one that you cannot. The royal family could, some aristocrats could, and so could a few yeomen who have lived undisturbed in a quiet corner of England for a couple of hundred years. But most of the people I know (and probably most of the people who read these words) will fail. We can often get six or seven, seldom the whole eight. And the human mind is so dishonest and so snobby, that we instinctively reject the eighth as not mattering, and as playing no part in our biological makeup. As each of us looks back into his or her past, doors open upon darkness. Two doors at first—the father and the mother—through each of these two more, then the eight great-grandparents, the sixteen great-greats, then thirty-two ancestors . . . sixty-four . . . one hundred and twenty-eight . . . until the researcher reels. Even if the stocks producing us interbred, and so reduced the total of our progenitors by using some of them up on us twice, even if they practiced the strict domestic economy of the Ptolemies, the total soon becomes enormous, and the Sykeses in it are nothing beside the Mrs. Jameses. On such a shady past as this—our common past—do we erect the ridiculous doctrine of racial purity.

In the future the situation will be slightly less ridiculous. Registers of marriage and birth will be kept more carefully, bastardy more cunningly detected, so that in a couple of hundred years millions of people will belong to old families. This should be a great comfort to them. It may also be a convenience, if governments continue to impose racial tests. Citizens will be in a position to point to an Aryan ancestry if their government is Aryan, to a Cretinist ancestry if it is Cretin, and so on, and if they cannot point in the direction required, they will be sterilized. This should be a great discomfort to them. Nor will the sterilization help, for the mischief has already been done in our own day, the mess has been made, miscegenation has already taken place. Whether there ever was such an entity as a "pure race" is debatable, but there certainly is not one in Europe today—the internationalisms of the Roman Empire and of the Middle Ages have seen to that. Consequently there never can be a pure race in the future. Europe is mongrel forever, and so is America.

How extraordinary it is that governments that claim to be realistic should try to base themselves on anything so shadowy and romantic as race! A common language, a common religion, a common culture all belong to the present, evidence about them is available, they can be tested. But race belongs to the unknown and unknowable past. It depends upon who went to bed with whom in the year 1400, not to mention Mrs. James, and what historian will ever discover that? Community of race is an illusion. Yet belief in race is a growing psychological force, and we must reckon with it. People like to feel that they are all of a piece, and one of the ways of inducing that feeling is to tell them that they come of pure stock. That explains the ease with which the dictators are putting their pseudoscience across. No doubt they are not cynical about it, and take themselves in by what they say. But they have very cleverly hit on a weak spot in the human equipment—the desire to feel a hundred percent, no matter what the percentage is in.

A German professor was holding forth the other day on the subject of the origins of the German people. His attitude was that the purity of the Nordic stock is not yet proved and should not be spoken of as proved. But it should be spoken of as a fact, because it is one, and the proofs of its existence will be forthcoming as soon as scholars are sufficiently energetic and brave. He spoke of "courage" in research. According to his own lights, he was a disinterested researcher, for he refused to support what he knew to be true by arguments that he held to be false. The truth, being a priori, could afford to wait on its mountaintop until the right path to it was found: the truth of Nordic purity that every German holds by instinct in his blood. In India I had friends who said they were descended from the sun and looked down on those who merely came from the moon, but they were not tense about it and seemed to forget about it between times, nor did they make it a basis for political violence and cruelty; it takes the West to do that.

Behind our problem of the eight great-grandparents stands the civilizing figure of Mendel. I wish that Mendel's name was mentioned in current journalism as often as Freud's or Einstein's. He embodies a salutary principle, and even when we are superficial about him, he helps to impress it in our minds. He suggests that no stock is pure, and that it may at any moment throw up forms that are unexpected, and that it inherits from the past. His best-known experiments were with the seeds of the pea. It is impossible that human beings can be studied as precisely as peas—too many factors are involved. But they too keep throwing up recessive characteristics, and cause us to question the creed of racial purity. Mendel did not want to prove anything. He was not a "courageous" researcher, he was merely a researcher. Yet he has unwittingly put a valuable weapon into the hands of civilized people. We don't know what our ancestors were like or what our descendants will be like. We only know that we are all of us mongrels, dark haired and light haired, who must learn not to bite one another. Thanks to Mendel and to a few simple exercises we can see comparatively clearly into the problem of race, if we choose to look, and can do a little to combat the pompous and pernicious rubbish that is at present being prescribed in the high places of the earth.

E. M. Forster, from *Two Cheers for Democracy*

THE QUIETENING OF CONSCIENCE

Despite the influence of certain thinkers, race prejudice developed into a regular doctrinal system during the eighteenth and nineteenth centuries. There was indeed a relatively brief period when it appeared as though the spread of principles of the French and American revolutions and the success of the antislavery campaign in England might lessen or even abolish such prejudice, but both the reaction that followed the Restoration and the industrial revolution in Europe at the beginning of the last century had direct and damaging repercussions on the racial question. The development of power spinning and weaving opened ever-wider markets to cotton manufacturers, and cotton was king, particularly in the southern part of the United States. The result was an increasing demand for servile labor; slavery, which was breaking down in America and might have vanished of itself, automatically became a sacrosanct institution on which the prosperity of the Cotton Belt depended. It was to defend this so-called special institution that southern thinkers and sociologists developed a complete pseudoscientific mythology designed to justify a state of affairs clean contrary to the democratic beliefs they professed. *For the quietening of consciences men had to be persuaded that the black was not merely an inferior being to the white but little different from the brutes.* (italics mine)

Juan Comas, from *The Race Question in Modern Science*

TOWARD A SOUTHERN MYTHOLOGY

The Negro race is a primitive race. The average Negro is a child in every essential element of character, exhibiting those characteristics that indicate a tendency to lawless impulse and weak inhibition. His childish weaknesses and improvidence and his disposition to live only for the things of today tend to bring him to dependence in sickness and old age, or lead him into excesses and neglect of his body that bring him to an early death.

Negro servants are generally good-natured in manner, often profusely polite, and ready with protestations of good faith. Like all impulsive individuals, they may do many acts of kindness or even of self-denial, and if properly treated under discipline may show faithfulness worthy of the highest praise. While these are all essentially the acts of a child, they are nevertheless significant of his possibilities. Prison guards and probation officers might well keep this in mind.

Charles McCord, from *The American Negro as a Dependent*

THE STORY OF CRISPUS ATTUCKS

It was a Negro citizen who was America's first casualty in her War for Independence. On the cold, snowy evening of 5 March 1770, in the city of Boston, trouble that had been brewing for many weeks between the citizens of Massachusetts and the British soldiers broke into open conflict. Leading an angry crowd armed with sticks and hard-packed snowballs was a giant Negro who worked on a whaling ship. Crispus Attucks was his name, and when the British soldiers opened fire on the people, he was the first to fall. His was the first life claimed in the American Revolution. And when in 1888, a monument was erected on Boston Common, a poem for the occasion by one John Boyle O'Reilly included these words, addressed to a fellow countryman:

Has he learned through affliction's teaching
   what our Crispus Attucks knew—
When Right is stricken, the white and black are counted
   as one, not two?

Wilma Dykeman and James Stokely,
from *Neither Black Nor White*

CRISPUS ATTUCKS
AS SEEN
BY THE DAR

WASHINGTON (CDN)—Crispus Attucks, popularly thought of as the first Negro killed in the American Revolution, was actually a rioter, according to the Daughters of the American Revolution.

"It's a misnomer to think of him as a part of the American Revolution," said a DAR aide at national headquarters.

"He actually took part in a riot which was held before the established date" of the American Revolution, 19 April 1775, DAR officials maintain, when the "shot that was heard around the world" was fired at the Battle of Lexington.

Attucks was killed during the Boston Massacre in 1770, when a group of American demonstrators, Attucks among them, was fired on by the British.

Some scholars consider him a significant figure in Negro and American history.

The DAR celebrates the beginning of the Revolution every year with a national convention in Washington. This year's conclave begins Monday.

The DAR is a group of 187,000 American women who can prove their lineal descent from a "man or woman who aided the cause of or fought in the movement for American independence," said Mrs. William Henry Sullivan, Jr., president-general of the DAR.

Someone at a press conference yesterday asked Mrs. Sullivan if the DAR, which had no Negro members, would admit a Negro, if she could prove lineage descent say, from Crispus Attucks.

A male DAR staff member piped up from the rear of the

room. "He was just a boy, and besides, he was never married."

The *World Book Encyclopedia* indicates that Attucks was nearly fifty when he was killed.

Betty Flynn, *New York Post,*
15 April 1968

THE AMERICAN INDIANS
AND AGRICULTURE

The potato, tobacco, maize, tomato, chocolate, tapioca, and a lot of other useful plants were cultivated in America long before 1492. All of which means that as farmers many of our prehistoric Indians were as good as any known.

We do not know which of the many early hunting tribes in the United States first took to farming, but the archaeologists are furnishing the information to reconstruct the picture. There are rock-shelter deposits in the Ozarks of Missouri and the rough country of Kentucky that tell us that most of the plants first cultivated there are still growing wild near these same primitive dwellings. It is surprising what a pile of debris in a rock shelter or the mouth of a cave can tell us about the lives of vanished peoples. For example, such debris in Menifee County, Kentucky, when examined and analyzed from the bottom to the top, or from the earliest to the latest layers, shows first a period of Stone Age hunting, followed by hunters who have taken to gardening as a sideline. Here and there appear the seeds of plants that formed a substantial part of their food. To prove this, the archaeologist analyzed some of the dried feces found in the debris. Some of the most common seeds in the debris, next above that belonging to the true hunters, are sunflower (*Helianthus annuus*), giant ragweed (*Ambrosia trifida*), goosefoot (*Chenopodium Sp.*), and marsh elder (*Iva ciliata*).

Clark Wissler, from *Indians
of the United States*

THE RAPE
OF THE PAST

*(As published by the United States
Government Printing office, 1958)*

Indians did not know how to read or write like white men and did not understand the colonists' custom of building permanent homes in groups and communities and of working hard to improve the land, to increase trade and manufacture, and to provide good schooling and orderly, peaceful living conditions for their families. The Indian tribes had an authority and organization that seemed to the colonists to be constantly changing. Their members moved from place to place, hunting and fishing; they did not like to work regularly at farming or home industries, and they fought very often among themselves.

Catheryn Seckler-Hudson, from *Federal
Textbook on Citizenship*

THE BLACK FAMILY:
A RACIST VIEW

The Negro never had a home or knew anything of the monogamic family and the proper rearing of children, as a social institution, within historic times.

. . . and the temperament of the Negro made it next to impossible to force upon him a well-ordered family life.

Charles McCord, from *The American Negro as a Dependent*

CHILDHOOD
IMPRESSIONS

The years as they pass keep revealing how the impressions made upon me as a child by my parents are constantly strengthening controls over my forms of habit, behavior, and conduct as a man. It appeared to me, starting into manhood, that I was to grow into something different from them; into something on a so much larger plan, a so much grander scale. As life tapers off I can see that in the deep and fundamental qualities I am each day more and more like them.

James Weldon Johnson, from *Along This Way*

ROMANTICIZATION: THE OTHER SIDE OF PREJUDICE

In some Indian tongues, one word serves for *happiness* and *beauty*. How significant this is! How it determines the direction of the Indian's activity, which, as we know, is the mere currency of his search for happiness. His search for beauty!

The touch of this is upon all his works. It is upon his dwellings, upon his pottery, upon his jewelry and ceremonials and dress. But most impressively of all, the touch of this preoccupation is upon his person. The bearing of the Indian is rhythmical and reticent, like his dancing and his music. His body is erect and fluent, symbol of his greatest striving: to achieve an inner harmony with the living world. The proud, massive power of his features is no less than the outward mark of that harmony that his race has won. The Indian girl is gentle, timid, musical in the flutter of her hands and the note of her voice. Her eyes are too open to meet the gaze of the stranger. They would pour all the limpidity of her soul upon him. She moves hidden in black shawls from the sun's passion that would exhaust her own. But when she is a woman and a mother, her slender grace spreads into buxom ease. She is still rather silent, but her form welcomes fellowship and work. She depicts the homely realism of Indian life. The slow, sure march of her mate, his indrawn lips and searching eyes suggest the majesty of long silences in prayer.

Waldo Frank, from *Our America*

IT IS IMPOSSIBLE
NOT TO BE
DISGUSTED

. . . it is impossible not to be disgusted—when one has seen even a little of the real Indian world—by our surreptitious efforts, on the one hand, to despoil and disperse the Indians and, on the other, our loud exploitation of literary Indian romance: the Mohawk Airlines, the Pontiac cars, the hotels Onondaga and Iroquois, and the Seneca cocktail lounges.

Edmund Wilson, from *Apologies
to the Iroquois*

LOVING
THE MEXICANS

There might be something wrong with me, but I could never help loving the Mexicans. All of them, good and bad, because they were human to a vivid degree. My principal regret about the years I wasted in the Southwest is that with the padrone complex and carrying the white man's burden, I had very little chance to be human with them. I could only look at them wistfully and come away sadly, wishing at times that I could be a Mexican.

John Houghton Allen, from *Southwest*

IT IS NOT
NEARLY ENOUGH

But it is not nearly enough to admire and use the talents of a foreign race, if one goes on despising its feelings and its spirit, merely fondling the vases, the lacquers, the works in ivory, bronze, and jade that it has produced. There is something more precious still, of which such masterpieces are only the proof, the recreation, and the relics—I mean life.

Paul Valéry, from *History and Politics*

IN MEMORIAM:
Dr. Martin Luther King, Jr.
(1929–1968)

I have a dream that one day men will rise up and come to see that they are made to live together as brothers. I still have a dream this morning that one day every Negro in this country, every colored person in the world, will be judged on the basis of the content of his character rather than the color of his skin, and every man will respect the dignity and worth of human personality. I still have a dream today that one day the idle industries of Appalachia will be revitalized, and the empty stomachs of Mississippi will be filled, and brotherhood will be more than a few words at the end of a prayer, but rather the first order of business on every legislative agenda. I still have a dream today that one day justice will roll down like water, and righteousness like a mighty stream. I still have a dream today that in all of our state houses and city halls men will be elected to go there who will do justly and love mercy and walk humbly with their God. I still have a dream today that one day war will come to an end, that men will beat their swords into plowshares and their spears into pruning hooks, that nations will no longer rise up against nations, neither will they study war any more. I still have a dream today that one day the lamb and the lion will lie down together and every man will sit under his own vine and fig tree and none shall be afraid. I still have a dream today that one day every valley shall be exalted and every mountain and hill will be made low, the rough places will be made smooth and the crooked places straight, and the glory of the Lord shall be revealed, and all flesh shall see it together. I still have a dream that with this faith we will be able to adjourn the councils of despair and bring new light into the dark chambers of pessimism. With this faith we will be able to speed up the day when there will be peace on earth and goodwill toward men. It will be a glorious day, the morning stars will sing together, and the sons of God will shout for joy.

Martin Luther King, Jr., from *The Trumpet of Conscience*

Robert Francis Kennedy (1925–1968)

. . . There is a new world about us—beset by hunger, energized by revolution, largely controlled by that half of the world's people who are under the age of twenty-five. In this world the United States—all of us, our children, and their children, must find our place for the future. It is not a world in which people can be judged by the color of their skins or their nationality—for its future will depend on finding and recognizing talent wherever it exists. It is not a world in which we can preserve all our advantages of wealth and position and comfort—but a world in which we must use those advantages for the benefit of others. It is not a world with which all our contacts can be clean and antiseptic, in which we can insist that all people conform to our ideas of what is right and fitting. Rather it is a world of awakened diversity, of hundreds of nations asserting their right to self-determination and full participation in world affairs. To deal with such a world—to make it safe for diversity—to assure true security to our children—we will have to learn to accept the diversity, to disdain all stereotypes, to cast off all excess intellectual and social baggage. We cannot be ready for diversity abroad—until we return to its acceptance at home.

Robert Francis Kennedy, speech
to Hebrew Immigrant Aid Society,
10 June 1965

THE MAN INSIDE [31]

They told me—the voices of hates in the land—
They told me that White is White and Black is Black;
That the children of Africa are scarred with a brand
Ineradicable as the spots on the leopard's back.

They told me that gulfs unbridgeable lie
In the no man's seascapes of unlike hues,
As wide as the vertical of earth and sky,
As ancient as the grief in the seagull's mews.

They told me that Black is an isle with a ban
Beyond the pilgrims' Continent of Man.

[31] To the memory of V. F. Calverton.

I yearned for the mainland where my brothers live.
The cancerous isolation behind, I swam
Into the deeps, a naked fugitive,
Defying tribal fetishes that maim and damn.

And when the typhoon of jeers smote me and hope
Died like a burnt-out world and on the shore
The hates beat savage breasts, you threw the rope
And drew me into the catholic Evermore.

We stood on common ground, in transfiguring light,
Where the man inside is neither Black nor White.

Melvin B. Tolson,
from *Rendezvous With America*

. . . with time all that is strange automatically becomes
familiar. And, therefore, as acquaintance grows, the stranger
tends, other things being equal, to move from "bad" to
"good."

Gordon W. Allport, from
The Nature of Prejudice

COLOR CONCIOUSNESS
IS RELATIVE

Physical difference in itself is not sufficient to produce race prejudice; another factor is needed. This may be one of a number of things: economic profit, political gain, or the existence of almost any problem in the environment of the white man. It is an *x* factor, with a wide variety of possible substitutions. (It is exactly because the possibilities are infinite that no one can find *the* cause.) This *x* factor is so chameleon-like as to be virtually impossible of elimination; that is a man could stub his toe in the presence of a Negro and develop race prejudice.

. . . it is not possible to eliminate the deadly combination —physical difference plus *x*—which produces race prejudice, by eliminating either one of the two in an *absolute* sense. So long as there is outstanding physical difference (and this may be either visually obvious or socially ordained when it is not obvious) the possibility for the birth of race prejudice will always exist.

Physical difference, however, can be eliminated in a *relative* sense. That is, skin color and facial features can become lost in a mass of other characteristics—qualities of both physique and personality—so as to lose their specialness as identifying features. Those physical characteristics that denote "race" become relatively insignificant when competing for attention with a hundred other aspects of personality. To create such a situation, segregation—both the legal segregation of the South and the actual segregation of the North—must be ended. When the Negro is separated as a group from the rest of society, he cannot be known in all his complexity. Only one thing is known about him for sure in this state of separation: he is a

Negro. And this fact, dominating all else, becomes the causal explanation for every aspect of his behavior.

The more contact there is between whites and Negroes, the vaster the number of sense impressions that flow back and forth, the more the physical characteristics that denote "race" become diluted in a sea of impressions of all kinds. Then, being dark skinned, or having thicker lips or a softer nose, becomes as minor an object of attention as the fact that someone is short or has freckles or is a Baptist. Then, even if the sense impressions are bad ones, even if two people find they are incompatible, the grounds are no more sought in "race" than they are in shortness or freckledness.

Color consciousness is relative. A black drop of ink on a white paper is startling, but when you begin filling the paper with other things, the drop becomes lost, though it is as black as before. And when the blackness or whiteness of skin becomes just a small part of many other, more relevant elements piercing our consciousness, it takes its deserved minor place. A Negro seen casually at a distance is mainly a black person. A Negro *known* is a person with dozens of different characteristics, one of the least important of which is blackness.

Howard Zinn, from *The Southern Mystique*

A WHITE GEORGIA MINISTER SPEAKS, 1943

The white race has never recognized the propriety of inter-marriage. It's a sin to marry a Negro or to mix with them, just as it's a sin to peddle dope instead of teaching school. Such a man throws away his opportunities and debases himself by failing to use his opportunity as a white man and sinks to a lower standard. He allows his creative capacity, his traditions, his descendants to be corrupted. He pronounces a curse on all his descendants. He no longer has pure white blood in his veins. He has produced a mule in the human family.

quoted by Charles S. Johnson, from *Patterns of Negro Segregation*

THE BARRIER

I must not gaze at them although
   Your eyes are dawning day;
I must not watch you as you go
   Your sun-illumined way;

I hear but I must never heed
   The fascinating note,
Which, fluting like a river-reed,
   Comes from your trembling throat;

I must not see upon your face
   Love's softly glowing spark;
For there's the barrier of race,
   You're fair and I am dark.

Claude McKay, from *Selected Poems of Claude McKay*

GALLUP POLL, 1970

Princeton, N.J., Sept. 9—Views on interracial marriage have undergone a dramatic change in the last five years, with a clear majority of people surveyed nationwide, 56 percent, now disapproving of laws that prohibit marriage between whites and blacks, the Gallup Poll reported today.

Following is a comparison of the latest findings with those from 1965, nationally and by Northern and Southern whites:

NATIONWIDE

	1965 %	1970 %
Approve	48	35
Disapprove	46	56
No opinion	6	9

SOUTHERN WHITES

	1965 %	1970 %
Approve	72	56
Disapprove	24	38
No opinion	4	6

WHITES OUTSIDE SOUTH

	1965 %	1970 %
Approve	42	30
Disapprove	52	61
No opinion	6	9

New York Times

WEDDING
IN MISSISSIPPI

JACKSON, Miss., Aug. 2—A twenty-four-year-old civil rights law clerk and a young black woman from a poor rural south Mississippi county were here married today, toppling a legal barrier against interracial marriage that had been on the books for more than one hundred years. It was believed to be the first such wedding in Mississippi.

Armed with a marriage license issued two days ago under a Federal Court order, dark-haired Roger Mills, a former Washington, D.C., law student from Indiana, and Berta Linson, twenty-one, a Jackson State College student from Hazelhurst, who now works as a file clerk in the same law office with Mills, exchanged vows in a formal ceremony at Central Methodist Church.

Following the wedding here today in the new brown brick church in the heart of a Negro commercial area in the downtown section, Mills said . . . that the interracial marriage was "not anything really different than what's been happening for years in Mississippi."

"The only thing that is new is this is the first time the state of Mississippi has ever sanctioned it."

New York Times, 3 August 1970

THE SEASON
OF CHANGE

It was the judge who first taught me that one has to earn one's beliefs; most liberals unfortunately think you can inherit them, like prejudices.

The judge's task was especially poignant because he was born to segregation and shared its values until he managed to pull himself out of the swamp of his heritage. The agonizing examination of conscience that this must require of a white man in the Deep South is probably beyond the understanding of an outsider. But there was a suggestion of what his evolution must have cost the judge, and how such a change may come to a white Southerner, in something the judge told me while he waited for the state legislature's latest attempt to frustrate his efforts to uphold the law—not the law of the state but the law of the nation. Louisiana, ruled by segregationists, had already tried to take over the schools to forestall the judge's order to integrate the first grades, and it was a tense time waiting for the next move. There had been threats against his life already and the police were guarding both his home and his office. I had to show proof of identity three times before I reached him in his office in the federal building. Our talk was interrupted several times by people who telephoned wishing to tell that "nigger-loving" judge what they thought of him. The judge coolly told them that they must have the wrong number. His face was unreadable.

His evolution on the surface was charted clearly in the reference books. He had been born to a poor family—his father was a plumber and had seven children—and a scholarship took him to the university for a law degree. But in the depression days, it took a lot of money to launch yourself as a lawyer and so he became a high school teacher and took another degree at night. He became assistant U.S. attorney in New Orleans and spent several years in Washington and in London during World War II. Then he returned to his hometown as U.S. attorney and a year later President Truman —"reposing special trust and confidence in the wisdom, uprightness, and learning of J. Skelly Wright, of Louisiana"— appointed him U.S. district judge for the eastern district of the state.

Thus he could be seen as the poor Irish-American boy who inherited the segregation background but then changed his way of thinking by discovering the world outside the Deep South. But such a picture is too glib and hardly does justice to the judge's loneliness in his hometown—a loneliness that drove him occasionally to talking to the people on the telephone to probe their feelings against him, listening keenly for any doubts, any uncertainty, that might eventually bring him allies. He said his own early struggle had given him a great sympathy for "underdogs," yet that seemed too glib an explanation of his conversion.

That day, in searching for what had changed him, the judge talked about his boyhood: "I was a normal child who probably called Negroes niggers, which was what we all called them. I don't know that I felt any particular sympathy for them, the kind that I feel now. When we were kids, the habit was to go through the colored sections and throw things at Negroes—rotten apples and things. I never threw anything but I was in the car with some kids who did. I remember a Mardi Gras when I saw some kids beat up a Negro. They looked for one by himself and beat him up. I remember that, but I don't know when the change came in me. I have noticed it on the bench but perhaps it was coming slowly all those years." Had his religion helped? "No, I don't think so. I'm a bad Catholic." He remembered being impressed by what Oliver Cromwell had said, that in matters of the mind we looked for no compulsion except light and reason. "That's how I feel today," said the judge.

He gave the impression of searching back in his memory

for the first time for what had given him "my mature and great sympathy for Negroes," and suddenly his memory seemed to throw it up, and he began to tell of one Christmas party in his office, and how amid the gaiety he looked out of the window at a blind people's building opposite and saw that the blind people were having a party too, but as they arrived they were being separated into black and white.

"They couldn't see to segregate themselves . . ."

He was recalling a memory of many years ago and yet he was so moved that he could not complete the story for several minutes. He turned his swivel chair so that his back was to me and there was a pause. Then he turned back and went on: "That upset me a great deal. That made a lasting impression on me. Perhaps that worked the change . . ."

W. J. Weatherby, from *Love
in the Shadows*

THE CHOICE

The first children I came to know in New Orleans were Negro children, and for a while it appeared that they would be the only children in the two schools the four little girls were attending. As one of them reminded me in a talk we had after her first few days of school: "I don't see anyone but the teacher all day. They said I would be seeing the white kids, but none have come yet, and the teacher, she says they may never come—all on account of me. But I told her they will."

In point of fact several white children were almost always at school during her long ordeal, though it took her time to become aware of their presence. For a time she *was* the first grade of a fairly large school, while a fluctuating handful of white children constituted the remnants of the other grades, the second through the sixth.

Two of these white children came from ministers' homes, one Baptist and the other Methodist. Four of them, two boys and two girls, came from a third home, a Catholic one with five other children, headed by an accountant.

"We are eleven, so we're a mob too," the wife of the accountant and the mother of their nine children once told me as we stood in her kitchen and looked at an angry crowd outside and not far away. She was counting those on her side because she knew those on the other side had become her enemies.

She lived near the school, near enough to see it from her backyard; near enough to see and hear the crowds from her front window. She was born in Louisiana, as were her parents, and their parents. She and her husband were "ordinary" people, or at least so it would once have seemed. That is to say, they lived with their children in a small, lower-middle-class area, their home like thousands about it, their life distinguished by little except its daily routine of care for one another and the children. They were both high school graduates.

Just before the crisis came upon their city they had no interest in politics and were against school desegregation. "We never really thought they would do it, and then we found that not only did they mean to go ahead, but ours was slated to be one of the schools." That was the way she summarized her surprise, her previous attitude of mild or unexcited opposition to what the newspapers less indifferently called "mixing."

In a matter of weeks this mother and her children were being subjected to a degree of danger and intimidation that rivals for violence any I've seen in the South. Her house was assaulted, its windows broken, its walls stained with foul inscriptions. Her husband's place of work was threatened and picketed. It became necessary for the police to protect her children as well as the little Negro girl whose lone entrance precipitated disorder in the streets and sporadic violence destined to last for months. In watching this Southern white lady walk through those mobs with her small children, one could not but wonder why she persisted. Why did she take on that challenge, and how did she endure it?

After years of interviews with her, I have had to guard against tampering with my recollection of this woman, against making her into someone she wasn't at the time she made the various choices—choices that in turn helped make her into the person she is *now*. This is a problem psychiatrists must always keep in mind. It is possible to forget the truth of the past when the present, with its visions and formulations, is the vantage point from which the conclusive determination is being made.

Here is how—word for word—she once described her attitude when the conflict of school desegregation, hovering over the city for months, settled upon her children's school.

"I couldn't believe it. First, I became angry at the nigras. I figured, why don't they leave well enough alone and tend to their own problems. Lord knows they have enough of them. Then, I thought I just couldn't keep four children out of school; not on one little nigra girl's account. So I thought I'd just send them and see what happens. Well, the next thing I knew, mothers were rushing in and taking their children out; and every time they did it, they would get cheered. The end of the first day of it there wasn't much of a school left.

"The next day I decided to give it one more try. I was going to stay away, keep my children away, but to tell the truth the idea of having four children home with me, squabbling and making noise and getting into trouble, was too much for me. So I thought I'd just stick it out and maybe things would quiet down, and then we'd all forget one little nigra and our children would go on with school.

"The crowd was there the next day and they were more of one mind now. They started shouting at each white mother that came to the building, and one by one they pulled back. It was as if the building were surrounded and only the police could get through, and *they* weren't doing anything. The mob let Ruby (the Negro girl) through, because they said they wanted her to be there alone. They screamed when the minister brought his girl, and I decided to withdraw. Well, I was walking back home, and I saw the back door to the building. They were so busy with the minister and shouting at the reporters, they weren't looking at the rear. So I just took the children there and let them go in. At that moment I thought, 'It's better than their being at home, and better than their listening to those people scream all day from our porch.' It was bad enough *I* had to hear it, and my baby too young for school.

"The *next* day I really decided to join the boycott. I couldn't see fighting them, and they weren't going away like I thought. Well, my husband stayed home a little later than usual, and we talked. I said no, no school for the kids, and he agreed. Then he said maybe we should try to move to another part of the city, so that the kids could continue their schooling. Then I said I'd try *one more day*. Maybe the mob would get tired and go away. After all, they had their way—there was only the children of a minister or two left out of five hundred families. I snuck the kids in, and later that day one of the *teachers* called, to ask me if I was sure I wanted to do it. She sounded almost as scared as me, and I think she would just as soon have had the whole school closed, so she could be spared listening to that noise and that filthy language.

"That night, I think, was the turning point. A few of the mob saw me leaving with the children, and started calling me the worst things I'd ever heard. They followed me home and continued. Thank God the police kept them away from the house, but I had the sickening feeling on the way home that I was *in* something, unless I got out real fast. In the morning I couldn't send them, and I couldn't *not*. One woman came here instead of to the school, to swear at me just in case I tried sending the children off. I guess she thought that just her being there would take care of me. Well, it did. I became furious; and I just dressed those children as fast as I could and marched them off. Later that day those women from the Garden District came, and they said they'd stand by me and even drive the children the one block, and I guess I soon was a key person in breaking the boycott.

"But I didn't *mean* to. It was mostly, I think, their language, and attacking me so quickly. I didn't feel any freer than the nigra. I think I gained my strength each day, so that I was pretty tough in a few months. After a while they didn't scare me one bit. I wouldn't call it brave; it was becoming *determined*. That's what happened, really. We all of us—my children, my husband, and me—became determined."

Of course I am giving you one section from hours of taped conversations. I knew her quite well when we had that talk, and it was not the first time she had given me an account of those experiences. When I listen to her voice today, I can almost feel her drifting—precisely that—drifting—and then coming to terms not only with her own past but with history itself. Choice was required: at some point her children either had to stay home or go to school. Each alternative has its advantages: a home without restless children, or a home unbothered by restless and angry outsiders—calling at midnight to predict death and destruction, shouting similar forecasts in the daytime.

We are still left with the matter of why this woman chose as she did, and how she managed the strength to make her choice stick fast so long.

Surely we may call that unassuming strength her courage. Not everyone, even among the so-called mature, will take on the possibility of death day after day with evident calm. In this woman's case her commitment, her course of courageous action, developed through a series of moments or accidents. Step by step she became an important participant in a critical struggle. Indeed, in looking back at her life and the situation she faced, we may forget that a historical event was once a crisis by no means settled. Had the boycott in New Orleans held fast, the forces at work there for segregation would have become stronger, perhaps decisively so for a long time. That is what I heard from people on both sides of the struggle as it was occurring.

Our Southern lady, like Conrad's Lord Jim, slipped into an important moment that became a determining force in her life as well as her country's history. Not only her views on segregation but her participation in community affairs and the goals she has for herself and her children are far different now than they "ordinarily" would have been. "I met people I never would have," she said to me recently, "and my sights have become higher. I think more about what's important, not just for me but for others; and my children do better at school because they're more serious about education."

What can one say about this woman's choice? Certainly there was no one reason that prompted it. I have talked with enough of her neighbors to realize the dangers of saying that her past actions or beliefs might easily differentiate her from others. Many of her nearby friends are decent, likable people. Before a mob they simply withdrew themselves and their children. This woman had also planned to do so. Yet she never did, or she never did for long or for good. She drifted. She tried to resolve the mixed feelings in her mind. She weighed her fear of a mob against her annoyance at her children's loss of schooling and their bothersome presence in the home. She was a hopeful person and she assumed—wrongly indeed—that the riots would end quickly. She is a sound, stable person, and once under fire she did not waver. She is the first to remind me that her husband's employers stood by him. Had *they* wavered, she is certain that she would have quickly withdrawn her children from the school. For that matter, were her husband different—that is, more of a segregationist, or generally more nervous and anxious—she might never have dared stand up to a mob's anger.

In sum, there were a number of reasons that helped this woman's courage unfold, each of them, perhaps, only a small part of the explanation, though each necessary. I suppose we could call her—in the fashion of the day—"latently" courageous. A crisis found her strong, and in possession of certain ideals. Those ideals gained power through a cumulative series of events that eventually became for one person's life a "point of no return." She puts it this way: "After a few days I knew I was going to fight those people and their foul tongues with every ounce of strength I had. I knew I had no choice but that one. At least that's how I see it now."

Robert Coles, from *Children of Crisis*

Epilogue

UNDER THE MASK

O bless this people, Lord, who seek their own face under the
mask and can hardly recognize it
Who seek Thee amidst cold and hunger that gnaw their bones
and entrails
And the betrothed laments her widowhood and the young
man sees his youth filched away
And the wife laments her husband's absent eye, and the mother
picks over rubbish to find the dream of her child.
O bless this people that breaks its bonds, O bless this people at
bay who face the bulimic pack of bullies and torturers.
And with them all the peoples of Europe, all the peoples of
Asia, all the peoples of Africa, all the peoples of
America
Who sweat blood and sufferings. And see, in the midst of these
millions of waves, the sea swell of the heads of my
people.
And grant to their warm hands that they may clasp the earth
in a girdle of brotherly hands
BENEATH THE RAINBOW OF THY PEACE.

Léopold Sédar Senghor, from "Prayer
for Peace," from *Selected Poems*

*This book was set in Janson and
Helvetica types by Brown Brothers
Linotypers, Inc. Printing and binding
are by The Haddon Craftsmen, Inc.*

Book designed by Ben Birnbaum